Counseling Theory and the Scriptures

The Conflicts and Compatibilities of Psychological Theory and the Bible

Roger Alliman, M.A.

Rick Surley, M.A.

All scripture references are from the
New King James Version
unless otherwise noted.

All italics and underlines
in biblical passages are the emphasis
of the authors.

Additional copies may be purchased at

www.counselingtheoryandthescriptures.com.

Copyright © 2012
Roger Alliman / Rick Surley
Colorado Springs, Colorado

Printed in the United States of America
All rights reserved. No part of this publication may be reproduced, stored in a retrieval system, or transmitted in any form or by any means—for example, electronic, photocopy, recording—without the prior written permission of the authors or publisher.
The only exception is brief quotations in printed reviews.

Dedicated
to
the many students, teachers, professors,
counselors, pastors
and interested believers
who, by faith,
trust that the God of all creation
has given his children
the guidelines necessary
for peaceful, productive,
and balanced living.

Contents

	Introduction	7
1.	Client-centered Therapy Carl Rogers	15
2.	Gestalt Therapy Fritz and Laura Perls	39
3.	Cognitive Therapy Aaron T. Beck	73
4.	Behavior Therapy B.F. Skinner / Ivan Pavlov	99
5.	Rational Emotive Behavior Therapy Albert Ellis	133
6.	Psychoanalytic Theory Sigmund Freud / Carl Jung	165
7.	Reality Therapy William Glasser	197
8.	Adlerian Psychotherapy Alfred Adler	221
9.	Solution-focused Brief Therapy Steve de Shazer / Insoo Kim Berg	251
10.	Existential Psychotherapy Rollo May / James Bugental Victor Frankl	269

Epilogue		307
Appendices		313
A-1	The New Birth	315
A-2	Tricotomist View of Man	317
A-3	Life in the Spirit	319
A-4	Man as Spirit, Soul and Body	321
B-1	Principles of Perception	327
B-2	Young Woman / Old Woman	329
B-3	A Boundaries Overview	331
B-4	What is Biblical Salvation	333
C-1	From Bondage to Freedom	337
C-2	Under the Surface	339
D-1	The Power of Sin	341
D-2	Put Off / Put On	345
D-3	A Counseling Model	349
E-1	Renewing the Mind from Irrational Beliefs	361
E-2	Renewing the Mind with Positive Confessions	365
F-1	Man and the Tabernacle	369
G-1	What Happens When Christians Die?	371
Notes		377

Introduction

In a most fundamental description, psychology is the scientific study of the human mind, its power and functions. The concepts of human psychology have deep roots in today's culture. From lecture halls to prisons, counseling clinics to church pulpits, from talk shows to the tabloids at your grocery store, there is little doubt that the world has a deep interest in who we are, how we think, what triggers certain actions and how two children can come out of a near-identical environment and be poles apart in their values, reasoning and motivating life paths.

Our purpose in writing *Counseling Theory and the Scriptures* is to provide the reader with guidelines that will be helpful in comparing some of the major counseling theories with what we believe the Scriptures present. We are not attempting to present the perfect counseling model for prospective students and counselors in the field. We hope to provide a valuable resource for students, counselors and those exploring the differences and similarities between psychological theory and Scripture. We view the theorists from a less technical position and more from a practical standpoint. We have attempted not so much to analyze their beliefs as to compare their views with a credible understanding of God's unfailing word.

We would be remiss in failing to address the existence of numerous contemporary theories and models. These include feminist therapy, narrative therapy, attachment therapy, biopsychosocial therapy, constructivist therapy, time-limited dynamic therapy and numerous addiction therapies. Our primary purpose was to deal with the foundational theories in which most contemporary therapies have their roots.

There are numerous counseling models, views, helpful books and materials that can be useful in helping prepare the contemporary Christian counselor, pastor and discipler who has a strong desire to adhere to and utilize the fundamental principles for living that are found in the Judeo-Christian Scriptures.

Within the Christian community you will find a vast array of resources: Larry Crabb, Jay Adams, Robert McGee, Charles Solomon, Dan Allender, Steve Arterburn, H. Norman Wright, John Eldredge, Neil Anderson and numerous other Christian writers have helped to better define the conflicts that exist between the Scriptures and much of contemporary psychology and philosophies for living.

Introduction

If counseling is to have success it must begin with the determination to give the client hope and encouragement. Those who struggle with the issues of life are generally at a point in their journey where they are at a loss to understand themselves, their circumstances, their feelings, their thought life and even their God. They are often desperately in search of someone who can help them find true meaning and understanding in light of their personal dilemma.

Much has been written on the impact of peers, siblings, family, community and cultural molds. Raymond Corsini offers a good description of the world's attempt to conform us to its image soon after our arrival on planet earth: "The search for significance and the consequent sibling competition reflect the values of the competitive society in which we live. We are encouraged to be first, to excel, to be popular, to be athletic, to be a 'real' man, to 'never say die,' to recall that 'practice makes perfect' and to 'dream the impossible dream.' Consequently, each child must stake out a 'territory' that includes the attributes or abilities that [they hope] will give...a feeling of worth."[1] Clearly, a proper biblical perspective on life has a far different view of worth and value as they relate to our view of self and the significance for which we search.

Our text is certainly far from exhaustive. There are a multitude of books on each of the theorists presented here and we recommend a visit to your local library if you have a desire to learn more about any particular theorist's views. We have tried to design our text as a tool for individual counselors, college and university schools of counseling and psychotherapy, church staff and others who desire to understand the importance of how our Creator intended for us to experience the fullness and joy that is a vital part of his plan and purpose.

As an introduction to the major theorists in this text it is helpful to comprehend the very meaning of why they are referred to as theorists: "A theory is a systematic way of organizing information into a set of meaningful relationships; empirical findings (facts) can be placed into some internally consistent framework. Hall and Lindsey (1970) hold that a theory serves three basic functions. First, a theory leads to observation of relevant facts.... If it is both comprehensive and verifiable, it generates testable hypotheses. A second function of a theory allows for the incorporation of empirical facts into a parsimonious and logically consistent framework. A third function of theory is that it helps simplify the task of observation by reducing...irrelevant facts."[2]

Although there are several views of what constitutes a category of theory, there is general agreement on the foundational categories. The additions to these classifications are largely in line with some of the more contemporary spin-offs that lend themselves to cate-

Introduction

gorization, particularly in the contemporary culture of the western world. For example Tosi, LeClair, Peters and Murphy present a broad foundation for theory: "The four broad categories of counseling theory are:
- Psychodynamic
- Existential-Humanistic
- Cognitive-Behavioral, and
- Family and Systems

"These are based upon quite different assumptions about the nature of human behavior and how to modify or change it."[3]

Adding to this basic category view, Ray Woolfe and Windy Dryden, in their *Handbook of Counselling Psychology*, broaden the four categories to a more contemporary listing. In part three, Perspectives on Practice, they list the categories as paradigms under the following headings:
- The Psychodynamic Paradigm
- The Humanistic Paradigm
- The Cognitive-Behavioral Paradigm
- The Existential-Phenomenological Paradigm
- Feminist Approaches to Counselling Psychology
- The Constructivist Paradigm
- The Systems Paradigm and
- The Eclectic and Integrative Paradigm.[4]

In a very practical sense, a theory is simply a system of ideas whose purpose is to explain something. Ideally, the theory is based on applications that are independent of the theory. However, in the end, it remains a theory. We find applications that would tend to marginalize the theory separating it from any kind of established validation as an absolute.

Although we would prefer to not be labeled, our view in today's Christian world would likely be considered evangelical with an absolutist's and positive view for the authority of Scripture. We approach the Scriptures with the view that they are everything God wanted to say to those upon whom his favor rests. Jesus Christ is indeed a divine part of the Godhead, one who took on the form of a man, lived a perfect and sacrificial life and died a cruel death on a cross as payment to his Father for the sins of the world. He was buried and rose again. Spiritual understanding will only be revealed to those who are born of and indwelt by the Holy Spirit of God.

We believe the Bible presents a principle for living that is applicable to all of humanity. For example, in its most basic message the Author of all of creation has made it clear that a "man reaps what he sows."[5]

Such a statement might be questioned by a curious reader and easily dispelled as a sound, but somewhat conditional directive. Placing such a statement in the realm of absolutes is only achieved by those who place their faith in a sovereign God who has never relinquished control of his creation to anyone or anything. In any thorough reading of the Scriptures we

Introduction

find story after story, from King David to the apostle Paul, that validates the principle of sowing and reaping and independently adds credence to its validity. In a minimal sense it is wisdom at its best to acknowledge that there is a force at work in the universe that is always in effect, much like the law of gravity. If we sow anger we will reap anger, if we sow love we will reap love, if we sow compassion we will reap compassion. God has given his children specific insight into their makeup and inherent potential. He has also made it clear what is required to find the joy and abundance that is available to those who are willing to understand and walk in his ways.

We offer this text with the realization that in the normal framework of things, we believe that the standard for counseling and psychological truth is to be found in the Scriptures. Every theory, new or old, must be held up to and properly weighed against the foundational beliefs that the God of the Scriptures, the one and only creator God of Abraham, Isaac and Jacob, is more than capable of providing answers to his children as we wrestle with life's issues, pains, struggles and trials. We are always mindful that *"all Scripture is inspired by God and is useful to teach us what is true and to make us realize what is wrong in our lives. It corrects us when we are wrong and teaches us to do what is right. God uses it to prepare and equip his people to do every good work."*[6]

Chapter One

Client-centered Therapy

Carl Ransom Rogers, Ph.D., was born in Oak Park, Illinois, the fourth of six children, on January 8, 1902. His father was a civil engineer and his mom a homemaker and devout, fundamentalist Christian. Because young Carl could read by the time he reached kindergarten, he started school in second grade.

He was raised in a very strict home and had many chores on his parent's farm, where his family moved when Carl was twelve years old. He became isolated, self-sufficient and self-disciplined. Rogers would later characterize himself as distant and aloof at that time in his life. He also became quite interested in the science of agriculture by reading his father's books on the subject. In fact, he would later major in agriculture in his undergraduate studies at the University of Wisconsin.

Because of his strict religious upbringing, Carl decided to change his major to religion and go into the ministry. During his studies, he was chosen from his class to travel to Beijing for the World Student Christian Federation Conference. He lived in China for six months and experienced new ideas that caused him to begin to doubt many of his religious beliefs. Rogers stated in his 1967 autobiography that "the possibility of the constructive improvement of life for individuals would probably always interest me, but I could not work in a field where I would be required to believe in some specified religious doctrine."[1]

After he graduated, Rogers married Helen Elliot, against his parents' wishes. They moved to New York City where he attended Union Theological Seminary, a liberal college for religious studies. He would later state that he took a seminar there that asked the question, "Why are you entering the ministry?" He wrote, "I might as well tell you that, unless you want to change your career, never take a class with such a title! [M]ost of the participants thought their way right out of religious work."[2]

Rogers changed his studies to clinical psychology at Columbia University and received his doctorate in 1931. Referring to that time in his life he stated, "Experience is, for me, the highest authority. The touchstone of validity is my own experience.... It is to experience that I must return again and again, to discover a closer approximation to truth as it is in the process of becoming in me. Neither the Bible nor the prophets—neither Freud nor research—neither the revelations of God nor man—can take precedence over my own direct experience."[3]

He started his clinical pursuit during this time at the Rochester Society for the Prevention of Cruelty to Children. There he discovered the research and theory of Otto Rank, which encouraged him to develop his own approach to therapy. At Rochester he would learn, "it is the client who knows what hurts, what direction to go, what problems are crucial, what experiences have been deeply buried. It began to occur to me that unless I had a need to demonstrate my own cleverness and learning, I would do better to rely upon the client for direction of movement in the therapeutic process. For effective counseling [to take place], the psychotherapist [must be] 'genuine and without a facade...and must be empathetic in understanding. As a result, the client begins to feel positive and accepting toward himself. [H]is defenses diminish [and] he becomes more open...and he finds that he is free to grow and change in desired directions."[4]

Rogers went on to teach at three universities, including The Ohio State University (1940-1945), the University of Chicago (1945-1957) and the University of Wisconsin (1957-1963). He was able to apply his theory and test the results during this time.

He would go on to apply his theory to group psychotherapy, education and in facilitating understanding between antagonistic factions arising from cultural, racial and religious differences. Toward the end of his life he was nominated for the Nobel Peace Prize for his work with national intergroup conflict in South Africa and Northern Ireland. Rogers was voted one of the most eminent psychologists of the twentieth century among clinicians, second only to Sigmund Freud. He died in 1987.

Philosophy

During the process of observing clients, Rogers found many examples of individuals who reinforced his theory. One of these clients was a young boy who had been seen by Rogers for some time and made no progress. Rogers had decided that he could not help the boy or his mother and was in the process of telling her so when she asked if he saw adults in his practice. She immediately began telling Rogers of her problems. As Rogers described it, "Real therapy began then, and ultimately it was highly successful [for her and for her son]."[5] This experience, and many more like it, would lead Rogers to conclude that it was the client who knew what the problem was and how to solve it. This belief became the basis for client-centered therapy.

Client-centered Therapy

Rogers was a pioneer in the field of therapy. He was the first to challenge the use of the term "patient" and begin calling those who entered therapy "clients." He explained his use of this term by saying, "The client is one who comes actively and voluntarily to gain help on a problem, but without any notion of surrendering his own responsibility for the situation."6

Over the initial years of his practice, he became increasingly convinced that the genuineness of the therapist, as well as the therapist's ability to be empathetic, was crucial for a positive outcome.

The centerpiece of this theory is Rogers' belief that human beings are inherently and fundamentally good. He made this clear when he stated, "[T]he basic nature of the human being, when functioning freely, is constructive and trustworthy.... We do not need to ask who will control his aggressive impulses; for as he becomes more open to all of his impulses...his need to be liked by others and his tendency to give affection will be as strong as his impulses to strike out or to seize for himself. He will be aggressive in situations in which aggression is realistically appropriate, but there will be no runaway need for aggression."7

A person's need to grow and develop is innate in all human beings, according to Rogers. Regarding this topic, Murdock states, "Person-centered theorists believe that the only motivation of human behavior is the tendency to grow to full potential in constructive, positive ways. Living beings strive to maximize the organism and avoid experiences that are detrimental to it. Person-centered theorists see no inherent aggressive or destructive tendencies in people, although aggression or assertion may sometimes be used as a means to grow, such as when an individual asserts himself to obtain something that enhances his existence."[8]

Rogers would make his views of the inherent goodness of man even more clear in his 1966 paper on client-centered therapy. "Contrary to those therapists who see depravity at men's core, who see men's deepest instincts as destructive, I have found that when man is truly free to become what he most deeply is, free to actualize his nature as an organism capable of awareness, then he clearly appears to move toward wholeness and integration."[9] Rogers saw this as the most basic of human processes. He called it *our actualizing tendency.*

Rogers further believed that humans, as well as all organisms, know and strive for whatever is good for them. Whether it is love, experience, food, acceptance or whatever else—humans will always evaluate it to determine if it contributes to one's growth and development. He called this *organismic valuing.* He would also write a great deal about the self. Murdock tells us, "As humans grow and experience the world, a portion of this experience becomes labeled as the self. All experiences that the person recognizes as 'me' and the values that are attached to them become what is termed the Self Concept."10

Rogers would go on to describe what he called the *ideal self*, describing it as the self we most want to be or the self-concept which the individual would most like to possess and upon which he places the most value.

Human beings, according to Rogers, instinctively value what he called *positive regard*. Concepts such as love, affection, attention and nurturance fall into this construct. Rogers believed that the need for positive regard of the self (positive self regard) is learned through experiencing it from others important to the individual. We experience things such as positive self-esteem, self-worth and self-image by experiencing the positive regard others show us.

According to Murdock, "[T]he need for positive regard motivates individuals to seek love from important others around them. When the individual perceives that some aspect of himself...is evaluated positively by someone important to him and other aspects are not, conditions of worth arise."11

Rogers called positive and rewarding conditions of worth *conditional positive regard*. Because humans need positive regard, this can be extremely powerful. It can cause us to shape ourselves in what society or family expects of us in order to gain approval. Over time we may be conditioned to accept ourselves only if we meet the standards of others—*conditional positive self regard* can occur. "[T]o the extent that our society is out of synch with the actualizing tendency, and we are forced to live with conditions of worth that are out of step with organismic valuing, and receive only conditional positive regard and self-regard, we develop instead an ideal self."[12] *Ideal* refers to something that is always out of our reach, the standard we can't meet.

Roger's reference to this ideal self would subsequently lead to what he called *incongruity*, which is the difference between the "I am" and the "I should." This, in turn, would lead the client to neurosis, or being out of synch with one's own self.

Foundational Precepts

Rogers believed that the client-centered approach made the client the expert. Clients do not require fixing, but are valued for what they bring to the session. The therapist should guide the client in a nondirective manner. There should be a major emphasis on not instructing the client and not leading them to do or not do certain things. Rather, the therapist should empower the client to discover their own solutions to their problems. If the therapist is successful at this approach, the client will experience being exceptionally understood. Rogers believed, "The curious paradox is that when I accept myself just as I am, then I can change."13

Rogers used a number of important concepts in describing his theory. He wrote about the need for the client to be accepted by the therapist unconditionally and nonjudgmentally. The client needs to feel free in exploring his thoughts and feelings, both positive and negative, without the danger of condemnation. Rogers called this *unconditional positive regard* to which he added, "It is real achievement when we can learn, even in certain relationships or at certain times in those relationships, that it is safe to care, that it is safe to relate to the other as a person for whom we have positive feelings."14

Rogers stressed the need of the client to be accurately understood. The therapist needs to understand the client's feelings from the client's perspective in order to grasp what his world is like. He called this *empathic understanding*. According to Rogers, this involves "temporarily living in the other's life, moving about in it delicately without making judgments."15

Rogers wrote that the therapist must be authentic and genuine, not presenting aloofness or a facade that he is the expert. The counselor must be transparent, without an air of authority or hidden knowledge. *Congruence* was the term used by Rogers to describe this concept. "The more the therapist is himself or herself in the relationship, putting up no professional front or personal facade, the greater is the likelihood that the client will change and grow in a constructive manner."[16]

Rogers believed that these three conditions would allow the client to grow and develop at their own rate and in their own way. These conditions allow the client to be energized and to grow in their own identity independently of what others think or believe about them. Rogers further believed that when a client sees a therapist who gives them unconditional positive regard, empathy and genuineness, that client will be energized and will grow in their own identity independently of what others think or believe about them.

Unconditional positive regard, empathic understanding and congruence are core conditions and the only requirements for sound therapy. Rogers believed that no other techniques were necessary or recommended, since technique was seen by Rogers as guiding and objectifying the client, instead of allowing him to find his own solutions.

Even the evaluative process of the client was unnecessary according to Rogers. It is the responsibility of the client to decide what to bring up and how much to explore any particular issue. Evaluation was seen as overly leading the client and setting up the therapist to be seen as an expert. In this way, Rogers was a pioneer in shifting the therapeutic focus from an emphasis on technique to that of relationship.

Although Rogers did not consider what he called *reflection* to be a technique, it is a well-known term coming from *Client-centered Therapy*. Reflection is simply mirroring back to the client what the therapist just heard him or her say. It is not just repeating words or phrases, but is reflected in such a way that the client knows and feels that the therapist has truly understood and identified what is being said. This reflecting must be genuine and congruent.

The Fully-functioning Person

Rogers described in detail in his 1961 work, *On Becoming a Person: A Therapist's View of Psychotherapy,* what he considered a fully-functioning, healthy person.

These individuals are open to experience, which Rogers considered to be the opposite of defensiveness. They live existentially, which means they live in the present, not in the future or the past. They are increasing in *organismic trust*, being guided by the *organismic-valuing process* and trusting in themselves to do what is right and natural. They have a clear freedom of choice, determining their own behavior. These individuals feel free when choices are available to them. They tend to be more creative and feel free in being creative, without feeling a need to conform. They can be trusted to act constructively. Even their aggressive behavior will be balanced by their intrinsic goodness. A fully functioning person living a rich, full life. "This process of the good life is not, I am convinced, a life for the faint-hearted. It involves the stretching and growing of becoming more and more of one's potentialities. It involves the courage to be. It means launching oneself fully into the stream of life."[17]

Rogers' Propositions

Rogers expanded his observations into a theory of personality and behavior that he described in detail. The following are known as Rogers' Nineteen Propositions:

1. Every individual exists in a continually changing world of experience of which he or she is the center.
2. The organism reacts to the field as it is experienced and perceived. This perceptual field is, for the individual, "reality."
3. The organism reacts as an organized whole to this phenomenal field.
4. The organism has one basic tendency and striving—to actualize, maintain, and enhance the experiencing organism.
5. Behavior is basically the goal-directed attempt of the organism to satisfy its needs

as experienced, in the field as perceived.

6. Emotion accompanies and in general facilitates such goal-directed behavior, the kind of emotion being related to the seeking versus the consummatory aspects of the behavior and the intensity of the emotion being related to the perceived significance of the behavior for the maintenance and enhancement of the organism.

7. The best vantage point for understanding behavior is from the internal frame of reference of the individual.

8. A portion of the total perceptual field gradually becomes differentiated as the self.

9. As a result of interaction with the environment, and particularly as a result of evaluational interaction with others, the structure of self is formed—an organized, fluid, but consistent conceptual pattern of perceptions of characteristics and relationships of the "I" or the "me," together with values attached to these concepts.

10. The values attached to experiences, and the values that are a part of the self structure, in some instances are values experienced directly by the organism, and in some instances are values introjected or taken over from others, but perceived in distorted

fashion, as though they had been experienced directly.

11. As experiences occur in the life of the individual, they are (a) symbolized, perceived and organized into some relationship to the self-structure, (b) ignored because there is no perceived relationship to the self-structure or (c) denied symbolization or given a distorted symbolization because the experience is inconsistent with the structure of the self.

12. Most of the ways of behaving that are adopted by the organism are those that are consistent with the concept of self.

13. Behavior may, in some instances, be brought about by organic experiences and needs that have not been symbolized. Such behavior may be inconsistent with the structure of the self, but in such instances the behavior is not owned by the individual.

14. Psychological maladjustment exists when the organism denies to awareness significant sensory and visceral experiences, which consequently are not symbolized and organized into the gestalt of the self-structure. When this situation exists, there is a basis for potential psychological tension.

15. Psychological adjustment exists when

the concept of the self is such that all the sensory and visceral experiences of the organism are, or may be, assimilated on a symbolic level into a consistent relationship with the concept of self.

16. Any experience that is inconsistent with the organization or structure of self may be perceived as a threat, and the more of these perceptions there are, the more rigidly the self-structure is organized to maintain itself.

17. Under certain conditions, involving primarily complete absence of any threat to the self-structure, experiences that are inconsistent with it may be perceived and examined, and the structure of self revised to assimilate and include such experiences.

18. When the individual perceives all his sensory and visceral experiences and accepts them into one consistent and integrated system, then he is necessarily more understanding of others and more accepting of others as separate individuals.

19. As the individual perceives and accepts into his self-structure more of his organic experiences, he finds that he is replacing his present value system—based so largely upon introjections which have been distort-

edly symbolized—with a continuing organismic valuing process.[18]

Conclusion

Carl Rogers' view of human nature is that of inherent goodness with an ability to understand oneself. He believed that a client was able to correctly identify what is causing happiness or unhappiness, and could determine what is good for himself and what is wrong with himself. Clients are asked to decide for themselves the direction therapy will take and when it will conclude. Persons who have a strong ability to explore themselves and their feelings make particularly good candidates for Client-centered Therapy. Those who need more direction, advice and problem solving from a therapist would be less suited for success with a client-centered therapist.

A Biblical Perspective

Person-centered theory has been extremely influential in the field of counseling and psychotherapy. Rogers was the first to major on the importance of the client-therapist relationship and the first to stress how important listening and empathy are in the counseling process. His view of human nature is that of inherent goodness with an ability to understand and correctly identify oneself. As Christians we respect the value and importance of relationship since our salvation, peace and security are built on a relationship with our heavenly Father through his only begotten Son, the Lord Jesus Christ.

Carl Rogers is also recognized in his efforts to challenge therapists to openly express empathy and compassion for those who are struggling with many of the difficult and painful issues that life can thrust upon even the most seemingly innocent.

As Christians, however, we would take issue with Rogers' view that sees humanity as inherently good. The Christian view of original sin and man's resultant fallen condition would not perceive the natural man as fundamentally good. Although Adam and Eve chose to go against God's command and eat from the forbidden tree, we must recognize that the tree from which they ate was the tree of the knowledge of both good and evil. One could assume God included good as a way of maintaining a degree of order and measured decency in the resulting fallen world. Emery Bancroft sheds light on the ultimate results of our first parents' fatal choice: "Man was originally created with a moral nature which was positively good...but with the power to choose evil. The inherent tendency to do good is supported by the scriptural statement that he was created 'upright.'... Sin originated in man's free act of revolt from God—the act of will which, although inclined toward God, was still capable of a contrary choice...the necessary condition for free moral development."[19]

The first man's fall from innocence brought grievous ramifications to himself, his wife and all those who were born into the fallen line of humanity. *As by one man sin entered into the world, and death by sin; and so death passed upon all men, for that all have sinned* (Romans 5:12, KJV).

Bancroft continues, "What theologians call the doctrine of 'original sin,' by which they mean that the results of Adam's sin, both legal and moral, have been transmitted to Adam's posterity, so that now each individual comes into the world as the inheritor of a nature that has been disempowered by sin.... Whether affirmed or contradicted by modern thought, the doctrine of Scripture shines like a sunbeam, that man is *conceived in sin and shaped in iniquity* (Psalm 51:5), that children are *estranged from the womb and go astray* (Psalm 58:3), that all are by nature *children of wrath* (Ephesians 2:3), that *the imagination of man's heart is evil from his youth* (Genesis 8:21), and that everyone requires to have *a clean heart* created in him (Psalm 51:10), since *that which is born of the flesh is flesh* (John 3:6), and *no man can bring a clean thing out of an unclean thing* (Job 15:14).

"If these passages do not show that the Bible teaches the doctrine of original, or transmitted and inherited sin, it is difficult to see in what clearer or more emphatic language the doctrine could have been taught. The truth of the doctrine may be challenged by those who repudiate the authority of Scripture; that it is a doctrine of Scripture can hardly be denied."[20]

A graphic view of man's fall from grace, the resulting human condition and God's redemptive process in the person of Jesus Christ is illustrated in Appendix A-1.

C.S. Lewis addressed the issue in his usual concise fashion: "The human spirit from being the master of human nature...had turned from God and become its own idol, so that though it could still turn back to God, it could do so only by painful effort, and its inclination was self-ward. Hence pride and ambition, the desire to be lovely in its own eyes and to depress and humiliate all rivals, envy, and restless search for more, and still more security, were now the attitudes that came easiest to it. It was not only a weak king over its own nature, but a bad one: it sent down into the psychophysical organism desires far worse than the organism sent up into it. This condition was transmitted by heredity to all later generations, for it was not simply what biologists call an acquired variation; it was the emergence of a new kind of man—a new species, never made by God, had sinned itself into existence. The change which man had undergone was not parallel to the development of a new habit; it was a radical alteration of his constitution, a disturbance of the relations between his component parts, and an internal perversion of one of them."21

Rogers' belief "that man is able to determine what is good for man, what is right and wrong," is contrary to Scripture. It is our opinion that Christian counseling, by definition, involves teaching and instruction. If this is true, then Rogers' view that we're to avoid instructing the client would be in conflict with what we consider to be the Christ-centered approach to therapy. Most people enter therapy seeking answers to their problems—answers that are based on truth rather the therapist's opinion. It is in God's word and the teaching and conviction of the Holy Spirit that truth is revealed. Truth for a Christian is the vehicle by which we define reality.

The Christian therapist is called to instruct and lead the client into the truth found in Scripture that will lead them out of their present problems and into the soundness of mind and heart that is received and trusted in cooperation with the indwelling Spirit of truth, joy and peace.

We would agree with Rogers that truth "discovered" has more of an impact than truth intellectually reasoned. As Christians, however, we would be prone to leave the uncovering of healing truth to the revelatory powers of God than to the inventions and often fatalistic discoveries of a person distressed by the pain and heartache of life.

Finally, we would like to address Roger's belief that, as individuals, we instinctively value positive regard, which includes concepts such as love, affection, attention and nurturing and that we tend to learn the value of positive regard through relationships with others. From this, he concludes that the relationship between therapist and client must be centered around the therapist's showing favor toward the client so that self-esteem, self-worth and self-image can be fostered. Rogers was so convinced that the therapist's ability to be empathetic was crucial for a positive outcome in therapy that it became a centerpiece for his theory.

We would certainly agree with Rogers that the relationship between client and therapist works best when there is mutual respect, positive regard and developing trust. However, it does not necessarily follow, as Rogers suggests, that this will automatically lead to success in therapy. We find that, in many cases, negative self-esteem and value are so deeply embedded in the client that it doesn't matter what the therapist thinks or feels about the client. The client knows the truth about himself, as do we all.

Further, assisting a client in building positive

regard based upon the therapist's relationship with him only makes the client more dependent on the therapist. This may make the client feel better about himself for a brief period of time, but those positive feelings often disintegrate when the client is forced to face the real world. Positive regard built on the opinions of others only serves to strengthen what the apostle Paul referred to as the flesh.

In Appendix A-2, A-3, and A-4 we outline the concept that man is composed of three parts—the body, soul and spirit. The flesh resides in the body and soul, affecting one's physical urges and one's ability to think, feel and make decisions that are healthy. We noted in the Appendix A series that the soul often cooperates with the power of sin working in the individual, and is in constant battle with one's spirit— which for the Christian is indwelt and empowered by God's Holy Spirit.

The flesh in a Christian attempts to develop a self-identity or self-image which is not centered around the believer's true identity in Christ but around one's self-interests. As this progresses in one's life, the Christian becomes tied to a false identity. He or she is living according to the flesh (Romans 8:1-17). The flesh, then, is all that we are apart from Christ as we function in self-sufficiency. The individual operates out of his own resources and does things his own way for his own ultimate benefit.

When we think of the battle that goes on between flesh and spirit, we usually think of the negative aspects of the flesh, or what we would call negatively programmed flesh. This is what most people come into therapy with—a flesh condition that is beating them down and causing them to feel anxious, worthless, incompetent, unloved, hopeless and unacceptable. When a person's will chooses to depend on his flesh, it always leads to self-sufficiency and distorts his view of God, self and others. When the client depends upon his or her own strength (the flesh) to cope with present pressures and past rejections, the result is ultimate conflict and frustration. This can lead to stress-related health problems, self-pity, withdrawal, performing for others, a need for control and anger.

In addition to negatively programmed flesh, many people go into therapy with a positively programmed flesh. This is a desire and need to appear strong, worthy, confident, secure, significant and successful. When the client depends on his or her own strength to meet these needs, pride, self-righteousness and judgmentalism can result. Positively programmed flesh causes the client to depend on himself and creates a distorted view of God, self and others just as strongly as does negatively programmed flesh.

As the therapist assists the client in developing a stronger positive regard, he or she may very well be encouraging the client to grow in his or her own strength or become dependent on others for that strength. Self-sufficiency, performance and independence from God are the by-products of positively programmed flesh. Positive regard may very well continue to foster these by-products rather than teaching the client to rely on Christ's sufficiency, his grace, mercy and dependence upon him.

Rogers stated that, "When I accept myself just as I am, then I can change." In reality, when a person accepts himself as God sees him, then lasting change can take place. Living in the flesh leads to death. Living in the Spirit leads to life. *I have come that they may have life, and that they may have it more abundantly* (John 10:10).

Chapter Two

Gestalt Therapy

An attempt to grasp the concepts behind gestalt therapy must begin with definitions. According to the Merriam-Webster online dictionary the definitions of gestalt, existential and phenomenology are as follows:

Gestalt—A structure, configuration, or pattern of physical, biological, or psychological phenomena so integrated as to constitute a functional unit with properties not derivable by summation of its parts.

Existential—Grounded in existence or the experience of existence;...having being in time and space.

Phenomenology—A philosophical movement describing the formal structure of the objects of awareness and awareness itself in abstract from claims concerning existence.

Defining these three terms can lead to more questions than answers. And generally speaking, much that has been written about gestalt methods and beliefs will leave the reader with vague insights to these answers but struggling to grasp the whole. An irony to be sure.

As with all disciplines there are numerous books. Websites, articles and stories abound. We have drawn from many of these sources to offer a brief, yet thorough, examination of their composite views.

We begin with this from Gerald Corey. "Gestalt therapy, developed by Fritz Perls and his wife, Laura, in the 1940s, is an existential/phenomenological approach based on the premise that individuals must be understood in the context of their ongoing relationship with the environment. The initial goal is for the clients to gain awareness of what they are experiencing and doing. Through this awareness, change automatically occurs. The approach is phenomenological because it is grounded in the notion that people are always in the process of becoming, remaking, and rediscovering themselves."[1]

Although nearly every definition of the term *existential* is general in its scope, the application to therapy does take on new meaning. Simkin and Yontef, common names in gestalt circles, help us to further define our terms. "The existential view of humankind is that people are endlessly remaking or discovering themselves. There is no essence to be discovered 'once and for all.' There are always new horizons, new problems, and new opportunities. Any concept of the absolute 'nature of man' is put in brackets. People operate in an unstated context of conventional thought that obscures or avoids acknowledging how the world is.... This, as a self-deception, creates such feelings as dread, guilt or anxiety. This self-deception is the basis of living inauthentically; it is not based on the truth of oneself in the world. Gestalt therapy provides a way of living authentically aware,...able to choose and organize one's existence in a meaningful manner."[2]

Fritz Perls was considered an enigma to those outside the world of gestalt. He was a paradox unto himself and not only brought new and questionable views to therapy circles, but accentuated those views with a personal approach for the therapist that quickly drew strong boundary lines throughout the counseling community. Corey offers the following: "Personally, Perls was both vital and perplexing. People typically either responded to him in awe or found him harshly confrontive and saw him as meeting his own needs through showmanship.... He was viewed variously as insightful, witty, bright, provocative, manipulative, hostile, demanding, and inspirational. Unfortunately, some of the people who attended his workshops became followers of the "guru" and went out to spread the gospel of Gestalt therapy."[3]

Susan X. Day gives us this insight into Perl's personality and history: "One of Fritz Perls's principal biographers described him as 'a bastard and a saint,' and by many accounts, it was an apt description.... As early as elementary school, he was characterized as a gifted but difficult student.... He pursued a degree in medicine...graduated in 1921 and practiced in Berlin as a neurophychiatrist.... In 1926 he went to Frankfurt and worked at the Institute for Brain Damaged Soldiers [and] met and married Laura Posner, a graduate student of Gestalt psychology.... In 1933 [they] fled Nazi Germany for Amsterdam [and] soon located to South Africa. There, the Perlses successfully established themselves as psychoanalysts, and later embarked on a trip to Vienna with the express purpose of meeting and aligning with Freud. [H]is visit with the declining Freud lasted only a few minutes and Perls left bitterly disappointed."[4]

As we look at the Perls philosophy, and attempt to hold it up to our own Christian beliefs on the nature of man and the driving force behind man's dilemma during his time on this planet, it should be no surprise that Perls had roots in some of the Eastern philosophical views. Hersen and Gross address this: "Frederick Perls [was] familiar with Eastern philosophy and principles of Taoism and Zen Buddhism, which is seen in Gestalt therapy's attention to what is rather than what should be, the importance of awareness, and the focus on the here-and-now."5

The authors add: "While the term gestalt itself has no direct translation into English, it is generally translated as configuration, structure, or whole.... The goal in Gestalt therapy is increased awareness and expanded experience of self."6

Gestaltists are quick to point out that students of counseling must first recognize the difference between gestalt therapy and gestalt psychology. The therapy is only a derivative of the psychology, as Les Parrott writes: "Gestalt therapy is built...on a theory of perception known as Gestalt psychology, which has proposed the radical hypothesis that the whole is psychologically greater than the sum of its parts. It maintains that psychological phenomena can be understood, not when broken down into primitive perceptual elements, but only when viewed as organized, structured wholes.... Even the stars in the sky are grouped into wholes, into constellations such as the Big Dipper and the Southern Cross, not simply because we enjoy painting pictures in the night sky, but because we possess this fundamental need to make things whole."7

Perl's wife Laura even expressed her disagreements with the very term gestalt. As Susan X. Day explains, "Laura Perls objected to the label Gestalt.... Why would she object? Laura Perls and others...don't see the direct connection between Gestalt psychology, which has to do with perception and cognition, and

Gestalt therapy, which deals with personality, psychopathology, and counseling."[8]

Organizing Principles

To recognize some of the basic principles behind Gestalt theory, one must first examine how the principles, or what many refer to as the gestalt laws, apply to the umbrella concepts. The Wikipedia posting on Perls gives us a glimpse of how those laws operate: "There are many organizing principles called gestalt laws. The most general version is called the law of pragnanz...in the sense of pregnant with meaning.... that we are innately driven to experience things in as good a gestalt as possible. 'Good' can mean many things here, such as regular, orderly, simplicity, symmetry, and so on, which then refer to specific laws. For example, a set of dots outlining the shape of a star is likely to be perceived as a star, not as a set of dots. We tend to complete the figure, make it the way it 'should' be, finish it.... The law of closure says that, if something is missing in an otherwise complete figure, we will tend to add it. A triangle, for example, with a small part of its edge missing, will still be seen as a triangle. We will 'close' the gap. See Appendix B-1. The law of similarity says we tend to group similar items together to see them as forming a gestalt, within a larger form."[9]

The following offers a few simple typographic examples taken from the same publication.

```
0 X X X X X
X 0 X X X X
X X 0 X X X
X X X 0 X X
X X X X 0 X
X X X X X 0
```

It is natural for us to see the o's as a line within the field of x's. Another law is the law of proximity. Things that are close together are seen as belonging together. For example:

```
* * * * * * * * *
* * * * * * * * *
* * * * * * * * *
```

This example clearly shows us that we are much more likely to see three lines of close-together *'s than ten vertical collections of three *'s each. Next we see an example of what is termed the law of symmetry:

[ ] [ ] [ ]

Despite the pressure of proximity to group the brackets nearest each other together, symmetry overwhelms our perception and makes us see them as pairs of symmetrical brackets.[10]

We can begin to see how Perls envisioned and developed his theories and the importance of a person's relationship with, and response to, their uniquely personal environment. Parrott breaks this into meaningful stages: "Perls believed that people develop in relation to their environment. During the earliest, the social stage, the infant depends upon others for nearly everything...an awareness of others but little awareness of self. During the psychophysical stage, we become more aware of what is self and what is nonself...the self and self-image develop through the process of adaptation, acknowledgment, and support.... In sum, the Gestalt view of human nature, which is further influenced by Eastern philosophy, is existential and humanistic."[11]

Problems Stemming from Human Nature

Perls was certainly correct when he addressed the fact that the foundation of a person's basic problems stem from human nature itself and the inherent lack of completion and wholeness that humans experience from birth. Corey explains: "Fritz Perls's conception of human nature is that clients are manipulative and avoid self-reliance and responsibility. Given this basic assumption, the Gestalt therapist's function is to confront and frustrate the client's escape from responsibility. A basic assumption...is that individuals have the capacity to 'self-regulate.' The more we attempt to be who or what we are not, the more we remain the same. [W]e change when we become aware of what we are as opposed to trying to become what we are not."[12]

Susan X. Day adds another insight. "According to Gestalt psychotherapy, people have problems because they are cut off from parts of themselves that they need for wholeness, integration, and balance. They may be alienated from their own feelings, their bodies, or other people. It is human nature to be whole, but life experience teaches us to fragment ourselves because some parts are unacceptable and will be punished.... The requirements of polite and productive society include continual suppression of parts of ourselves.... In Gestalt thought, when people are successful at cutting needs and feelings out of awareness automatically, they become rigid, confined, and stuck in unfulfilling habits. These habits can control behavior and thoughts.... Gestalt therapy consists of reintegrating split-off parts of the self and the world."[13]

Gestalt Therapy

Bringing the definitions and thoughts that accompany

the terms gestalt, existential and phenomenology into a therapy approach requires insight into how all of this relates to what a person is experiencing at a particular moment and how that experience relates to the circumstances and environment that are described as now—not past, not future but now. Helping us move this theory into some form of practical application brings us to a central theme in gestalt therapy—awareness. As Parrott writes, "Gestalt therapists believe that we are a composite whole made up of interrelated parts, none of which—body, emotions, thoughts, sensations, and perceptions—can be understood outside the context of the whole person. At the same time, we are also part of our own environment and cannot be understood apart from it. The implication is that we are creatures of our environment, and that as such, we are neither 'good' or 'bad.' Gestaltists further believe we have the potential to be fully aware of all sensations, thoughts, emotions, and perceptions, and we are capable of making choices because of this awareness. Only then will we have the capacity to govern our own lives effectively, to choose how to respond to external and internal stimuli, for instance, so that we are acting on our world rather than reacting to it. Counselors trained in Gestalt therapy also believe that we cannot truly experience the past and the future; we can only experience ourselves in the present."[14]

In their book on modern therapies, Virginia and

Arnold Binder, along with Bernard Rimland, help us to equate how awareness is essential as a primary form of experiencing the moment, the now. *Awareness is a form of experiencing. It is the process of being in vigilant contact with the most important event in the individual/environmental field with full sensorimotor, emotional, cognitive, and energetic support.... Owning [is] the process of knowing one's control over, choice of, responsibility for one's own behavior and feelings (lit. ability to respond, to be the primary agent in determining one's own behavior). Without this the person may be vigilant to his own experience and life space, but not to what power he has and what he does not have.*"[15]

Susan X. Day helps us to bring a practical understanding to the gestalt philosophy with a quote from another text written by Clarkson and Mackewn. She notes, "Awareness is 'the capacity to be in touch with your own existence, to notice what is happening around or inside you, to connect with the environment, other people and yourself; to know what you are feeling or sensing or thinking; how you are reacting at this very moment.'"[16]

Boundary Disturbances

Delving further into the practical application of the

gestalt therapy paradigms we find a series of processes that help to describe the methods a person might use to color, or even alter, their personal perception of healthy boundaries as they relate to others and their own circumstantial environment.

Individuals are often closed to inner awareness or live in a world where they have developed a distorted view of their needs and emotions. In that process they develop barriers to an awareness that is healthy, often acting in line with the rules of behavior that they have learned. For example, Perls felt that a person who is nearly always in agreement with those around him or her is being disrespectful to themselves, their personal interests and views. These become distorted views of their own healthy boundaries. These are referred to as boundary disturbances or interruptions of contact. Five of those processes are well addressed by Hersen and Gross, and by Susan X. Day as noted:

Introjecting

Hersen/Gross—[Involves] erroneously experiencing something from the environment as if it is part of the self.... Introjecting may become a person's way of dealing with the world and relationships.... Early introjects can be destructive as parental messages like, "You are worthless."

Day—Taking in others' views and values to the point where they seem like your own.

Projecting

Hersen/Gross—[D]isowning a feeling, behavior, attitude, or trait of one's own and attributing it to another or the environment. [A] person who is not able to be angry...may inaccurately perceive another person as angry at him or her.

Day—Assigning undesired parts of yourself to others, especially when you feel guilty or angry. If it seems that everyone else is obsessed with material success, for example, you may yourself harbor a guilty wish for wealth.

Retroflecting

Hersen/Gross—[This] describes energy that would naturally move into action or expression being contained and held in so that the action or expression is prevented. [The] feelings that would be directed toward another person may circle back and be directed toward oneself.... A classic example is a person in an abusive relationship who feels he or she is to blame for the abuse.

Day—Directing an action or thought toward yourself rather than toward others.... If you usually assuage negative feelings by eating comfort food rather than by asking your friends to comfort you, you may be engaging in retroflection.

Confluence

Hersen/Gross—The attempt to deny existence of the self/environment boundary.... A person who is generally confluent may talk in terms of "we" excessively, go along with others, or agree with everything others say—a chameleon personality.

Day—Agreeing in opinion and feeling with someone else to the point where the boundary between you is blurry.... A healthy course is to delight in the differences that keep the relationship interesting.

Deflecting

Hersen/Gross—[B]ehavior that dilutes or reduces the intensity of contact. Examples are avoiding eye contact, laughing off what one says, circumlocution, and understating one's true feelings.

Day—Turning aside direct contact with another person or...you sometimes deflect conversation away from a highly charged topic onto a milder one, or deflect attention away from yourself onto another person or topic.[17]

The Goal of Gestalt Therapy

Among the many unique beliefs that Perls brought to the profession are those centered around the role of the therapist. Perls felt strongly that the therapist/patient relationship should be perceived as a critical part of successful therapy. Day writes, "The person of the therapist is paramount in Gestalt practice.... Perls believed that clients should get in-the-moment feedback from counselors, so that they realize how they are viewed by mature others. Thus, Perls would encourage the counselor to act bored, irritated, or impatient if that's the way he or she felt. In flagrant violation of some dearly held therapeutic rules, Perls even fell asleep while clients talked."[18]

Simkin and Yontef address the importance of process over content in the therapist role: "The goal is for clients to become aware of what they are doing, how they are doing it and, at the same time, to learn to accept and esteem themselves.... Gestalt therapy focuses on process (what is happening) rather than content (what is being discussed). Process refers to the observable development of behavior that occurs during the therapy hour. The emphasis is on what is, rather than on what was, might be, could be or should be.... The objective of Gestalt phenomenological exploration is awareness or insight. Insight is the patterning of the perceptual field in such a way that the significant realities are apparent; it is the formation of a gestalt in which the relevant factors fall into place with respect to the whole."[19]

There are certain principles that pertain to perception and cognition in gestalt thinking. Often graphic illustrations are used to help the student or client see what is meant by the variable in experience and perception. See Appendix B-2 for more on this.

Back to the Foundations

Having had a brief introduction into what Gestalt therapy is and touching on some of the rules and guidelines of the approach, let us now discuss other foundations that will assist us in bringing together the why and the what-for of gestalt thinking.

Hersen and Gross delve into the important role of *field theory*: "The Gestalt therapy method is guided by three philosophical foundations.... The first of these is field theory, a concept...that defines the field as a dynamic interrelated system in which every part influences every other part, so that nothing exists in isolation.... Perls insisted that an individual be understood in the context of an environment, and [that] the psychotherapist considers all elements of the field as the possible focus of therapeutic attention. That may include socioeconomic, political and cultural factors, and how they interact with and influence psychological issues.

"The second philosophical foundation is *phenomenology*. [This is] bracketing off preconceived biases, theories, and interpretations, and attending as much as possible to what is being experienced directly through the senses, unmediated by assessment and judgment. The therapist's task is to be with what is, and to describe what is observed, rather than explaining or interpreting.

"The third philosophical foundation is *dialogue*. [This] invites the therapist to be available for an 'I-Thou' way of relating that is nonhierarchical, and has the qualities of immediacy, directness, presence, and mutuality. [T]he therapist attempts to bring his or her genuineness and authenticity to the encounter,.... to engage honestly,.... to feel the patient's side of the relationship as well as his or her own, and to confirm, acknowledge, and see the other's whole being."[20]

Corey adds the following: "Field theory...is grounded on the principle that the organism must be seen in its environment, or in its context, as part of the constantly changing field. [E]verything is relational....

All of nature is seen as a unified and coherent whole, and the whole is different from the sum of its parts.... Gestalt practice attends to a client's thoughts, feelings, behaviors, body, and dreams. The emphasis is on integration, how the parts fit together, and how the individual makes contact with the environment.... The present is the most significant tense in Gestalt therapy."[21]

Simkin and Yontef provide additional insight: "Field theory is a method of exploring that describes the whole field of which the event is currently a part...a whole in which the parts are in immediate relationship and responsive to each other and no part is uninfluenced by what goes on elsewhere in the field.... The person in his or her life space constitutes a field."[22]

Hersen and Gross offer this example to help draw the concept into greater focus: "Humans do not passively perceive objective external reality, but rather that we are active organizers of perception. Two of the laws of perception [are] the natural tendency to: 1) perceive a figure against a background, and 2) to complete a figure or gestalt—[in order] to achieve closure.... If you are hungry you might enter a room and walk right past a beautiful flower arrangement, only noticing the food set out on the table. Once you have eaten, that figure is closed, and you may then notice the flowers."[23]

Processes and Techniques

One of the word pictures that Perls observed invoked the image of peeling an onion, with each layer of the onion representing a different level of the client's makeup. Perls labeled each layer to clarify the process. Susan Day lists Perls' examples:

The phony layer—People...manipulate situations according to habit, and behave inauthentically in social settings.

The phobic layer—People feel fearful and helpless, but they keep the feelings hidden.

The impasse layer—People feel that they are stuck and often seek help, wanting someone else to take over and tell them what to do.

The implosive layer—It's at this level that the phony identity begins to collapse in upon itself. People feel that they are dead inside, or cut off from their former selves.

The explosive layer—Clinging to an inauthentic version of self takes up a lot of energy, and when that self is finally abandoned, the energy is quickly freed as though in a combustive reaction....[24]

It is worth noting that the impasse layer noted above is not uncommon in the therapy environment. Clients often perceive themselves at an impasse—or stuck in an area of their life that puts them beyond reach of their own ability to support and deal with the issues confronting them. The Gestalt therapist offers assistance by offering situations that help them to fully experience their condition of being stuck.

Gestalt therapy addresses the development of psychological issues from many different views, but always within the whole of the person's environment. The person can lose touch with the environment in one extreme, or can lose connection with self in the other extreme. The terms "top-dog" and "under-dog" are common terms that Perls used to identify the conflict between what a person thinks he should do (top-dog) and what the person wants to do (under-dog). Day writes that "The most important problems for Gestaltists are conflicts within the individual, such as those between top-dog and under-dog, or between the person's social self and natural self, or between the disowned parts of the person and the catastrophic expectations that keep the person from expressing polarities that may meet with disapproval or rejection.... Polarities within each of us include adult versus child, worried versus carefree, responsible versus wild, loving versus hateful, intellectual versus emotional, strong versus weak, generous versus stingy...minority versus mainstream...or lesbian versus straight.... If you are centered...you will be aware of which side needs attention (or expression) at the moment, and you will maintain homeostasis, which is balance or equilibrium.... In this way, we creatively adjust to inner and outer environments; we go with the flow.... The battle between top-dog and under-dog is Perls' substitute for the superego-id conflict imagined by Freud. The two dogs in our psyches represent warring polarities."[25]

In addition to these processes, there are more common techniques that are related to gestalt therapy. Two of these are role playing and the empty-chair technique. Day explains: "Role playing is an experiment in which the client or clients take on different perspectives and act them out in session. The goal is to resolve unfinished business and integrate polarities by arousing emotions, discovering needs, and shifting one's point of view.... Perls was inspired by many role-playing methods, including the empty-chair technique created by J.L. Moreno.... Two chairs are used, with each one assigned a character, attitude, emotion, or quality. The client moves back and forth between the two chairs, alternately speaking from the perspective of each."[26]

Day quotes from Perls himself as noted in *The Gestalt Approach* from 1973: "If the therapist were limited in his work only to asking three questions, he would eventually achieve success with all but the most seriously disturbed of his patients. These three questions...are 'What are you doing?' 'What do you feel?'

'What do you want?' We could increase the number by two, and include these questions: 'What do you avoid?' 'What do you expect?' All five of these are healthily supportive questions.... The patient can only answer them to the degree that his own awareness makes possible.... They give him a sense of self because they are directed to his self. His verbal answers to them may come from the intellect, but his total response...comes from his total person and is an indication of his total personality. Aside from the pat answers...there will nearly always be some additional reaction—a confusion, a hesitation...a shrug of the shoulder...a bit of embarrassment, a wish not to be bothered...an eager leaning forward, and so on. Each one of them is an indication of the self and of the patient's style.... Eventually there will be a click in the patient's awareness...the first big step he makes in therapy.... The therapist cannot make discoveries for the patient; he can only facilitate the process in the patient."[27]

The Direction of Change

After all the years since Perls moved gestalt thinking to a new level, opinion is still mixed on the practicality of the approach and the role of the therapist in the counseling process. The pros and cons are readily available in books and on the internet.

"People, according to Gestalt therapy, are responsible (response-able), that is, the primary agent in determining their own behavior. When people confuse responsibility with blaming and shoulds they pressure and manipulate themselves.... Gestalt therapy believes in the importance of a clear distinction between what one chooses and what is given. People are responsible for what they choose to do."[28]

In their book *Modern Therapies*, written in the 1970s, editors Binder and Rimland quote Beisser's work on Gestalt therapy: "Change occurs when one becomes what he is, not when he tries to become what he is not. Change does not take place through a coercive attempt by the individual or by another person to change him, but it does take place if one takes the time and effort to be what he is—to be fully invested in his current positions.... The Gestalt therapist rejects the role of 'changer'. [C]hange can occur when the patient abandons, at least for the moment, what he would like to become and attempts to be what he is."[29]

Among Gestaltists there is a consistent effort to work with the client on the present and existing experience. To avoid the immediate is to extract a key element from the integrity of both the counseling relationship and the counseling process. "In therapies in which the therapist undertakes to directly modify the patient's behavior, the immediate experience of the patient and therapist are not honored. This is what separates Gestalt therapy from most other therapies.... Beck...Ellis...and Glasser all try to modify the patient's irrational or irresponsible or unreal attitudes. They judge what is irrational.... In Gestalt therapy there are no 'shoulds.' Instead of emphasizing what should be, Gestalt therapy stresses awareness of what is. What is, is."[30]

This difference from Beck and Ellis largely centers on who the agent of change is in the client/therapist relationship: "Although many patients come to therapy to be changed, they do not want to make real changes themselves—they want the therapist to do it for them. They resist growth and invest energy in the failure of the therapist.... The problem is not that the patient manipulates his environment, but that he manipulates others to help him stay a cripple more comfortably.... In these new talk therapies the therapists still act as change agents, believing they know better than the patient how he should be.... All of this elevates the therapist at the expense of the patient.... The patient is thus not responsible for himself and cannot know himself, but rather has a disease or disability that the therapist will cure or eliminate.... GT involves a whole different framework; it is not just another talk therapy, another behavior therapy, or another encounter therapy. It is a new framework within which therapists have to create their own style of working. GT is more an attitude than a set of techniques."[31]

Many critics of the gestalt approach can't move beyond the personality of Perls himself and his view of the therapist role. Separating Perls from the therapeutic approach however is not easily achieved. Susan X. Day notes, "Many of the harshest criticisms of Gestalt psychotherapy are aimed at Fritz Perls himself. Perls was flamboyantly narcissistic and loved to shock people.... Perls's personality is not Gestalt psychotherapy."[32]

Others are troubled by the self-centered emphasis on both the client and the therapist as a model for therapeutic ethics. Parrott relates that aspect of the approach to timing and our culture in the early stages of its development. "It is a matter of intense debate as to whether or not Gestalt therapy is capable of leading to more responsible ethical and moral behavior in the larger social context. Since it is the view of Gestalt therapy that our wants and needs assume a position of absolute primacy, our accountability to others is inevitably of secondary importance. [S]elf-sufficiency is the preeminent virtue.... The turbulence of the late 1960s and the early 1970s, with the focus in these years on 'doing your own thing,' welcomed Gestalt therapy with open arms, and the approach was propelled into widespread recognition."[33]

The following is taken from a book published in 1984. The reference to Perls' prophecy as "three decades ago" could now be stated as nearly six decades ago. The statement still carries a degree of relativism to the impact of gestalt thinking in modern psychotherapy circles. "Fritz Perls prophesied three decades ago that Gestalt therapy would come into its own during the 1960s and become a significant force in psychotherapy during the 1970s. His prophecy has been more than fulfilled. In 1952, there were perhaps a dozen people seriously involved in the movement. In 1983 there were scores of training institutes, hundreds of psychotherapists who have been trained in Gestalt therapy, and many hundreds of nontrained or poorly trained persons who call themselves 'Gestaltists.' Thousands of people have been exposed to experiencing Gestalt Therapy—many with quite favorable results—others with questionable or poor outcomes."[34]

Suffice it to say there is a steady and ardent base of supporters for Gestalt therapy to include those who hold to Perls' foundational beliefs.

Corey states the basic goals of the therapy in a concise and orderly fashion: "The basic goal of Gestalt therapy is attaining awareness and, with it, greater choice.... Gestalt therapy is basically an existential encounter out of which clients tend to...

- Move toward increased awareness of themselves.
- Gradually assume ownership of their experience...to satisfy their needs without violating the rights of others

- Become more aware of all of their senses
- Learn to accept responsibility for what they do
- Move from outside support toward increasing internal support
- Be able to ask for and get help from others."[35]

Finally, this statement, also from Corey, regarding the agent of change in a counseling session since Gestalt therapy is inclined to dissuade therapists from teaching their clients, preferring the therapist help the client in learning the truth of their environment and actively moving toward self-discovery as well as the discovery of truth as it relates to what is. Corey suggests, "Why should therapy exclude giving information, making suggestions, cognitive processing, explanations, interpretations, and coaching on the therapist's part?"[36]

As a crowning touch to this controversial therapeutic approach, Parrott quotes Prochaska (1979) in a concluding exclamation of the purpose of the gestalt aim: "One of the most significant goals of Gestalt therapy is helping individuals assume responsibility for themselves rather than relying on others to make decisions for them. [T]he 'ideal outcome of Gestalt therapy, is the clients' discovery that they do not and never really did need a therapist.' "[37]

A Biblical Perspective

For the Christian therapist, Gestalt therapy is more than perplexing. Seldom will we find the mix of eastern thought, polarizing influences, atheistic bias, and a process of self absorption so prevalent.

The quote we used by Simkin and Yontef that Gestalt thinking must begin with "Any concept of the absolute 'nature of man' is put in brackets, is a vivid example."

As believers in the authority of God's word, we must go back to times prior to Perls and Gestalt to see that self-awareness is nothing new. Our first parents were the first to experience self: *She took of its fruit and ate. She also gave to her husband with her, and he ate. Then the eyes of both of them were opened* (Genesis 3:6-7). It doesn't take a great imagination to see that a major part of the results from eating of the tree of the knowledge of good and evil included a corrupt and polluted self-awareness.

As we look closely at the conflicts between gestalt theory and the Scriptures, it also becomes apparent that there are major conflicts between the views of Perls and many of the other contemporary theories of counseling. For example, the Perls habit of falling

Gestalt Therapy

asleep while clients talked would likely not meet with the approval of the therapist who leaned toward the Rogerian view of building a strong, personal, empathetic, client/therapist relationship.

Gestalt presses the client toward taking responsibility for feelings and behavior. There is a challenge to embrace the power to make life-changing choices and to exercise a rightful control over life processes. This is in contrast to Skinner, for example, who felt that choices were an exercise in futility and the results of life are determined by the experiences that come our way.

As Christian counselors, we must always place concepts and views under the light of biblical truth. One of the positive features of gestalt theory is the idea of having the client move from what they would like to become and accept what they are right now. Although the gestaltist has a different purpose in this, for Christians it is imperative that we embrace who we are as a child of the living God and a valuable part of the body of Christ. Laying that foundation of truth gives our clients a powerful tool in challenging the destructive beliefs that carry the guilt, shame and insecurities that become layers of the proverbial onion in a damaged belief system.

The Bondage of Self

In a biblical sense, self awareness can lead to bondage because of the power of the flesh and indwelling sin. Many theological commentators use the apostle Paul's statements in Romans 7 to show how this awareness can become so focused on self that it distorts the truth about the battle we face as believers in Christ.

It is worth repeating the passage of Scripture we referred from Romans 7. Note how often Paul refers to himself as he struggles with the law of sin in his life: *"For what I am doing, I do not understand. For what I will to do, that I do not practice; but what I hate, that I do. If, then, I do what I will not to do, I agree with the law that it is good. But now, it is no longer I who do it, but sin that dwells in me. For I know that in me (that is, in my flesh) nothing good dwells; for to will is present with me, but how to perform what is good I do not find. For the good that I will to do, I do not do; but the evil I will not to do, that I practice. Now if I do what I will not to do, it is no longer I who do it, but sin that dwells in me"* (Romans 7:15-20).

We find the apostle coming to grips with the futility of his own self life. In this case he is struggling in his flesh against the indwelling power of sin that is a law—operating 24/7 against his own desire to do things God's way. Over the course of five verses in the passage Paul uses "I," "me" or "my" twenty-four times.

Finally, moving past the personal guilt and failure associated with performance, he is relieved to humbly recognize that the battle against the power of sin in his life is only overcome by the indwelling Spirit. As one friend notes, "Paul is reduced to God!" His joyful realization can only be expressed with *"O unhappy and pitiable and wretched man that I am! Who will release and deliver me from [the shackles of] this body of death? O thank God! [He will!] through Jesus Christ (the Anointed One) our Lord!"* (Romans 7:24-25, AMP).

We find the same examples in the battles faced by the Israelites in the Old Testament. Whether our battles are physical or spiritual, the solution always rests in our jealous and protective God who has provided the resources necessary for our success. *"This is what the L*ORD *says to you: 'Do not be afraid or discouraged. [T]he battle is not yours, but God's.... You will not have to fight this battle. [S]tand firm and see the deliverance the L*ORD *will give you. [D]o not be discouraged. [T]he L*ORD *will be with you'"* (2 Chronicles 20:15-17, NIV).

Who is the agent of change in Christian counseling? It is the indwelling power given to God's children in the person of his Holy Spirit. As counselors, we are dependent on this. The client must be taught that God is worthy of our trust. We must all learn to trust in, and rely on God's person and power.

Living Out our True Identity

It is worth repeating, and adding our comments to the notes from Beisser's work on Gestalt therapy referred to earlier and referenced in Note 29 of this chapter. Beisser wrote, "Change occurs when one becomes what he is, not when he tries to become what he is not. Change does not take place through a coercive attempt by the individual or by another person to change him, but it does take place if one takes the time and effort to be what he is—to be fully invested in his current positions.... The Gestalt therapist rejects the role of 'changer'. [C]hange can occur when the patient abandons, at least for the moment, what he would like to become and attempts to be what he is."

For the Christian, this statment should be seen as a powerful exclamation point to highlight the importance of understanding who we are *in Christ,* and how to make that true identity a part of our daily living and world view. The Apostle Paul stated, *For me to live is Christ [His life in me]* (Philippians 1:21 Amp). By faith we are called to trust in the fact that the very life of Christ not only indwells us, but is in fact the essence of our spiritual identity. Paul made a similar statement in another letter to the church: *For you died to this life, and your real life is hidden with Christ in God. And when Christ, who is your life, is revealed to the whole world, you will share in all his glory* (Colossians 3:3-4 NLT). Believers, of all people, must abandon what we would like to become in the sense of becoming a "good Christian," and we must learn to be and live based on who we already are according to God's word. *But you are a chosen people, a royal priesthood, a holy nation, God's special possession, that you may declare the praises of him who called you out of darkness into his wonderful light* (1 Peter 2:9 NIV).

Proper Boundaries

The student of gestalt thinking can often recognize the view that there are times when a clear need requires the establishment of boundaries for certain clients. Although the gestalt purist does not take the position of teacher, there can be suggestions that certain here and now emotions or behaviors are a result of the lack of proper boundaries in important relationships.

Can the effective Christian counselor teach the need for boundaries. Yes! Many of the issues we see in marriage counseling, for example, are a direct result of the lack of boundaries on the part of one, or both, of the clients. Often the need for boundaries on the part of one person is triggered by dominant control violations in another person. See Appendix B-3 for an example of how boundaries can be addressed in relationships.

Many who enter counseling are in a pattern which they cannot, or will not, break. Dr. Bill Gillam, a psychologist in Fort Worth, Texas, believes that most clients are emotionally "stuck." He feels that life experiences from childhood on can disable a person from moving on in their emotional maturity. Until they work through some of their disabling belief systems they cannot develop a healthy paradigm for meaningful relationships.

Working through the bondage of those beliefs can indeed be like peeling an onion, one layer at a time.

As Christian counselors, teachers and disciplers in the body of Christ and the family of God, we can never lose sight of the fall of mankind that brought us the human condition. We urge our readers to read through Appendix B-4 to refresh their understanding of God's simple plan of faith that leads to our freedom from the past.

Chapter Three

Cognitive Therapy

In our chapter on rational emotive behavioral therapy (REBT) we discuss the call for Christians to renew our minds. This biblical challenge gives us the responsibility of changing the way we feel and act by changing how we think, learning to tell ourselves the truth, especially when it comes to identity and self-worth. Our diagram in that chapter indicates how incorrect thinking can lead to negative emotions and cause destructive behavior.

Responsible for the early concepts of cognitive therapy (CT) and still very much active in the development and study of the theory is Aaron T. Beck. Beck's theory falls into the same model as Albert Ellis' REBT since the primary goal of both is to change the beliefs that psychologically cause dysfunction in the lives of people. Both men felt the best way to help clients move out of negative emotions and behavior was to help them modify their flawed belief systems.

Beck was born in Providence, Rhode Island, the youngest of five children born to Russian immigrants who were very devoted to their Jewish religion. Putting himself through college he earned degrees in English and political science. He earned his doctorate in psychiatry from Yale Medical School. Nancy Murdock writes, "After flirting with a career in neurology, he turned his attention to psychiatry and was classically trained as a psychoanalyst. Early in his career Beck was engaged in the science of psychotherapy, attempting to test Freud's hypothesis that depression was anger turned inward. Instead he found that depressed individuals sought the approval of others."[1]

Beck's career includes serving as a neuropsychiatrist at Valley Forge Army Hospital and a lengthy career at the University of Pennsylvania Department of Psychiatry. He is a senior member of the Institute of Medicine of the National Academy of Sciences, and, with his daughter Judith S. Beck, Ph.D., serves at the Beck Institute for Cognitive Therapy and Research. For more information on Dr. Beck, please see www.beckinstitute.org and www.academyofct.org.

Like Ellis, Beck was trained in psychoanalysis but was soon discouraged as he began to track results with clients suffering from depression. He found that when he began to uncover his client's gloomy view of themselves and their world and helped them to think in a more truthful way, their response was to feel better emotionally which triggered better behavior. Beck became convinced that true psychological change could be achieved by correcting faulty core beliefs.

What Is Cognitive Therapy?

In many ways the concept behind cognitive therapy is not new. As editor Jay L. Lebow noted in his work on contemporary approaches to theory, "The Stoics have been a major inspiration for rational emotive behavioral therapy and cognitive therapy with their emphasis on the connection between interpretation and emotional pain or distress. As Epicetetus wrote, 'People are not disturbed by things, but by the view they take of them' (quoted in Ellis, 2005, p. 171). Marcus Aurelius affirmed, 'If thou are pained by any external thing, it is not this thing that disturbs thee, but thine own judgment about it. And it is in thy power to wipe out this judgment now' (quoted in Bedrosian & Beck, 1980, p. 127). These ancient words are still at the core of contemporary cognitive therapy."[2]

A more contemporary and clarifying description of cognitive therapy can best be portrayed by Beck himself: "Cognitive therapy is one of the few forms of psychotherapy that has been scientifically tested and found to be effective in over three hundred clinical trials for many different disorders. In contrast to other forms of psychotherapy, cognitive therapy is usually more focused on the present, more time-limited, and more problem-solving oriented. Indeed, much of what the patient does is centered around solving current problems. In addition, patients learn specific skills that they can use for the rest of their lives. These skills involve identifying distorted thinking, modifying beliefs, relating to others in different ways, and changing behaviors."[3]

In explaining some of the theory behind the cognitive approach Beck continues, "The way we perceive situations influences how we feel emotionally. When people are in distress, they often do not think clearly and their thoughts are distorted in some way. Cognitive therapy helps people to identify their distressing thoughts and to evaluate how realistic the thoughts are. Then they learn to change their distorted thinking. When they think more realistically, they feel better."[4]

There are, of course, many who disagree with Beck and cognitive therapy as a viable psychotherapy. Murdock notes that "Psychoanalytic folk tend to dismiss CT as surface oriented, dealing with symptoms rather than the important issues.... A common criticism of CT is that it is too simple and mechanistic."[5]

Murdock goes on to point out, however, that many

behaviorists have altered their views. "[I]n a recent survey 69% of the members of the American Association of Behavior Therapy reported that they use cognitive techniques (Craighead, 1990).... Cognitive therapy is perhaps the most well-researched counseling approach in existence, with an overwhelming amount of empirical support for its effectiveness with a variety of client problems."[6]

In their book on counseling and psychotherapy, David and Diane Sue note that Beck, in supporting his view that certain innate factors make certain individuals prone to depression writes, "Emotional behaviors such as shyness, anxiety, fear, or other emotional qualities observed in a child often persist into adulthood. These tendencies or vulnerabilities can become strengthened or weakened during interaction with experiences or environmental conditions.... For example, some individuals may be predisposed to respond to common childhood rejection experiences with intense emotion and 'catastrophic beliefs' regarding the events. They may develop a negative self-image and believe they are unlovable. If repeated exposure to rejection during a vulnerable childhood period occurs, the beliefs may be structuralized into a schema, a pattern of thinking or believing."[7]

Is Cognitive Therapy the Same as Rational Emotive Bahavior Therapy?

In reading the later chapter on Rational Emotive Behavior Therapy the reader might be inclined to question the differences in theory between Ellis and Beck. Lebow addresses that issue in concise fashion: "There are a number of differences between Beck and Ellis.... Ellis' approach is fundamentally a philosophical one; a person's suffering decreases as he or she develops a different life perspective. This philosophy led him to a more educative treatment approach in which teaching his humanistic philosophy was central. Beck, in turn, is connected to science.... In a therapy setting, he would not directly challenge a problematic belief, as Ellis might; instead, he would explore the full ramifications of the thought and might work with the patient to develop experiments to gather evidence that would support or refute the validity and the usefulness of the belief. A second way the two differ is that Ellis believed that a core principle of demandingness, in the form of shoulds and musts, underlies most or all psychopathology. Ellis emphasized universal principles rather than making a direct connection between specific thought profiles and specific disorders, as Beck did."[8]

Although there are many similarities in the two men's theories, there are fundamental differences in the way they relate and interface with their patients. Gerald Corey points out, "REBT is often highly directive, persuasive, and confrontive; it also focuses on the teaching role of the therapist. In contrast, Beck uses a Socratic dialogue by posing open-ended questions to clients with the aim of getting clients to reflect on personal issues and arrive at their own conclusions. CT places more emphasis on helping clients discover their misconceptions for themselves and generally applies more structure than REBT.... Ellis views the therapist largely as a teacher and does not think that a warm personal relationship with clients is essential. In contrast, Beck (1987) emphasizes that the quality of the therapeutic relationship is basic to the application of cognitive therapy.... Cognitive therapists are continuously active and deliberately interactive with clients."[9]

Automatic Thoughts and Schema

In an interview with a journalist in the spring of 2008 which was reprinted in Beck's online newsletter *Cognitive Therapy Today*, in response to an inquiry about the origins of CT, Beck noted, "In the early 1960s, after numerous clinical observations regarding automatic thoughts and cognitive distortions...I noted that depressed people had many negative beliefs about themselves and their futures. This...shaped the way the individuals interpreted and distorted their experiences. It was these negative interpretations that led to sad feelings, social withdrawal, and especially, suicidal ideas. Modifying beliefs in therapy reduced or eliminated these distorted interpretations, and symptoms of depression similarly reduced or disappeared."[10]

In references to writings from Judith Beck, Ph.D., director of the Beck Institute and daughter of Aaron Beck, Nancy Murdock writes, "Automatic thoughts (ATs) are a normal feature of our cognitive process. They are swift, evaluative statements or images that exist alongside our more conscious thoughts. Automatic thoughts tend to occur in shorthand rather than in full sentence form and often seem to just pop up out of nowhere (hence their name). Depending on their content, these thoughts can be functional or distressing, but in either case, they tend to be reasonable to the thinker. Usually, we are not particularly aware of our automatic thoughts; we are more likely to be aware of the emotion associated with them. In reality, automatic thoughts are the result of our core and intermediate beliefs.... Specifically, clients' automatic thoughts, intermediate beliefs, and core schemas are associated with depression, anxiety, and a variety of other kinds of psychological dysfunction. Automatic thoughts are brief, telegraphic statements or images that are related to core beliefs or schemas."[11]

Although you will note the reference to core beliefs

in the above remarks, there is only brief mention of the more recent development of the term schema. However in most recent references to the term, this more contemporary or second-generation term is clearly paralleled with core beliefs. David and Diane Sue combined the terms, noting that "A schema, or core belief, is an underlying cognitive structure that allows individuals to automatically process information about themselves, others, and events. If an individual has a rejection schema, situations such as missing a bus, dealing with an unfriendly salesperson, or differences in opinion with a friend may be interpreted as signs of rejection. Incoming information is often distorted so that it can fit within a particular schema. Schema are not conscious, but can be identified through introspection and are similar to the irrational beliefs in rational emotive therapy."[12]

Beck himself seems to place an importance on schema drawing the parallel to core beliefs. An important focus of the therapy session involved the restructuring of the schema from what was considered faulty core beliefs to more normal and healthy beliefs. These faulty core beliefs would likely include the person's personal view of themselves, their family of origin and their childhood environment.

Leahy and Dowd in a section of their writing headed *The Role of Schemas* make reference to how Beck related schema to the characteristics of depression: "I have postulated the existence of structures (schemas) to account for the repetitiveness of the same type of thinking in a given individual with each recurrence of the depression and for the striking similarities of the nature of the thinking pattern from one depressed individual to another (Beck, 1963).... The schemas that are prepotent in depression seem to be relatively dormant when the depression is not present (Beck, 1967), although specific experiences of deprivation or defeat may activate them even during nondepressed periods. During depression the negatively toned schemas emerge from the predepressive personality of the patient."[13]

There seems to be general agreement that automatic thoughts are harbored between the conscious and the subconscious. There also seems to be a degree of consensus that the client must exert effort, often with the assistance of the therapist, to access these thoughts. Lebow offers a comprehensive interpretation that, when visualized, can offer a more complete picture of how the therapist might see the interactive process of events, automatic thoughts and schemas: "Automatic thoughts can be seen as occupying the top of a pillar in which the underlying assumptions (or 'if-then' propositions) are in the middle and the schemas constitute the foundation. These are not always thoughts and may take the form of images (A.T. Beck, 1987)..... As a vehicle of interpretation, patients' automatic thoughts filter the incoming information and determine the emotional and behavioral response."14

A Biblical Perspective

As we read through the volumes written on cognitive therapy we cannot miss the fact that healthy and rational thinking must have its foundation in truth if it is going to have an impact on the belief system of an individual struggling with faulty belief structures. Truth, of course, may have a very large degree of relativism when it reflects on circumstances or other people's motives. When it is dealing, however, with the identity, value and worth of a Christian it takes on new dimensions. In responding to the disciple Thomas' inquiry about knowing the way to where he was going, Jesus said, "I am the way, the truth, and the life. *No one comes to the Father except through Me* (John 14:6). This is one of the most profound verses in all of Scripture. Jesus didn't say he would show Thomas the way. He didn't say he would tell Thomas the truth. He didn't say he would take Thomas to a place with a better life. He said *he is* the way, *he is* the truth, *he is* the life, because he, being God incarnate, is the source of all three. He is the only way through which humanity has access to God the Father. He embodies all truth in that he is the manifestation of God's message to his people. He is eternal life. He is the great "I Am."

As we relate this to a healthy core belief system, we begin with the question "Can there be such a thing as absolute truth?"

Norm Geisler in his *Encyclopedia for Christian Apologetics* states, "The nature of truth is crucial to the Christian faith. Not only does Christianity claim there is absolute truth (truth for everyone, everywhere, at all times), but it insists that truth about the world (reality) is that which corresponds to the way things really are.... According to theories of relative truth, something may be true for one person, but not for all people. Or, it may be true at one time, but not at another. According to the absolutist view, what is true for one person is true for all persons, times, and places."[15]

Here is the critical point relating truth to core beliefs: Most of our lives are lived based on what we believe. We can confess our views, we can offer our opinions, but we live by what we believe.

There has always been an attack on truth—absolute truth. This is not new, although it may seem new to us in the twenty-first century. The Scriptures tell us that the world, the flesh and the devil are enemies of the truth: *You shall know the truth, and the*

Cognitive Therapy

truth shall make you free (John 8:32). The Christian therapist must learn to rely on the power of truth to effect core belief systems in a way that will bring freedom to the recipient. Although we must be careful to not allow formulas to become cure-alls, we can trust in biblical examples as guides to change faulty core beliefs. See Appendix C-1 to help visualize the following process:

1. Bondage to a faulty core belief can lead us down the path of—"I am unworthy to be loved."
2. Truth is presented—"You are deeply loved by God."
3. Trust is a choice I make to learn to rely on truth.
4. Obedience is my response by acting upon what I am learning to trust in.
5. Understanding is God's response by revelation to my response of trust and obey.
6. Freedom is the result that releases me from the faulty core belief and its bondage.

I pray that your hearts will be flooded with light so that you can understand the confident hope he has given to those he called—his holy people who are his rich and glorious inheritance (Ephesians 1:18, NLT).

Ellis and Beck seemed to grasp that only truth can effectively change a core belief. But we must be diligent in taking a firm stand on the absolute truth as presented in God's word. *A time is coming when people will no longer listen to sound and wholesome teaching. They will follow their own desires and will look for teachers who will tell them whatever their itching ears want to hear. They will reject the truth and chase after myths* (2 Timothy 4:3-4, NLT). One of the great myths in contemporary culture is that truth is relative—relative to circumstances, paradigms and perspectives. But let's consider what that kind of relative thinking suggests.

If you and I are facing one another across a desk and I place a pencil to my right on the desk and say to you, "Can you see the pencil I have placed on the right side of the desk?" You might respond, "No, the pencil is on the left side of the desk from my perspective." If you believe in relative truth you might conclude that both of us are correct.

But if we are seeking truth we must put the statement in the context of the one who makes it. By taking the person who made the statement out of the equation, truth becomes relative to anyone's view. This is precisely what the world tries to do with God's truth—take it out of the culture and make it relative to anyone's perspective.

John 3:19-21 says, *This is the crisis we're in: God-light streamed into the world, but men and women everywhere ran for the darkness. They went for the dark-*

Cognitive Therapy

ness because they were not really interested in pleasing God. Everyone who makes a practice of doing evil, addicted to denial and illusion, hates God-light and won't come near it, fearing a painful exposure. But anyone working and living in truth welcomes God-light so the work can be seen for the God-work it is (MSG).

We come back to the question, What is truth? Just as importantly, What is faith? Philosophers have argued for centuries about what truth is. The reason many can't decide what truth is, is because they don't like where the answer takes them. They're not ready for the answer for one reason—because of who said it. Pilate, in confronting Jesus, questioned truth: *Jesus answered, 'My kingdom is not of this world. If My kingdom were of this world, My servants would fight, so that I should not be delivered to the Jews; but now My kingdom is not from here.' Pilate therefore said to Him, 'Are You a king then?' Jesus answered, 'You say rightly that I am a king. For this cause I was born, and for this cause I have come into the world, that I should bear witness to the truth. Everyone who is of the truth hears My voice.' Pilate said to Him, 'What is truth?'* (John 18:36-38).

Pilate sarcastically implies that there is no such thing as absolute truth. (Sound familiar?) From Pilate's perspective, the context of "Who said it?" had no meaning in his life. His truth was relative to his circumstances.

For believers, God's Word is the truth that enables us to define reality. Without the absolute and established Word of God, we are reduced to the infinite and baseless views of philosophers and academics who are trapped in the endless irrationality that is a product of self love.

Bondage and Faulty Beliefs

Bondage is the result of patterns of thinking and belief systems that are carried over from our fallen nature, and it affects areas of our spiritual, mental, physical and emotional lives. Deception about God, self and others, generational ties, unresolved rebellion, guilt and shame are symptoms of bondage. We still tend to grasp and hold onto the things that the world has to offer. Being in bondage implies that we are blind to our sinfulness and impotent to change those things of which we are aware.

However, we no longer have to live in bondage, judging ourselves and others according to the natural tendencies that held us as slaves in our fallen nature. We now, as believers, have a new nature—one of perfect union with our heavenly Father, making it possible to judge ourselves and others according to how he sees us—perfected for all time.

Rebellion is an easily recognized product of bondage and describes the universal human inclination to willfully choose personal desires rather than the will of God. In Deuteronomy 30, we are commanded to choose life rather than death. As with Adam and Eve, this life and death issue is not only spiritual, but emotional and psychological. When we choose the world's ways over God's ways, spiritual death takes place. In the same manner, choosing the world over God causes an emotional and psychological death that breeds turmoil and unrest in our lives. Even though God wants us to have abundant life, we too often choose to follow our own choices and desires, largely in conflict with God's will.

The operative word here is choice. We often make willful decisions and follow them with certain behaviors or acts. If these behaviors are reinforced and rewarded, they develop into habits. As habits are reinforced and overlap, they develop into lifestyles of unconscious choices and perceived needs. At this point, they seem to develop a life of their own and become another layer of bondage. The force of habit begins to control us to the point that we are often unable to control our choices by simple acts of the will.

But God has given us his word, and by yielding to it, we can break the control that bondage and rebellion have over us.

Thoughts, Beliefs and the Heart

There are many views on the possible distinctions between thoughts, beliefs and the heart. Clearly the Scriptures teach us that the heart is closely tied to our core belief systems. *With the heart a person believes (adheres to, trusts in, and relies on Christ) and so is justified (declared righteous, acceptable to God), and with the mouth he confesses (declares openly and speaks out freely his faith) and confirms [his] salvation* (Romans 10:10, AMP).

A psychologist friend feels that when it comes to our identity, value and self-worth, truth and faith should be looked at only in the very uncomplicated perspective that truth is what God says, and faith is acting like God tells the truth. Faith is to move in trust in the same direction that the evidence is pointing. Faith is a choice we make without having all the proof we think we need.

The issue for the Christian becomes quite simple: How do we move from core beliefs that are faulty, ending in forms of destructive behavior to a renewed core belief system that is based on truth and results in constructive behavior? What is the process?

In Appendix C-2 we apply the illustration of an iceberg as an aid to presenting this process. An interesting aspect of icebergs is that, on average, only fifteen percent of it is actually above the waterline, leaving eighty-five percent of the iceberg below the waterline. Comparing that to a distressed client sitting in our office, we are faced with the fact that the cause of most of the problematic issues with which our client is dealing come from areas that are not only below the surface but are very, very deep below the surface. The originating cause of much of their turmoil is so deep that they are often beyond the client's awareness.

As you study the illustration, you can visualize the process of moving from the depths to the surface: false beliefs create lie-based thoughts which trigger unhealthy emotions, ending in destructive behavior.

The process of change begins with truth—God's truth about his people—our identity, our value and our worth. When we learn to believe God's truth about ourselves, our thought life begins to parallel what God says about us, and our emotions become healthy. Over time our behavior becomes constructive. *As he thinketh in his heart, so is he* (Proverbs 23:7, KJV).

There are some in CT, as with REBT and psychoanalysis, who lean toward the view that our behaviors are generally determined. Some would believe that even when we exercise the freedom of choice, that this freedom is an illusion, incompatible with freedom as we know it. Jones and Butman address this issue: "In none of the behavioristic conceptions of the person do we have true limited freedom. All of these models are thus 'dangerous' in that they propose a view of human persons in which we are mechanisms of some sort or another, beings which always do what they must do.... Such views demean our true nature and undermine our sense (which reflects reality) of our responsibility for our actions. Only a theistic view of persons that asserts that we are created for moral accountability has an adequate grounding for a full conception of limited freedom. Cognitive-behavioral therapy has a high view of the person's capacity for change through 'self-control' and related processes."[16]

Taking Charge

God has promised the believer spiritual, emotional and psychological freedom through an understanding and practice of the truth. The power of this freedom needed and often desired by the Christian is found within. As believers, we recognize the need for help in areas of our thought life, emotions, bodily cravings and desires. God's word challenges us to exercise the freedoms we have in each of these areas. *Fix your thoughts on what is true, and honorable, and right, and pure, and lovely, and admirable. Think about things that are excellent and worthy of praise. Keep putting into practice all you learned and received from me—everything you heard from me and saw me doing. Then the God of peace will be with you* (Philippians 4:8-9, NLT).

The believer is called and challenged to take charge of his/her thinking. The Bible has made it clear that there are four potential sources of wrong thoughts: the power of sin that is ever present, the flesh, the sinful world system and Satanic suggestion or accusation.

As believers we must learn to take charge of our thinking by refusing those thoughts that are triggered by the world, the flesh and the devil, and to aggressively choose to fix our thoughts on what is true. *You must put off falsehood and speak truthfully* (Ephesians 4:25, NIV). *You must rid yourselves of all such things as these: anger, rage, malice, slander, and filthy language from your lips* (Colossians 3:8, NIV). *Demolish arguments and every pretension that sets itself up against the knowledge of God, and take captive every thought to make it obedient to Christ* (2 Corinthians 10:5, NIV).

In the same way it is incorrect and ultimately destructive to accept feelings of hopelessness and despair and to act on those feelings or to allow a strong physical attraction to become an intent for action. The believer has no reason for hopelessness. We must reject hopelessness and affirm the truth of the Scriptures. *Count yourselves dead to sin but alive to God in Christ Jesus* (Romans 6:11, NIV).

Freedom is the power we are given through God's

grace and promise. This freedom, however, must be exercised through our beliefs and aggressive choices. *It is God who works in you to will and to act according to his good purpose* (Philippians 2:13).

Practical Applications

Many who trust in and use a cognitive approach in their therapy develop practical steps that can be applied to the therapeutic process for all Christians. As part of a practical track Lebow suggests:
- Defining the Terms—When patients describe themselves in negative ways... they may be asked to define what they mean when they say they are a "failure" and what they mean by "success."
- Examining the Evidence—to marshal all of the evidence that both supports and refutes a belief.
- Testing the Thoughts—Just because an individual holds a belief strongly does not mean that it is true.
- General Alternatives—Patients can be asked to generate alternative explanations or hypotheses.
- Positive Reframing—See if a positive meaning be made of a negative situation.

- Examining the Feared Fantasy—Examining fears...serves to reduce anxiety and to increase the sense of self-efficacy.[17]

Another practical approach for counselors is suggested by authors David and Diane Sue under the heading *Interventions and Probes*:

- Monitor their thoughts, especially as they relate to depressive feelings.
- Understand the connection between their thoughts, emotions and behaviors.
- Identify the underlying dysfunctional beliefs.
- Use scientific thinking by evaluating the evidence regarding connection between their negative thoughts and their mood.
- Change their thoughts. Substitute more realistic thoughts or interpretations.

The Sues include this definition, "[C]ognitive probes...involve having the client imagine that the upsetting event is currently occurring. They are then asked what they are thinking. This method is generally successful in uncovering the automatic thoughts."[18]

For the believer or unbeliever, automatic thoughts are spontaneous thoughts that enter the mind instantly, often triggered by a visual or mental stimulus or circumstance.

For example, when an authority figure seems to brush off a suggestion from his employee Jack, an automatic thought might flash across Jack's mind such as, "He couldn't care less about my ideas." At the bottom of this iceberg there may be a history of inadequacy, inferiority and insecurity. Those core beliefs immediately trigger the negative emotions of failure, weakness and anger. Over time Jack has developed a mentality that when he is not in total control in a relationship, he feels totally out of control in the relationship. Anger has become his learned behavior.

Karen walks into a room filled with people. She catches the eye of one or two friends across the crowded room. As she heads their way one turns to the other and in a whisper-like motion says something, and they both laugh. An automatic thought floods Karen's total being. A pattern of rejection throughout her childhood has programmed negative data into her core belief system. Acceptance and love are at issue here. "They're laughing at me. Is it my dress, my hair or being late? They have never really accepted me. What a loser I must be! Oh, there's my dumb neighbor. I'll just go talk to her."

For Jack and Karen, cognitive therapy could be helpful to distinguish disturbing thoughts and learn to evaluate how reasonable and realistic the thoughts are, especially as they relate to the truth God has given his children and how that truth should be applied to our views of personal value and worth.

Changing some of our deepest core beliefs and bringing them in line with God's Word will strongly impact our emotional strength and security, resulting in positive, constructive behavior. It all begins with our deepest core belief systems.

With the heart a person believes (adheres to, trusts in, and relies on Christ) (Romans 10:10, AMP).

Chapter Four

Behavior Therapy

Behavior Therapy is a treatment model that was researched and developed by a wide range of pioneers who believed that in order for therapy to be successful, it must focus on behavior rather than on feelings or cognitions. "Its philosophical roots can be found in the school of behaviorism, which states that psychological matters can be studied scientifically by observing overt behavior, without discussing internal mental states."[1]

Those who are proponents of behavior therapy would say that psychological and emotional problems originate with one's learning unadaptive behavioral methods as a way of problem solving. Behavior therapists believe that behavior is a response to stimulation. Therefore the goal of therapy is to modify one's unadaptive stimulus-response.

Because so many individuals play a part in the

development of *behaviorism*, it is very difficult to single out only one who is the primary contributor to the theory.

History

The cornerstone of behavior therapy is the beginnings of conditioning. This was initiated by Ivan Sechenov, who is known as the father of Russian physiology.

His hypothetical structure, developed about 1863, considered the functions of the brain in terms of the reflex arc, which had three components: sensory input, process and efferent outflow. Sechenov stated, "All behavior consisted of responses, with interactions of excitations and inhibitions operating at the central part of the reflex arc. Using this model, Russian scientist Ivan Pavlov embarked on a series of classical experiments with dogs who were conditioned to various stimuli. These experiments demonstrated many of the phenomena later to be extended to all types of learning. The translation into English of the works of Bekhterev and Pavlov in 1927 furnished the impetus for adoption of a behavioristic approach to the study of psychology in the United States."[2]

Generally speaking, behavior therapy was established in three specific points of origin. Joseph Wolpe, in South Africa, formed his approach for viewing behavioral problems. B.F. Skinner, Ogden Lindsley and Harry C. Solomon began their research in the early 1950s in the United States. S.J. Rachman and Hans Eysenck ran their research primarily in the United Kingdom. "Each had their own distinct approach to viewing behavior problems. Eysenck in particular viewed behavior problems as an interplay between personality characteristics, environment, and behavior. Skinner's group took more of an operant conditioning focus. The operant focus created a functional approach to assessment and interventions focused on contingency management such as the token economy and behavioral activation."[3]

Another point of view regarding the subject was developed by Pavlov, who was trained in biology and medicine and was a contemporary of Sigmund Freud. Pavlov was awarded the Nobel Prize for medicine in 1904 for his study of the digestive system of dogs. He became intrigued with his observation that a dog deprived of food began to salivate when his assistants who fed the dog walked into the room. From these studies he established the laws of *classical conditioning*, which was the first type of learning to be discovered and studied within the behaviorist tradition, hence the term "classical."

Modern behavior therapy is based primarily on the principles of classical conditioning developed by Pavlov and *operant conditioning* developed by B.F.

Skinner. Corsini noted, "Behavioral influence in therapy has evolved in two directions, one based on Pavlovian concepts of learning which has as its major focus emotional learning, and Skinnerian methodology with its emphasis on observable behavior and change through contingent reinforcement. The former has developed in the outpatient setting, is usually a one-to-one therapy regimen, and is applicable to neurotic problems, while the latter has developed in inpatient settings, such as state hospitals and institutions."[4]

Operant conditioning tends to be more applicable in the classroom setting and in hospital settings, where token economies can be beneficial. This form of behavior therapy is commonly known as *behavior modification*. Classical conditioning, on the other hand, tends to be more appropriate in outpatient settings where the treatment of such disorders as chronic pain, anger management, stress-related behavior problems, eating disorders, substance abuse, depression, obesity and anxiety disorders can more readily take place.

Philosophy

Unlike psychodynamic therapies, behavior therapy does not focus on understanding or uncovering the client's unconscious motivations that cause his or her maladaptive behavior. Rather than attempting to find

Behavior Therapy

out why their clients behave the way they do, the behavior therapist's goal is to simply teach their client how to most easily change their own behavior. "Behavior therapy is a type of psychotherapy that focuses on changing undesirable behaviors. Behavior therapy involves identifying objectionable, maladaptive behaviors and replacing them with healthier types of behavior.... The therapist analyzes the behaviors of the patient that cause stress, reduce the patient's quality of life, or otherwise have a negative impact on the life of the patient. Once this analysis is complete, the therapist chooses appropriate treatment techniques."[5]

In the process of teaching the client how to control their behavior, it is important for the behavior therapist to immediately work on forming a closely bonded relationship with the client. This is especially important in behavior therapy because it is a therapeutic process that requires collaboration and the empowerment of the client to take an active role in the process. "Obviously the process of behavior therapy is not one of straightforward reconditioning of the patient. The therapist cannot impose conditioning or relearning on anyone, for the most potent of techniques is useless without the cooperation and motivation of the patient. The therapeutic techniques to be used, whatever they may be for a given person, must be embedded in the context of a 'working relationship' between the therapist and the patient. A working relationship is one in which the therapist and patient are working together toward a commonly agreed-upon goal. If this is not accomplished then, in the vast majority of cases, therapy will be ineffective."6

At the basis of the philosophical beliefs inherent in behavior therapy is the view of determinism. This doctrine states that every event, every act and every decision we make is the inevitable consequence of antecedents that are independent of the human will. In fact, behavior therapy absolutely denies the entire idea of free will, theorizing that humans always behave in ways that are dependent upon preceding events.

Also inherent in behavior therapy is the belief that conclusions regarding the effectiveness of therapy must rely upon observation. That is, those conclusions are based solely on practical experience, without regard to theory or system. Behavior cannot be separated from the particular event in which it occurred. Environment and context are critical in evaluating behavior. The behavior therapist must evaluate the functionality of the behavior—what is the consequence of any given behavior? He must view behavior based on what is statistically predictable. What is conceivable? What is plausible? What is apt to occur or be true the majority of the time?

Behavior therapy treats the person as a unified whole, rejecting a mind-body dualism. And behavior therapy evaluates the logical or natural interaction between two stimuli, as in classical conditioning or between a behavior and a consequence, as in operant conditioning.

Foundational Precepts

As previously noted, the two primary conditioning theories that comprise the foundational precepts for what we call behavior therapy are classical conditioning, developed by Pavlov and operant conditioning, developed by Skinner.

Classical conditioning theory was developed using experimentation with dogs. Pavlov presented his dog with food and measured its salivary response. He then began ringing a bell just prior to presenting the dog with food. In the beginning, the dog did not salivate at the ringing of the bell. However, after several rounds of this presentation—first the bell, then the food—the dog began to salivate when the bell sounded. The dog had learned to associate the sound of the bell with the presentation of the food. In other words, the sound of the bell became equivalent to the presentation of the food.

Stimuli that animals or people react to without needing to be trained are known as *unconditioned stimuli* (US). In Pavlov's experiment, the food was the unconditioned stimuli. Typical experiments with animals use food or pain, such as electrical shock. Obviously, animals do not need to learn to react to electric shock, just as Pavlov's dog did not have to learn to react to food.

Stimuli that animals or people react to after learning about them are known as *conditioned stimuli* (CS). These are stimuli that have been associated with an unconditioned stimulus. Once Pavlov's dog learned to associate the ringing of the bell with the presentation of the food, the sound of the bell became a conditioned stimulus.

In humans, such things as grades and money are examples of conditioned stimuli. These are things that we must learn to like or dislike. If a person does not know or understand the meaning of a grade on a piece of paper, making an "A" or an "F" will be meaningless to them. Similarly, a person who does not use money as a way of buying things would find a piece of money meaningless until the association was made between money and obtaining something that person wants. Obviously, people work hard to gain both of these conditioned stimuli.

The specific model for classical conditioning is this: The unconditioned stimulus elicits an *unconditioned response* (UR). A *neutral response* (NR) is introduced and it elicits no response of interest. The neutral response is repeatedly paired with the unconditioned

Behavior Therapy

stimulus. Over time, the neutral response is transformed into a conditioned stimulus so that when the conditioned stimulus is presented by itself, it elicits a *conditioned response* (CR).

In classical conditioning, no new behaviors are learned. Instead, an association is developed between the unconditioned stimulus and the conditioned stimulus, so that the animal or person responds to both events or stimuli in the same way.

Concepts Related to Classical Conditioning

There are specific *laws of learning* that stem from data gained during experimentation in the laboratory using classical conditioning techniques. According to Goldstein, "The following are some of the variables that have been extensively explored and are found to be reliably reproducible with high predictability. These are the more important laws in understanding the underpinnings of behavior therapy as practiced today.

Conditioning—In classical conditioning, learning is demonstrated by the acquisition of a conditioned response.... A stimulus that already has the capacity to elicit a response, an unconditioned stimulus, is presented in close temporal contiguity with a neutral stimulus, which ordinarily elicits no response, or, in some cases, a different response. With repetitive pairings of the neutral stimulus and the unconditioned stimulus, the neutral stimulus develops the capacity to elicit a response similar to the one elicited by the unconditioned stimulus and at this point is called a conditioned stimulus.

Extinction—After a conditioned response is established, it is, except under special circumstances, subject to elimination through repetitive presentations of the conditioned stimulus without the unconditioned stimulus or through repetitive performances of the response without reinforcement. Both of these procedures bring about extinction.

Generalization—When a response has been conditioned to a particular conditioned stimulus, stimuli similar to the conditioned stimulus also have the power to evoke the conditioned response. This phenomenon is referred to as stimulus generalization. The response varies in strength, depending upon the similarities of the generalized stimulus to the conditioned stimulus. As the stimulus becomes less similar, the strength of the response becomes weaker.... When an extinction procedure is applied to a generalized stimulus, extinction occurs more rapidly than extinction to the conditioned stimulus.... The more dissimilar it is to the conditioned stimulus—the more rapidly extinction occurs. If after extinguishing the response to a generalized stimulus, the experimenter again presents the original conditioned stimulus, he finds that the conditioned response has been weakened. This phenomenon, called generalization of extinction, is of considerable importance in understanding clinical techniques used in the extinction of neurotic behavior.

Counterconditioning—Extinction occurs in classical conditioning when the unconditioned stimulus is withheld. The elimination of the conditioned response can be further facilitated if, in addition to withholding the unconditioned stimulus, the experimenter presents another unconditioned stimulus in its place. When that elicits an unconditioned response incompatible with the conditioned response, then counterconditioning is said to occur.... Not only does counterconditioning speed elimination of conditioned responses, but it also results in eliminating the conditioned response under special circumstances in which extinction would not do so. Again, this phenomenon has particular relevance to clinical application.[7]

While classical conditioning forms an association between two stimuli, operant conditioning as developed by Skinner, forms an association between a behavior and a consequence. This has sometimes been called *response-stimulus* (RS) or conditioning because it forms an association between the animal's or person's response (behavior) and the stimulus that follows (consequence).

Operant conditioning involves the use of consequences to change or modify behavior, hence the term behavior modification. Operant conditioning is different from classical conditioning in that operant conditioning deals with the modification of voluntary behavior or operant behavior.

Operant behavior operates on the environment and is maintained by its consequences, while classical conditioning deals with the conditioning of respondent behaviors which are elicited by antecedent conditions. Behaviors conditioned via a classical conditioning procedure are not maintained by consequences.[8]

There are four contexts in which operant conditioning occurs. The first is known as *positive reinforcement* and occurs when a behavior is strengthened by the consequence of experiencing a positive condition. For example, a hungry chicken pecks on a button in its cage and receives food. The food is a positive outcome for the hungry chicken. The chicken pecks the button again, and again receives food. Positive reinforcement has taken place. The chicken's behavior of pecking the button is strengthened by the consequence of receiving food.

The second context in which operant conditioning occurs is known as *negative reinforcement*. This occurs when a behavior is strengthened by the consequence of stopping or avoiding a negative condition. For example, a hungry chicken is placed in a cage and immediately receives a mild electrical shock to its feet. The shock is a negative condition for the chicken. The chicken pecks the button and the shock stops. The chicken receives another shock, pecks the button again and the shock stops. The chicken's behavior of pecking the button is strengthened by the consequence of stopping the shock.

The third context in which operant conditioning occurs is called *punishment* or *positive punishment*. It occurs when a negative condition such as introducing a mild shock decreases or weakens a behavior. For example, a chicken pecks a button in its cage and receives a mild electrical shock to its feet. The shock is a negative condition for the chicken. The chicken pecks the button again and once again receives a shock. The chicken's behavior of pecking the button is weakened by the consequence of receiving a shock.

The final type of operant conditioning is known as

extinction. It occurs when neither a positive or negative condition is experienced by the subject, so that the particular behavior is weakened or done away with completely. For example, our chicken pecks the button in its cage and nothing happens. Neither a positive nor negative condition exists for the chicken. The chicken pecks the button again, and once again, nothing happens. The chicken's behavior of pecking the button is weakened or extinguished by the consequence of not experiencing anything positive upon pecking the button, nor anything negative. It should be stated that as we use these terms, it is important to understand that "[T]he terms 'positive' and 'negative' are not used in their popular sense, but rather: 'positive' refers to addition, and 'negative' refers to subtraction. What is added or subtracted may be either reinforcement or punishment. Hence positive punishment is sometimes a confusing term, as it denotes the addition of punishment (such as spanking or an electric shock), a context that may seem very negative in the lay sense."9

Concepts Related to Operant Conditioning

Just as there are laws of learning related to classical conditioning, these laws exist with operant conditioning as well. In addition to what has already been described, the following are concepts which relate to operant conditioning that stem from data gained during experimentation in the laboratory.

Conditioning—Learning occurs through a different sequence of events with operant conditioning. The essential element distinguishing operant conditioning from classical conditioning is that in operant conditioning the unconditioned stimulus follows some predetermined behavior when it occurs spontaneously. Thus presentation of the unconditioned stimulus is contingent upon occurrence of a response. In such a procedure, the unconditioned stimulus is designated the reinforcing stimulus or reinforcement. A simple example is the increasing rate of bar pressing by a rat when food (reinforcement) consistently and immediately follows the bar presses.[10]

Reinforcement—Any event that strengthens or increases the behavior that follows. Reinforcement, is a consequence that causes a behavior to occur with greater frequency.[11]

Avoidance Learning—When certain behavior results in the cessation of an aversive stimulus, avoidance learning takes place. For example, when a person shields his eyes from sunlight, he is avoiding the aversive stimulation of the pain of light in his eyes.

Noncontingent Reinforcement—This refers to the delivery of reinforcing stimuli regardless of the organism's aberrant behavior. Aberrant behavior refers to behavior that deviates from the normal or expected behavior. The idea is that the target behavior decreases because it is no longer necessary to receive the reinforcement.[12]

Partial Reinforcement Effect—In most life situations, behavior is not constantly followed by reinforcement. When the reinforcement is withheld during some laboratory trials of operant conditioning, the learned response is far more resistant to extinction. By gradually reducing the ratio of reinforced to unreinforced trials, the experimenter can teach the subject to emit the conditioned response sometimes thousands of times without reinforcement.... For example, since gambling slot machines are programmed on a partial reinforcement schedule, the behavior of putting in coins persists, even after long periods of no reinforcement, attesting to the power of partial reinforcement in retarding extinction.[13]

Behavior Therapy

Therapeutic Interventions

A number of interventions have grown out of behavior therapy. These interventions include, but are not limited to, Aversion Therapy, Relaxation Training, Systematic Desensitization, In-Vivo Desensitization, Flooding, Assertiveness Training, and Eye Movement Desensitization and Reprocessing (EMDR). These interventions were developed from classical and operant conditioning theory.

Aversion Therapy—Kantorovich, in 1929, is most often credited with the first clinical use of this approach in the treatment of alcoholics. This is often a controversial form of behavior therapy and uses punishment, often in the form of electric shock, loud noises and other stimuli such as medications or mixtures that cause nausea and vomiting. This intervention has been used in the treatment of unwanted homosexual behavior, alcoholism and other drug addictions, pedophilia and other sexual compulsions, as well as compulsive eating. It should be noted that aversion therapy is rarely used when there are other viable alternative treatment methods available. Aversion therapy employs operant conditioning principles.

Relaxation Training—Jacobson developed a progressive relaxation procedure in 1938, later to be known as deep muscle relaxation, that is used to assist patients in becoming increasingly relaxed and stress free when required for therapeutic purposes or to relieve stress and anxiety. This technique involves the systematic tensing and relaxing of muscle groups throughout the body, starting with the hands and arms, then tensing and relaxing the facial muscles, moving progressively down the body. This includes the neck, shoulders, upper and lower back muscles, the chest, stomach and abdomen, hips, buttocks, legs and feet. Also important to the process is the use of controlled breathing, taking a deep breath and exhaling, imagining blowing the tension and anxiety out and away from the body. This is first learned in a prone position. With practice, the patient moves into using the technique without first tensing their muscles, then using the technique sitting in a chair. With more practice, the patient becomes increasingly aware of how their body is feeling and how much anxiety or tension they are experiencing, and they learn to better control their tension or anxiety wherever they are. Relaxation techniques are used as a prerequisite to learning systematic desensitization techniques, assertion training, biofeedback, hypnosis and meditation.

Systematic desensitization—In 1958, Joseph Wolpe developed a technique by which anxiety and phobias could be reduced by using relaxation as a counter-conditioning agent. Wolpe believed that "If a response antagonistic to anxiety can be made to occur in the presence of anxiety-evoking stimuli so that it is accompanied by a complete or partial suppression of the anxiety responses, the bond between these stimuli and the anxiety responses will be weakened."[14]

Systematic desensitization involves gradually exposing a patient to an anxiety-provoking stimuli until the anxiety response is extinguished or eliminated. Patients must first learn relaxation techniques before beginning systematic desensitization. Patients are then gradually exposed to a situation they fear, either in role-playing or in reality (in vivo). The therapist will employ relaxation techniques to assist the patient in coping with their fear reaction and eventually eliminate the anxiety altogether. "Systematic desensitization is a technique...in which the patient is taught relaxation and, when in as profound a state of relaxation as is feasible, is asked to imagine a series of scenes relevant to a particular theme. The least distressing scene is presented first and repeated until the patient reports an ability to imagine it calmly. Moving in order from the least distressing up to the most distressing scenes, the remainder of the scenes are presented in a like manner until the scene which was originally most disturbing is imagined calmly."[15]

Specific phobias are one class of mental illness often treated through the use of systematic desensitization. When the patient is experiencing irrational fear of an object, such as driving an automobile, riding in an elevator or being near a snake, they tend to avoid it. Escaping the phobic object reduces the patient's anxiety, and this escaping behavior is reinforced through negative reinforcement, a concept defined in operant conditioning. The goal of systematic desensitization is to overcome this avoidance pattern by gradually exposing the patient to the phobic object until it can be tolerated.

In Vivo Desensitization—Various means of confronting a feared situation can be used by the therapist. In vivo desensitization is a means whereby the therapist takes the patient to the feared situation while the patient is using relaxation techniques. The patient may visit an elevator and ride in it while being as fully relaxed as possible. Or ride in an automobile, if that produces a fearful response, while practicing a relaxation technique. "Animals or small objects may be actually brought closer and closer while the patient relaxes; such problems as claustrophobia may be approached incrementally. Behavior therapists have driven patients to bridges, used closets, kept a pigeon in the office, used slides and movies, taken patients onto roofs, and asked secretaries and other people working nearby to play roles for the sake of in vivo desensitization."[16]

While imagery, visualization or actually going to a site that provokes fear and anxiety for the patient were used to expose patients to fear-provoking stimuli in the precomputer era, now the therapist has at his disposal virtual reality techniques or computer simulated exposure. These methods have begun to be employed in lieu of in vivo exposure.

Flooding—Flooding is an accelerated version of systematic desensitization in which the patient is exposed to the fear-provoking stimuli that they fear the most, not allowing the patient to move from the least fearful to the most fearful exposure gradually.

This technique differs from systematic desensitization in that no counterconditioning agent, such as relaxation, is used. It works on the principles of classical conditioning, where patients change their behaviors to avoid negative stimuli. According to Pavlov, we learn through associations, so if we have a phobia, it is because we associate the feared object or stimulus with something negative or fear provoking. "Flooding consists of intense and prolonged exposure to the actual anxiety-producing stimuli, [usually from two to three hours]. Remaining exposed to feared stimuli for a prolonged period without engaging in any anxiety-reducing behaviors allows the anxiety to decrease on its own [a state known as protective-inhibition, occurring in most individuals within twenty to forty minutes]. In flooding, patients are prevented from engaging in their usual maladaptive responses to anxiety-arousing situations.... Flooding tends to reduce anxiety rapidly. [It] is frequently used in the behavioral treatment for anxiety-related disorders, phobias, obsessive compulsive disorder, post-traumatic stress disorder, and agoraphobia."[17]

Assertiveness Training—Assertiveness training is a form of behavior therapy that is designed to help the patient maintain an appropriate balance between passivity and aggressiveness.

The purpose of assertiveness training is to teach individuals appropriate strategies for identifying and acting on their desires, needs and opinions while remaining respectful of others. "People who lack social skills frequently experience interpersonal difficulties at home, at work, at school and during leisure times. Many people have difficulty feeling that it is appropriate or right to assert themselves. Assertion training can be useful for those who cannot express anger or irritation, who have difficulty saying no, who are overly polite and allow others to take advantage of them, who find it difficult to express affection and other positive responses, or who feel they do not have a right to express their thoughts, beliefs and feelings.... Most assertion training programs focus on clients' negative self-statements, self-defeating beliefs, and faulty thinking."[18]

Assertiveness training promotes the use of *I statements* as a way of assisting the patient in expressing their thoughts and feelings. Whereas *I statements* can rarely be argued with by others, *you statements* can easily be challenged and are not often received well by others. *I statement*s include statements such as I feel..., I would like..., I need..., I believe... or I think. On the other hand, *You statements* include statements such as You always..., You never..., You won't..., or You can't.

Patients learn to start sentences with "I feel" rather than making accusatory or threatening statements.... "Another rule of thumb is to state directly what is wanted rather than evade by [asking] questions.... Another useful rule of thumb is to direct your patient to 'stand on your feelings'; in an interaction the person being spoken to can never effectively deny how the patient feels."[19]

Assertiveness training enables the patient to experience respect of self and others, yet be direct, firm, persuasive and persistent in accomplishing a win-win solution. Honesty and diplomacy are key sets of skills that assertive people need and use. Assertive behavior is usually understanding, open, direct, caring, calm, focused and kind.

Specific areas where assertiveness training is useful include conflict resolution, realistic goal setting, stress management, low self-esteem or self-confidence, lack of autonomy and codependency.

Eye Movement Desensitization and Reprocessing—Referred to as EMDR, this form of exposure therapy was developed by Francine Shapiro in 1995.

This procedure is a comprehensive, integrative

psychotherapy approach that involves integrating a wide range of procedural elements along with the use of rhythmic eye movements and other stimulation designed to treat traumatic memories and stress. The populations that may benefit from EMDR include those suffering from post-traumatic stress disorder, including rape victims, combat veterans, victims of crime, sexual abuse victims, rape survivors, accident victims and those suffering from panic, depression, addictions and phobias. EMDR has also been reported to be beneficial in the treatment of stage fright, divorce trauma, fear of public speaking, low self-esteem and even a fear of dentists.

EMDR uses an eight-phase approach to address the experiential contributors of a wide range of pathologies. These phases are as follows:

"The first phase involves taking the client's history.... This involves conceptualizing and defining the client's problem and identifying and evaluating specific outcome goals. Specific targets are selected, such as dysfunctional memories that set the groundwork for the pathology, present situations that trigger the disturbance, and specific skills and behaviors necessary for adaptive future action. The second phase is the preparation phase, which involves establishing a therapeutic alliance. The therapist explains the EMDR process and its effects, discusses any concerns or expectations the client may have, initiates relaxation procedures, and creates a safe climate where the client is able to engage in emotive imagery. In the assessment phase the therapist identifies the components of the target and establishes a baseline response before processing begins. This assessment includes identifying a traumatic memory that results in anxiety, identifying the emotion and physical sensations associated with the traumatic event, evaluating the subjective unit of disturbance scale of images, identifying a negative cognition that is associated with the disturbing event, and finding an adaptive belief (or positive cognition) that would lessen the anxiety surrounding the traumatic event. In the desensitization phase [fourth phase], the client visualizes the traumatic image, verbalizes the maladaptive belief (or negative cognition), and pays attention to the physical sensations. Exposure is limited, and the client may have direct exposure to the most disturbing element for less than one minute per session. Then other associations arise. During the process, the client is instructed to visually track the therapist's index finger as it is moved rapidly and rhythmically back and forth across the client's line of vision from 12 to 24 times [or twenty to thirty seconds]. The client is instructed to block out the negative experience momentarily and breathe deeply and to report what he or she is imagining, feeling and thinking. The installation phase consists of installing and increasing the strength of the positive cognition the client has identified as the replacement for the original negative cognition.... The object is to associate the traumatic event with an adaptive belief so that the memory no longer has the power to result in anxiety and negative thinking. After the positive cognition has been installed, the client is asked to visualize the traumatic event and the positive cognition and to scan his or her body mentally from top to bottom and identify any bodily tension states. The body scan is completed when the client is able to visualize the target event and, at the same time, experience little bodily tension and be able to experience the positive cognition. It is essential that adequate closure be brought to the end of each session. The therapist reminds the client that he or she may experience disturbing images, emotions and thoughts between the sessions. The client is asked to keep a log or journal and record any disturbing material.... Clients are expected to make use of relaxation, guided imagery, meditation, self-monitoring and breathing exercises [between appointments]. Reevaluation is the last phase of treatment, which should be implemented at the beginning of each new session.... The clinician using EMDR assists the client in reaccessing previously reprocessed targets and reviews the client's responses to determine if the treatment is progressing. This last phase of EMDR includes several behavioral processes: reconceptualization of the client's problems, establishing new therapeutic goals, engaging in further desensitization, continuing the work of cognitive restructuring, continuing the self-monitoring process, and collaboratively evaluating the outcome of treatment."[20]

There are other methods of behavior therapy practiced which are too numerous to mention here. However, the behavior therapies discussed in this section are the primary therapies used by most behavior therapists today.

A Biblical Perspective

Although certain methods in behavior therapy can be very effective for the Christian counselor, there is a general conflict in the application of biblical counseling and the behavioral fundamentals.

Behavior therapy focuses on direct behavior rather than cognitions, which is counter to sound biblical instruction. Like most psychological theories, it never addresses the biblical role of sin and the self-centeredness of the flesh.

The fact that most behavioral approaches deny the concept of free will is contrary to the biblical call for the believer to exercise their free will and take charge of their mind and emotions.

God has promised the believer freedom through a knowledge and practice of the truth. He has given the believer the power to make the right choices as they relate to truth. *You shall know the truth, and the truth shall make you free* (John 8:32).

The area of spiritual freedom needed by the Christian is found within. Every believer recognizes the need for cleansing and deliverance in the areas of thought life, emotions and bodily desires. *The weapons of our warfare are not carnal but mighty in God for pulling down strongholds, casting down arguments and every high thing that exalts itself against the knowledge of God, bringing every thought into captivity to the obedience of Christ* (2 Corinthians 10:4-5).

We are exhorted by God to cast down and to bring into captivity our thought life. This clearly infers that we have the power to do so by a choice of our will. *Whatsoever things are true, whatsoever things are honest, whatsoever things are just, whatsoever things are pure, whatsoever things are lovely, whatsoever things are of good report; if there be any virtue, and if there be any praise, think on these things* (Philippians 4:8). Again, the believer is exhorted to take charge of his or her thinking.

There are three possible sources of damaging thoughts and, as believers, we must never lose sight of where potentially destructive thoughts can originate:

Behavior Therapy

a. The power of sin that indwells us. See Appendix D-1. *For from within, out of the heart of men, proceed evil thoughts, adulteries...and defile the man* (Mark 7:21,23).

b. The sinful world system. *For all that is in the world — the lust of the flesh, and the lust of the eyes, and the pride of life — is not of the Father, but is of the world* (1 John 2:16).

c. Satanic suggestion or accusation. *Has God indeed said, You shall not eat of every tree of the garden?.... You will not surely die.... You will be like God, knowing good and evil* (Genesis 3:1-5).

We are exhorted to take charge of our thinking by refusing those thoughts that are wrong and to aggressively choose to think on thoughts that are biblical examples of God's ways:

- *Wherefore putting away lying* (Ephesians 4:25, KJV).
- *Put off.... anger, wrath* (Colossians 3:8).
- *Let us, who are of the day be sober, putting on the breastplate of faith and love* (1 Thessalonians 5:8).
- *Put on the whole armor of God* (Ephesians 6:11).

Scripture is clear that a Christian has the inherent power and ability to put on positive, constructive thoughts and to put off aberrant thoughts, emotions and behavior. See Appendix D-2.

The believer is exhorted to take charge of his or her thinking and emotions. It is just as wrong, if not more so, to accept the feelings of hopelessness and to act on those as it would be to accept a wrong bodily desire and act on it. The believer has no reason to be hopeless and must reject all hopelessness, affirming the truth of the Scriptures.

And certainly, the believer is exhorted to take charge of his or her bodily desires. *Likewise you also, reckon yourselves to be dead indeed to sin, but alive to God in Christ Jesus our Lord. Therefore do not let sin reign in your mortal body, that you should obey it in its lusts. And do not present your members as instruments of unrighteousness to sin, but present yourselves to God as being alive from the dead, and your members as instruments of righteousness to God* (Romans 6:11-13).

Our loving, powerful and creative Father has promised us freedom. This freedom, however, is wrapped in our entitlement and privilege to make aggressive choices. When we so choose, then God works in and through us, by his power, to exercise our freedom to live in and by his truth. *It is God who works in you to will and to act according to his good purpose* (Philippians 2:13, NIV).

With the believer's ability to make choices that

lead to positive behavior, we must never lose sight of what has led the client to the choices he has made that led to his present condition. In short, we cannot simply focus on behavior or emotions.

We have attempted to illustrate what we are presenting through a graphic that will assist the reader in understanding how the presenting problem has developed, as well as the process that can lead to a positive solution. This can be a useful counseling model with appropriate clients. See Appendix D-3.

Determinism and Free Will

Determinism is woven into the fabric of many of the major theorist's beliefs. In its most basic premise, determinism says, "Everything I do is dependent upon previous events in my life, independent of my free will."

One encyclopedia of Christian apologetics states that "there are two basic kinds of determinism: naturalistic and theistic. Naturalistic determinism is most readily identified with behavioral psychologist B.F. Skinner. Skinner held that all human behavior is determined by genetic and behavioral factors. Humans simply act according to what has been programmed into them.

"All who accept strong forms of Calvinistic theology hold to some degree of theistic determinism. Jonathan Edwards related all actions ultimately to God as first cause. *Free choice* for Edwards is doing what one desires, and God is the Author of the heart's desires. God is sovereign, in control of all and so ultimately the cause of all.... Nondeterminists respond that a self-caused action is not impossible.... Free choice is not, as Edwards contends, doing what one desires (with God giving the desires). Rather, it is doing what one decides, which is not always the same thing.... God can control by omniscience as well as by causal power."[21]

Skinner was noted for what he often referred to as *radical behaviorism*. As an atheist, he was influenced by Darwin and held the belief that behavior is determined by its consequences. At one time he was reported to have made the statement, "I did not direct my life. I didn't design it. I never made decisions. Things always came up and made them for me. That's what life is."[22]

Determinism is a view that many Christians would see as running in direct conflict with how a sovereign God works in his children's lives based on how the Scriptures record the workings of that relationship. From the Garden of Eden through God's dealing with Israel and the church, we are called to exercise our freedom to make choices based on God's purpose and plan for humanity. We have been given a book that clearly outlines his plan for more abundant living during our time on this planet. We have been told that we will reap what we sow and the choice comes with the freedom he has bestowed upon us.

Today I have given you the choice between life and death, between blessings and curses. Now I call on heaven and earth to witness the choice you make. Oh, that you would choose life, so that you and your descendants might live! (Deuteronomy 30:19, NLT).

Chapter Five

Rational Emotive Behavioral Therapy

Albert Ellis, Ph.D., practiced as a psychoanalyst from 1947 to 1953 and grew increasingly doubtful about the effectiveness of psychoanalysis, concerned that no amount of "talk-therapy" would help his clients if they failed to take action against their habitual thoughts, feelings and behaviors. He came to believe that neurosis was "just a high-class word for whining."[1] By late 1953, he had stopped calling himself a psychoanalyst and began developing Rational Emotive Therapy (RET), later to become Rational Emotive Behavior Therapy (REBT). Ellis explained, "I started to call myself a Rational Therapist in 1955, then later I used the term Rational Emotive. Now I call myself a Rational Emotive Behavioral Therapist."[2]

Ellis' ideas about rational therapy grew out of his intense shyness and the methods he used to overcome it. By the age of nineteen, he was painfully shy and eager to change his behavior. He determined that the best way to overcome his shyness was to make himself sit on a park bench near his home and talk to every woman who sat on it. In one month he had approached over one-hundred thirty women. "Thirty walked away immediately. I talked with the other 100 or so, for the first time in my life, no matter how anxious I was. Nobody vomited or ran away. Nobody called the cops."[3]

Though he got only one date from the plan, his shyness was overcome. Ellis would later say that "the best years of your life are the ones in which you decide your problems are your own. You don't blame them on your mother, the ecology or the President. You realize that you control your own destiny."[4]

He also overcame a fear of public speaking by making himself speak in public as often as he could and eventually became an accomplished public speaker. He realized that he had overcome his fear by overcoming his irrational thoughts. REBT, then, is an action-oriented therapy aimed at creating emotional and behavioral change by challenging self-defeating thoughts.

After developing his theory and making it public, he considered himself hated by the psychological and psychiatric communities. "They thought my approach

Rational Emotive Behavioral Therapy

was superficial and stupid and resented that I said therapy did not have to take years."[5] However, in 2003, the American Psychological Association named Dr. Ellis the second most influential psychologist of the twentieth century, second only to Carl Rogers. Ellis died at the age of ninety-three on July 24, 2007. His obituary noted that he was both irreverent and charismatic, calling him "the Lenny Bruce of psychotherapy."[6]

Thinking Rationally

Rational Emotive Behavior Therapy is a therapeutic approach to treatment that deals with both the emotional and behavioral aspects of human disturbance, but places special importance on the client's ability to think rationally. According to Ellis, "[O]ur psychological problems arise from our misperceptions and mistaken cognitions about what we perceive—from our emotional under reactions or overreactions to normal and unusual stimuli, and from our habitually dysfunctional behavior patterns, which enable us to keep repeating nonadjustive responses even when we 'know' that we are behaving poorly."[7]

Ellis discovered that no matter how much insight his clients gained, nor how well they understood the events stemming from their childhood, they were rarely able to free themselves from their disabling symptomology. Insight seemed to help very little in bringing about healing to the client. Ellis described this phenomenon by observing that, "People got insight into what was bothering them, but they hardly did a damn thing to change."[8]

Ellis also discovered that clients were very often unable or unwilling to surrender the few basic irrational premises that invariably seemed to underlie their disturbed symptoms. He concluded that "humans are self-talking and self-evaluating animals, who frequently take their simple preferences—such as their desire for love, approval, success and pleasure—and mistakenly define them as needs. People have motives and thoughts of which they are largely unaware."[9]

He determined that these main irrational beliefs are not difficult to discover. They can be listed under a few simple headings. Once understood, they can be quickly uncovered by a therapist who understands the rational-emotive way of classifying them.

Philosophy

The philosophic origins of REBT go back to the stoic philosophers. As previously noted, it was Epictetus who said that "Men are disturbed not by things, but by the views which they take of them."[10] And Marcus

Aurelius noted, "If you are distressed about anything external, the pain is not due to the thing itself, but to your own estimate of it; and this you have the power to revoke at any moment."[11]

REBT holds that there are no acceptable reasons why we must make ourselves mentally or emotionally ill, no matter what type of negative or hurtful events come our way. Ellis once said that "for the most part, you construct your own depression. It wasn't given to you. Therefore, you can deconstruct it."[12]

The theory gives full tolerance to the feelings of strong negative emotion such as sorrow, anger, guilt or remorse, yet states that when we experience self-defeating and unhealthy emotions such as panic, depression, worthlessness and rage, we are usually being unrealistic and illogical in our beliefs and self-talk.

No matter what type of situation we find ourselves in, we all have opinions, judgments or evaluations about it. We may not necessarily come up with the correct interpretation of the situation, but we are always thinking and concluding something about our life experiences. If we paid close attention, we would realize that we are continually thinking and talking to ourselves about our circumstances. Our emotions follow and our behavior follows those feelings. What we end up doing will depend on how we felt about what we told ourselves about the event. Thinking, therefore, produces feelings, which in turn, generate behavior.

According to Ellis, "[E]motional disturbance occurs when an individual commands, insists or dictates that he must have his wishes or desires satisfied. Thus, he or she demands that they succeed at important tasks and be approved by significant others; they insist that others treat them fairly and ethically; and they command that the universe be more pleasant and less difficult than it often is."[13]

Ellis believed that there are three musts that hold us back: I must do well, you must treat me well and the world must be easy. The objective of REBT is to teach people to recognize these inaccuracies in their thinking and arrive at a more realistic view of themselves and their surroundings.

Foundational Precepts

The main foundations of REBT can be stated as follows:

    1. Man is born with a unique potential to be distinctly rational and straight thinking and to learn from his mistakes. On the other hand, he has the potential to be irrational and confused in his thinking.

    2. Man's absolute tendency toward irrational thinking and intolerance of others is

Rational Emotive Behavioral Therapy

frequently exacerbated by his culture, in general, and his family of origin in particular.

3. Man tends to perceive, think, emote, and behave simultaneously and interactionally. He rarely, if ever, perceives or acts without also thinking and he rarely feels or emotes without first thinking as well.

4. A primary REBT hypothesis is that therapies, such as rational-emotive-behavioral treatment, which are highly cognitive, active-directive, and discipline-oriented are likely to be more effective, in a briefer period of time, than therapies which include less cognitive-active-disciplining methodologies.

5. Contrary to the heavy emphasis given to transference by psychoanalytic therapists, the rational-emotive-behavioral therapist does not believe that a deep or warm relationship between the counselee and the counselor is a sufficient condition for effective change. He believes, instead, that it is highly desirable for the client and therapist to have good rapport.

6. Like the behavior modification therapist, the rational therapist uses a variety of techniques with his client—including role-

playing, assertion training, desensitization, humor, support, and suggestion.

7. REBT holds that virtually all serious emotional problems with which humans are beset directly stem from their empirically invalid thinking; and that if disturbance-creating beliefs and ideas are vigorously and persistently disputed they can be eliminated and will ultimately cease to reoccur.

8. REBT asserts that ordinary psychological insight rarely, if ever, leads to major personality change: According to REBT theory, this type of 'insight' is largely misleading and nonproductive. For it is not the activating event(s) of the individual's prior life that cause his dysfunction, but his irrational belief systems about the events.[14]

Ten Irrational Beliefs

Rational therapy holds that certain core irrational ideas, which have been clinically observed, are at the core of most emotional and psychological disturbances. These irrational beliefs are as follows:

1. The belief that it is an absolute necessity to be loved or approved of by virtually every significant other person in one's life rather

than understanding that love and approval are good things to have in one's life, but that they are not necessities.

2. The belief that one should be thoroughly competent, adequate, and achieving in all possible respects if one is to consider oneself worthwhile and adequate rather than understanding that one can accept himself or herself as a person regardless of their performance.

3. The belief that certain people are bad, wicked, or villainous and that they should be severely blamed and punished for their villainy rather than understanding that people do bad things and that upsetting oneself will not change that reality.

4. The belief that it must be awful and catastrophic when things or people are not the way one would like it, or them, to be rather than understanding that a person may be disappointed when things or people do not cooperate, but they do not need to view this as catastrophic.

5. The belief that human unhappiness and misery is externally caused and that people have little or no ability to control their sorrows and disturbances. That this misery is forced on us by outside events and circum-

stances rather than understanding that it is one's thoughts (not externals) that cause one's feelings and a person can learn to control their thinking.

6. The belief that if something is or could be dangerous or unpleasant, a person should be concerned about it and should keep dwelling on the possibility of its occurring rather than understanding that worrying about things that might go wrong will not stop them from happening.

7. The belief that it is easier to avoid life's difficulties and responsibilities rather than understanding that avoiding problems is only easier in the short term and that avoiding them only gives a person more time to worry and fret.

8. The belief that we absolutely need something or someone stronger or greater than ourselves on which to rely, something or someone to lean on rather than learning to trust one's own judgment.

9. The belief that one's past history is an all-important determiner of one's present behavior and that because something once strongly affected one's life, it should continue to have a similar effect rather than understanding that the past does not have

Rational Emotive Behavioral Therapy

to influence a person in the here and now.

10. The belief that human happiness can be achieved by inertia and inaction rather than realizing that we tend to be the happiest when we are vitally absorbed in creative pursuits, or when we are devoting ourselves to people or projects outside ourselves.[15]

The ABC Format

REBT is a theory of personality and a method of psychotherapy that states that when a highly charged Emotional Consequence (C) follows a significant Activating Event (A), the activating event may seem to, but actually does not, cause the consequence. Instead, emotional consequences are largely created by—the Individual's Belief System (B). When, therefore, an undesirable consequence occurs, such as severe anxiety, this can usually be traced to the person's irrational beliefs. When this belief system is effectively Disputed (A), by challenging it rationally, the disturbed consequences disappear and eventually cease to reoccur. According to Ellis, "We teach people that they upset themselves. We cannot change the past, so we change how people are thinking, feeling and behaving today."[16]

Imagine that a person lives by a general rule that

he or she must succeed at everything they do, and that if they do not succeed, they are not worthwhile. Further imagine that this person studies very hard for an exam, but fails it anyway. This event, coupled with their rule for living, will tell them that they must not be a worthwhile person; they must be a failure. Or imagine that a person believes that if they are to have an adequate self-esteem, they must be accepted and approved of by every important person in their life. Then, unexpectedly, a close friend snubs them at a party. By definition, this person has to feel unworthy and unlovable. We can see that the rules we live by become extremely important in our lives, as they dictate how we react to the events that take place on a day-by-day basis.

Most self-defeating rules are a variation of one or more of the Ten Irrational Beliefs listed previously. In order to describe a belief as self-defeating or irrational, it must distort reality, it must block a person from achieving his or her goals and purposes, it must create emotions that persist, distress and immobilize and it must lead to behavior that harms ourselves or others.

Identifying Irrational Beliefs

In order to identify irrational beliefs, a person has to be very intentional. Whenever a person experiences an unpleasant, debilitating emotion such as anger, shame, depression, fear, guilt or worry (to name a few) that person needs to write out their perception or memory of the unpleasant emotion (Emotional Consequence). Because it is at the emotional level that a person will usually realize that they are accepting an irrational belief, one should describe with as much detail as possible their emotional reaction, unpleasant as it may be, to the event itself.

Next, the person needs to write out what the event actually was (Activating Event). What happened that actually led to the emotional reaction? What seemed to *trigger* the chain of events that led to the emotional consequence? Was it something that someone else did? Was it something that the person himself did or did not do? Was it something that someone thought? Was it related to some sense of failure or rejection? The client must write in as much detail as possible exactly what happened.

Finally, what exactly is the self-talk being accepted as truth at point B (Belief System)? This can be difficult to determine, since it may seem that the thought about the event is almost automatic. But always remember that it is not automatic at all—an emotional reaction never takes place unless it is preceded by a thought or a belief. Identify that thought. Gerald Kranzler, in his book *You Can Change How You Feel,* summarizes it this way: "Your own strong, negative emotions are signals that something is wrong. Usually that 'something' is some irrational nonsense that you believe. If you wish to identify what it is that you are saying to yourself when you feel upset: (1) describe as accurately as you can how you feel, (2) describe that activating event that led to the feelings, and (3) record your self-talk—what you can recall saying to yourself or what you must have been saying to yourself. Look especially for highly evaluative, judgmental, demanding sentences; or catastrophizing, whining sentences; or for over-generalizations."

Kranzler goes on to say: "If you wish to change your irrational beliefs and self-verbalizations, then it would be a good idea to go on to the next step, Step D, to Dispute the nonsense you are telling yourself. Almost all irrational self-verbalizations include various evaluative words such as 'should' and 'ought'; or the catastrophizing words 'It's awful!', 'It's terrible!', and 'I can't stand it!'; or over-generalizations such as 'I will never be able to do it', and 'I am a bad person.' When you do find self-verbalizations such as these, dispute them by asking questions such as: 'Where is the evidence of proof? Why is this so? How can this be?' When you have convinced yourself that there is no evidence to prove your irrational self-talk, substitute more rational self-talk that would result in milder, more facilitative feelings."[17]

A Biblical Perspective

Although Dr. Ellis significantly decreased, and even reconsidered, his opposition to religion later in his life, he maintained atheistic views until his death. He strongly believed that "all manner of religion is essentially childish dependency."[18] I, Rick, had the privilege of hearing Dr. Ellis speak on two occasions during my Master's program, and on both occasions he spent the first twenty minutes or so telling his audience why he believed there is no God. He expressed the opinion that religious restrictions are needless and often harmful to emotional health and that religion contributed to psychological distress. Later in his life, he would describe himself as a "probabilistic atheist,"[19] saying that while it was impossible to be certain that there is no god, the likelihood that a god exists is so small that it was not worth his, or anyone else's, attention. During his later years, Dr. Ellis realized that religion can play a positive role in one's psychological health if it is associated with a loving god.

Religion's Role in the Life of the Christian

Isn't it amazing that even an atheist can sometimes get it right when it comes to the things of God? The first point we wish to make about Dr. Ellis' beliefs regarding atheism is the fact that religion does, indeed, very often lead to "restriction and harmful emotions in people's lives"—even in the life of the Christian. The apostle Paul, for example, grew up in the Jewish culture and became a Pharisee. Judaism was his religion. Yet after meeting Christ on the road to Damascus, Paul gave his life to the Lord. Paul's religion, like ours, depended largely upon his culture. If you are raised in Pakistan, for example, you would probably be raised Muslim. If raised in Israel, as Paul was, you would probably be raised Jewish. However, the truth of Christ is a reality no matter what culture you are raised in, or what religion is predominant in one's culture.

Clarification can be found on this topic in a statement believed to have been made years ago by C.S. Lewis: "Christianity is not a religion," he said. "It is a relationship!" It is our opinion that Jesus would agree with this statement. His goal for us is that he live his life in and through us. Yet many of us live with restricted and damaged emotions, as Dr. Ellis said. We live out our Christianity under the burden of legalism, believing that we must obey rule upon rule in order to gain God's approval. Guilt and self-judgment are the by-product when we fail, as we always will; whereas pride and perfectionism seem to take over for the many who temporarily succeed. When we think of religion, we think of legalism. When we think of legalism, we think of laws.

If you read the gospels carefully, you will find that Christ took on the religious leaders of his time at every opportunity. He was not fond of religion or its leaders either. Jesus said that life in him is what leads to freedom and joy: *My yoke is easy and my burden is light* (Matthew 11:30, NIV).

So how does one reconcile these two ways of thinking? Let's first establish the more common elements in the misuse and misunderstanding of the law and how it relates to the body of Christ.

Paul's Message Concerning the Law

Paul explains to us that even though we thought the purpose of the Law was simply to show us the right things to do to be accepted by God (religion), in reality it was to serve as our personal tutor, designed to show us how desperately we need Christ. He teaches us that we are no longer under this tutor because of our new relationship to God in Christ.

Therefore the Law has become our tutor to lead us

to Christ, so that we may be justified by faith. But now that faith has come, we are no longer under a tutor. For you are all sons of God through faith in Christ Jesus (Galatians 3:24-26, NASB).

Paul further teaches us how this tutor accomplishes its job: *The Law came in so that the transgression might increase* (Romans 5:20, NASB).

Is Paul actually saying that God gave the law so that we would experience greater sin? Yes! Paul actually says that the law was given so that as we go on sinning, we see our inadequacy in keeping the law and realize our need for the Savior. Paul goes on to tell us how our tutor performs this work: *When we were controlled by our old nature, sinful desires were at work within us, and the law aroused these evil desires that produced a harvest of sinful deeds, resulting in death* (Romans 7:5, NLT).

So the law was given to arouse our sinful passions and show or teach us our need for Jesus Christ. Simply stated, *The law was not intended for people who do what is right. It is for people who are lawless and rebellious, who are ungodly and sinful, who consider nothing sacred and defile what is holy, who kill their father or mother or commit other murders* (1 Timothy 1:9, NLT).

Paul was attempting to assist us in understanding that the moral law of God was presented to the human race as a list of requirements designed to put us in right standing with God. But behind the law was a deeper underlying purpose: to actually drive us into and expose deeper sin so that we might recognize that we are absolutely powerless to live up to God's standard for righteous living. God's purpose for the law was not to teach us how to be good but rather to mirror our real sin problem—a sin problem that separated us from him.

My Doing or his Doing?

In his letter to the Corinthians, Paul makes a remarkable statement. He tells us, *Not that we are adequate in ourselves to consider anything as coming from ourselves, but our adequacy is from God, who also made us adequate as servants of a new covenant, not of the letter but of the Spirit; for the letter kills, but the Spirit gives life* (2 Corinthians 3:5-6, NASB).

Writer Steve McVey brings this into focus. "Paul states one of the most fundamental and revolutionary concepts of the entire Christian message: God never made us adequate to be servants to the Law. Prior to our coming to Christ, the only relationship between ourselves and our Creator was one based upon our obligation to fully and completely obey God's written law. The ancient Jews saw obedience to the moral Law of God as the path by which they could make themselves acceptable to Him. But now, says Paul, we relate to God based on the indwelling of the Holy Spirit. Before, under the law, it was *my* doing in living for God. Now, under the new covenant, it is *His* doing, because I am living in Him, and He in me. He lives His life through me. My *doing* flows from my *being*, not the other way around."[20]

Paul states in his letter to the Galatians: *We [Jews] know very well that we are not set right with God by rule-keeping but only through personal faith in Jesus Christ. How do we know? We tried it—and we had the best system of rules the world has ever seen! Convinced that no human being can please God by self-improvement, we believed in Jesus as the Messiah so that we might be set right before God by trusting in the Messiah, not by trying to be good. Have some of you noticed that we are not yet perfect? (No great surprise, right?) And are you ready to make the accusation that since people like me, who go through Christ in order to get things right with God, aren't perfectly virtuous, Christ must therefore be an accessory to sin? The accusation is frivolous. If I was 'trying to be good,' I would be rebuilding the same old barn that I tore down. I would be acting as a charlatan. What actually took place is this: I tried keeping rules and working my head off to please God, and it didn't work. So I quit being a 'law man' so that I could be God's man. Christ's life showed me how, and enabled me to do it. I identified myself completely with him. Indeed, I have been crucified with Christ. My ego is no longer central. It is no longer important that I appear righteous to you or have your good opinion, and I am no longer driven to impress God. Christ lives in me. The life you see me living is not 'mine,' but it is lived by faith in the Son of God, who loved me and gave himself for me. I am not going to go back on that. Is it not clear to you that to go back to that old rule-keeping, peer-pleasing religion would be an abandonment of everything personal and free in my relationship with God? I refuse to do that, to repudiate God's grace. If a living relationship with God could come by rule-keeping, then Christ died unnecessarily* (Galatians 2:15-21, MSG).

Paul was clear regarding our new way of relating to God once we have asked Christ into our lives as Lord and Savior. Yet it is unfortunate how many of us today come to Christ bringing the old covenant mentality with us. We continue to believe that our acceptability to God and our standing with him is based on how successfully we keep his laws. We see ourselves, in Paul's terms, as *servants of the letter*. But Paul's response to this kind of thinking is, *the letter kills*. We will strangle the life and vitality out of our walk with Christ if we approach our relationship with him on the basis of our obedience to the law.

Any attempt to successfully be obedient to the law of God is destined to fail. Therefore, religion will always fail us. It will fail us, not because moral obedience is unimportant, but because it is unattainable outside of a life lived in a growing love relationship with the person of Christ.

Rational Biblical Thinking

The second thing we wish to examine is what the Bible has to say about thinking rationally. Dr. Ellis describes in great detail his belief that humans must learn to think rationally—but it may surprise most readers to find that the Bible made this quite clear long before Ellis proposed his theory.

Outside of the Christian paradigm, which sees God as the foundation for all truth, we are inclined to ask the question, "What is the standard by which I am to measure my irrational thinking and perceptions that create my negative emotions and potentially destructive behavior?" God created man to be pure in thought and to know the truth taught by God himself. Irrational thinking started with the acceptance of the teaching of someone other than God. The author of irrational thinking is the archenemy of God, Satan himself. His works are designed to hold people captive and separated from the life offered them through knowing the truth. His names include the father of lies, the deceiver and the accuser of the saints. Therefore, the biblical name for irrational thinking is deception. We are deceived when we accept a lie to be the truth. Acting on that lie results in distorted living and distorted relationships that bring harm and disharmony to our lives.

If you have experienced a spiritual birth through Jesus Christ, you have the opportunity to come out of deception and into truth. In fact, Paul instructs us to do so. *This I say, and affirm together with the Lord, that you walk no longer just as the Gentiles also walk, in the futility of their mind, being darkened in their understanding, excluded from the life of God because of the ignorance that is in them, because of the hardness of their heart* (Ephesians 4:17-18, NASB).

It is extremely important that believers learn to think clearly and rationally.

Renewing the Mind

Rational thinking is simply a person's ability to shape his own life by the control of his thought process. As believers, we must learn to control our thoughts, which operate in the mind, and control our feelings, emotions and behaviors. As believers, we must learn to replace negative, harmful, destructive thoughts with the positive, healthy, transformed thoughts given to us by God himself.

Rational thinking becomes what the Bible calls

the renewing of our minds. *Therefore I urge you, brethren, by the mercies of God, to present your bodies a living and holy sacrifice, acceptable to God, which is your spiritual service of worship. And do not be conformed to this world, but be transformed by the renewing of your mind, so that you may prove what the will of God is, that which is good and acceptable and perfect* (Romans 12:1-2, NASB).

This Scripture is an exhortation to us to be constantly transformed by the renewing of our minds and to thus become conformed to the image of Christ. In this respect, rational thinking does not mean that we are to be unemotional, mechanical, boring or uncreative. In fact, the opposite is true. Thinking rationally means thinking appropriately and accurately (as God thinks) about ourselves, about events in our lives and about situations that we face on an everyday basis. When we think rationally and appropriately, we are in touch with reality and are developing thoughts and attitudes that are consistent with the truth of God. When we think rationally, we are able to express feelings and emotions freely and spontaneously.

Choosing To Believe the Truth

The secret to this method of rational thinking is to put truth into our minds, value systems and assumptions.

Rational Emotive Behavioral Therapy

The Bible tells us that knowing the truth sets us free. The truth as it is taught by Scripture is a way of life which leads to wholeness, restores functioning and offers freedom from emotional stress. The renewing of our minds allows us to alter the way we think, which, in turn, will alter our emotions, beliefs, attitudes and behaviors. We are responsible for, and capable of, changing the way we feel and act—simply by changing the way we think. *For as he thinks within himself, so he is* (Proverbs 23:7, NASB).

All of us have asked ourselves, "Why do I feel the way I do?" Usually we want to blame something or someone else for our problems. "It's my spouse, or my employer or my government—if only they would change, then things would be all right!" There are things we would all like to see changed. However, changing circumstances will not result in lasting relief from our problems because our problems spring from unrealized root causes stemming from irrational thinking.

The following is a diagram that illustrates how an event triggers our thought process, which produces emotion or feeling which, in turn, produces action or behavior.

Event >> Thought >> Emotion >> Behavior

An event is incapable of causing us to feel or act in

a particular manner. When we say, for example, "He really made me angry," we are making an inaccurate statement. In reality, what he did triggered a thought process in me, which created an emotion, in this case anger, which probably led to some sort of behavioral response. We choose to feel and act as we do, based on what we think.

Since our beliefs are based on past experience, which usually stems from how we have thought about circumstances in the past, the process sometimes appears to be automatic—making it seem as though the event caused the emotion or the behavior. In this regard, the process becomes cyclical, with behavior reinforcing certain thoughts, which reinforce certain emotions and so forth. This cyclical response becomes a belief system which involves our values, opinions and memories of past experiences, therefore making the process feel automatic. Until we identify the thoughts that are part of our belief system creating the irrational thinking, we will continue to feel and act irrationally—keeping ourselves in bondage.

Once we identify the irrational thoughts that are causing the problem and replace them with the truth of God's word, we will begin to experience relief from the bondage. By substituting the old ways of thinking with renewed ways of thinking, we can transform our lives to reflect the logic and rationality of God himself. See Appendices E-1 and E-2.

Christ has come to set us free from our bondage to guilt, shame, failure and rejection. Through him, we allow new life and a new paradigm to enter our thought process. New life comes into our minds from God when we think his thoughts. Walk no longer in the futility of your mind, *being darkened in [your] understanding, excluded from the life of God because of [your] ignorance...and hardness of heart.... But you did not learn Christ in this way, if indeed you have heard Him and have been taught in Him, that, just as truth is in Jesus, in reference to your former manner of life, you lay aside the old self, which is being corrupted in accordance with the lusts of deceit, and that you be renewed in the spirit of your mind, and put on the new self, which in the likeness of God has been created in righteousness and holiness of the truth* (Ephesians 4:17-24, NASB).

We are not forever doomed to live with harmful emotions and their resulting problems. If we tell ourselves lies, we will believe lies. If we tell ourselves the truth, we will believe the truth. If we tell ourselves we're a failure and can't do anything correctly, we will come to believe it. And, if we believe it, we will begin to act as though it were true.

We all go through life taking in data from various sources. Much of this data is not based on truth. It may be data that has convinced us that we're a failure or not a good person. Maybe it is data that has us convinced that we are not as successful as we should be or that we are socially out of the loop. Soon we believe the lie, "I am a failure," and we even begin to feel and act like a failure. Here is the real problem: when I give authority to that kind of lie, I give the devil the legal right, the ground, to wrap that lie in a system of deceit that makes it look like the truth—to myself and others. This is a stronghold. This is bondage.

The weapons of our warfare are not carnal, but mighty through God to the pulling down of strongholds; Casting down imaginations, and every high thing that exalts itself against the knowledge of God, and bringing into captivity every thought to the obedience of Christ (2 Corinthians 10:4-5, KJV).

Strongholds are why our beliefs are so important to our mental and emotional stability. Untruths are the direct cause of harmful emotions, destructive behavior, and some psychological disorders. That is why we are instructed to renew our minds so that God's transforming power in our lives will be personally realized.

Illustrations

Why can one person experience a negative event in their life and react differently than another person who experiences the same event?

Rational Emotive Behavioral Therapy

Take, for example, a young child sitting on the beach on a sunny day. He is playing in the sand with his toys and building a sand castle. Everything is perfect and he is having a wonderful time. Then, unexpectedly, a large wave comes out of the ocean and rolls over the little child, destroying his sand castle, putting him underwater and throwing him into a state of panic. The child screams in terror, and his mother comes running to him and picks him up to comfort him. The child refuses to go near the water for the rest of the day.

As you walk on down the beach, you come upon a second child sitting on the same beach on the same sunny day. She too is playing in the sand with her toys when, unexpectedly, another large wave comes out of the ocean and rolls over her, destroying her sand castle. But this little girl's reaction is different. This child is excited about the waves crashing down on her and runs down to the water waiting with anticipation for the next wave, hoping that it will be even bigger.

How do we explain these different responses to the same circumstances? Is it the way the children were raised? Is it their nature that caused the reaction or their personality? Is it their mood at the time of the incident? It may be surprising, but none of these explanations are valid. Howard Young notes, "What is valid is the fact that no outside event or circumstance can emotionally distress us or make us feel badly unless we allow it. And conversely, no outside event or circumstance can make us feel good emotionally. Our emotions are determined by our perception of the event—by our point of view! It is an opinion or belief about the event that determines our reaction, not the event itself. There is no way another <u>person</u>, <u>situation</u> or <u>event</u> can make us feel angry, depressed, nervous, anxious, guilty, shameful, worthless or inferior unless we allow ourselves to experience these emotions! We are responsible for creating our own emotional reactions. People, therefore, are not disturbed by events, but by the views they have of those events."[21]

We are people created in the image of God, who can, through renewed thinking, be in control of our feelings and behaviors. We will be on the road to freedom when we take the first step and identify distorted thinking for what it is. Once we have identified the irrational thought we can replace it with the truth of God's word. See Appendix E-2. Once we learn to recognize it and put it in its place, it is possible to be free from guilt, depression, anxiety, resentment, anger, fear and self-consciousness. What we believe is all important to emotional and mental health.

God's truth is the only barometer that should be used in defining our worth. When we look to our own performance or at the opinions of others in order to define who we are, we will find ourselves in a never-ending bondage to guilt, shame, rejection and failure.

God's purpose is to bring healing to all who will come to him through Jesus Christ and receive the truth and to experience our new selves and his new life within.

REBT's Void

Although we can find a degree of parallel in some of the principles that REBT presents, the biblical perspective clearly fills an ever-present void.

Certainly the view that emotions follow thinking and beliefs has a biblical foundation just as the view that love and approval are good things to have in one's life. But the statement that love and approval are not necessities is contrary to God's ways. Much of our need for him in our life is based on our need for love and acceptance, which are to be primarily found in him.

Assuredly all Christians can learn to control their thinking as suggested in the REBT list of beliefs. But the realization that we can do all things through Christ who strengthens us helps give the believer the foundation of support and power that is often needed to make those choices.

And certainly learning to trust one's own judgment takes on a promising confidence when we are dependent on the mind of Christ and the support and nurturing of a loving heavenly Father who is intent on working toward our well-being.

Chapter Six

Psychoanalytic Theory

What are the unseen forces that drive the inner workings of man? What motivates the human tendencies of self-preservation? Where do the dark desires that tease our mind originate? Where do the forces that drive sexual desire, revenge, self-promotion and deceit originate? These are just a few of the basic issues that man has pondered throughout human history. A major intersection of man's search for those answers began to take shape toward the close of the nineteenth century. Darwin's evolutionary theory had had a heavy impact on the scientific and intellectual community, and man was beginning to be seen as just one part of a complex natural order of living humans and nonhumans.

Into this mix a brilliant and curious Austrian, Sigmund Freud, was cast. A financially struggling father and indulgent mother motivated Freud to become a resolute student, mastering Hebrew, Latin, Greek, French, English, Italian and Spanish. Highly stimulated by Darwin's theories, he entered medical school before he finished high school.

Educated, inquisitive and motivated, Freud became the inspirational force behind the development of new theories regarding the makeup and motivations that determine the thoughts and actions of human behavior.

The *Internet Encyclopedia of Philosophy* states that "Sigmund Freud, the father of psychoanalysis, was a physiologist, medical doctor, psychologist and influential thinker of the early twentieth century.... Freud elaborated the theory that the mind is a complex energy-system, the structural investigation of which is the proper province of psychology. He articulated and refined the concepts of the unconscious, infantile sexuality and repression, and he proposed a tripartite account of the mind's structure—all as part of a radically new conceptual and therapeutic frame of reference for the understanding of human psychological development and the treatment of abnormal mental conditions. Notwithstanding the multiple manifestations of psychoanalysis as it exists today, it can in almost all fundamental respects be traced directly back to Freud's original work."[1]

Freud spent much of his career developing his theory of psychoanalysis. His theory of basic human nature and development, although challenged by many, became the standard by which most contemporary theorists still measure and formulate new views. "By providing the first truly comprehensive and scientific theory of human nature and behavior, as well as the first systematic method of inquiry and approach to psychotherapy, Freud filled a void in human thinking."[2]

Although Freud was committed to and focused on his own theories, he worked closely for a time with both Alfred Adler and Carl Jung who, after regular challenges to Freud's views, went on to develop their own theories and therapeutic approaches.

Much of Freud's understanding of human makeup and motivation was the result of emotional experiences in his own life. Nancy Murdock writes, "Freud was a pessimist, and thus psychoanalysis presents a rather gloomy view of human nature. Arguing against those who characterized human nature as inherently positive, Freud maintained that 'unfortunately what history tells us and what we ourselves have experienced does not speak in this sense but rather justifies a judgment that belief in the 'goodness' of human nature is one of those evil illusions by which mankind expect their lives to be beautified and made easier while in reality they only cause damage.'"[3]

Freudian Theories

Primary to Freud's beliefs is his view that motivation is the functioning force behind all behavior. William Wallace notes, "According to Freud (1940/1964/1923/1925), all behavior is motivated. We are impelled to act when psychic energy, aroused by bodily needs or impulses seeking expression and tension release, is reflected in the form of an instinctual object choice or wish."[4]

Freud believed there were unconscious powers and influences that were the driving forces behind much of a person's behavior. Quoting Murdock, "Freud hypothesized that humans have instinctual urges that are innate, resulting from their evolutionary heritage. These instincts must be expressed or the individual will become dysfunctional (Freud actually used the word ill; 1940/1964, p. 150)."[5]

Adding to this, "Freud distinguished three structural elements within the mind, which he called id, ego, and super-ego. The id is...the instinctual sexual drives which require satisfaction; the super-ego is that part which contains the 'conscience,' namely, socially-acquired control mechanisms which have been internalized, and which are usually imparted in the first instance by the parents; while the ego is the conscious self that is created by the dynamic tensions and interactions between the id and the super-ego and has the task of reconciling their conflicting demands with the requirements of external reality. It is in this sense that the mind is to be understood as a dynamic energy-system. All objects of consciousness reside in the ego; the contents of the id belong permanently to the unconscious mind; while the super-ego is an unconscious screening-mechanism which seeks to limit the blind pleasure-seeking drives of the id by the imposition of restrictive rules."[6]

One might conclude from Freud's concepts that much of our makeup as humans is unwavering in its drive to live out what has been largely programmed into our conscious and subconscious thinking. Freud seemed to believe that although the conscious mind has decision-making power, it is motivationally driven by the conflicting drives and desires of the id and super-ego.

Gerald Corey states the following: "The Freudian view of human nature is basically deterministic. According to Freud, our behavior is determined by irrational forces, unconscious motivations, and biological and instinctual drives as these evolve through key psychosexual stages in the first 6 years of life."[7]

The Internet Encyclopedia of Philosophy agrees: "Freud's theory of the unconscious, then, is highly deterministic.... Thus instead of treating the behavior of the neurotic as being causally inexplicable...Freud insisted, on the contrary, on treating it as behavior for which it is meaningful to seek an explanation by searching for causes in terms of the mental states of the individual concerned.... This suggests the view that freedom of the will is, if not completely an illusion, certainly more tightly circumscribed than is commonly believed, for it follows from this that whenever we make a choice we are governed by hidden mental processes of which we are unaware and over which we have no control."[8]

The view that freedom of the will is more an illusion than reality certainly puts one in a position that then requires the belief that emotional health can only come through the restructuring of "hidden" mental processes.

William A. Wallace takes a similar view: "The ultimate goal of psychoanalysis is reorganization, a form of ego development that promotes the integration of dissociated psychic material and results in a basically changed, firmly established structure of personality."[9]

Of course a high degree of complexity is added to this process when we take into account the defensive structures that have been developed, often over many years, that not only help the client to better cope with the hidden conflict, but also lead the client into areas of denial to avoid dealing with the conflict going on below his level of clear consciousness.

Although many writers and theorists cite logical and effective methods of avoiding the internal confrontation of these conflicts, the *Internet Encyclopedia of Philosophy*, as with many theorists, places one method at or near the top. "A key concept introduced here by Freud is that the mind possesses a number of 'defence mechanisms' to attempt to prevent conflicts from becoming too acute, such as repression (pushing conflicts back into the unconscious)."[10]

The *Internet Encyclopedia of Philosophy* addresses the effects of repression with this explanation: "Freud's account of this is as follows: when a person experiences an instinctual impulse to behave in a manner which the super-ego deems to be reprehensible...then it is possible for the mind to push this impulse away, to repress it into the unconscious.... Repression is thus one of the central defence mechanisms by which the ego seeks to avoid internal conflict and pain, and to reconcile reality with the demands of both id and super-ego.... However, the repressed instinctual drive...cannot be destroyed when it is repressed—it continues to exist intact in the unconscious, from where it exerts a determining force upon the conscious mind, and can give rise to the dysfunctional behavior characteristic of neuroses."[11]

Nancy L. Murdock helps us to better understand the complexity of Freud's view of this process. "Freud...recognized the conscious awareness of the individual. To the consternation of many, however, he denied it as the source of most behavior. Instead, he saw most behavior as stemming from the unconscious, so that what we typically think of as driving our behavior (our conscious thought) is only the tip of the iceberg."[12]

Making this applicable to real life is not easy. However, many of us have heard or used the term Freudian slip when a slip of the tongue revealed something seen as the expression of an unconscious aspect of the mind. Freud connected these 'slips' to his views of repression. Freud also proposed that dreams are merely the concealed or camouflaged fulfillment of unconscious desires.

Freud believed that most repressions took place in early childhood, through age five, and that most were in some way tied to sexual development. This, he believed, leads to later neurosis as the subject matures. William Stewart notes that, "Freud deduced that what was being repressed were disturbing sexual experiences, real or in fantasy, and that repressed sexual energy and its consequent anxiety finds an outlet in various symptoms that serve as ego defenses. He maintained that many of the impulses forbidden or punished by parents are derived from innate instincts. Forbidding expression to these instincts merely drives them out of awareness into the unconscious. There they reside to affect dreams, slips of speech or mannerisms and may also manifest themselves in symptoms of mental illness."[13]

Psychoanalytic Therapy

The ultimate conclusion of Freud's theory was a logical progression. Thus, "the task of psychoanalysis as a therapy is to find the repressions which cause the neurotic symptoms by delving into the unconscious mind of the subject, and by bringing them to the forefront of consciousness, to allow the ego to confront them directly and thus to discharge them."[14]

Gerald Corey explains it this way in his writings on psychoanalytic therapy: "[There is] a conflict among the id, ego, and superego over control of the available psychic energy. [Its function] is to warn of impending danger."

Corey went on to tie impending danger to anxiety. He states there are "three kinds of anxiety: reality, neurotic, and moral. Reality anxiety is the fear of danger from the external world.... Neurotic anxiety is the fear that the instincts will get out of hand and cause one to do something for which one will be punished. Moral anxiety is the fear of one's own conscience.... When the ego cannot control anxiety by rational and direct methods, it relies on indirect ones—namely, ego-defense behavior."

Corey goes on to list what he determines are the ego-defense mechanisms that help the individual cope with anxiety and prevent the ego from being overwhelmed: "Among the common ego defenses he lists are: repression, denial, reaction formation, projection, rationalization, and regression."

Corey concludes, "[T]wo goals of Freudian psychoanalytic therapy are to make the unconscious conscious and to strengthen the ego so that behavior is based more on reality and less on instinctual cravings or irrational guilt."[15]

Certainly Freud unleashed an army of adherents to his philosophy of the human condition and man's efforts to correct and override the hidden causes of destructive human thinking and behavior. Or does Freud's view tend to compound the complexity of the very issue he is attempting to correct?

Wallace notes that Freud himself may have had reservations about the effectiveness of his views. "Freud made rather modest claims for his therapy. He never presented it as a panacea for all psychic ills or offered it as a modality to perfection."[16]

Freud and Religion

Freud's development of his theories for psychoanalysis were certainly influenced by his early medical training, his close association with Darwinian theory and his gradually evolving pessimism.

Jones and Butman, in their Christian review of *Modern Psychotherapies,* make reference to an analysis by Vitz and Gartner (1984a, 1984b) regarding their view of Freud's understanding of religion noting that his views reveal "some interesting weaknesses in the theory. They argue that if one presumes God is an illusion, then the 'projection of a father figure' understanding of religion makes sense. But if one starts with a presupposition that God exists, psychoanalysis does equally well in explaining atheism!"

Jones and Butman expand on that view asking, "How would the denial of a real God happen psychologically if psychoanalysis is true? If God is a heavenly 'father,' then disbelief in God must clearly be attributable to the Oedipal period of development. During this period, the child feels infantile rage at the same-sex parent who competes with the child for the love of the opposite-sex parent. If the child does not adequately resolve that unconscious rage at the parent during the genital stage, the unconscious rage might be played out as atheism in adulthood—what better way to get back at (or murder) a father figure than to simply not believe in him! Since one can only go so far in rejecting the earthly parent, a deeper rage, an even more primitive aggressive impulse, can be vented on God by denying his very existence.... Such a philosophical and scientific commitment allows no room for anything supernatural, for the kind of general or special revelation so central to the Christian faith, nor for a more constructive perspective about our spiritual urgings for deeper meaning and significance in life. Freud's system is a closed system of cause and effect."[17]

Freud and the Scriptures

A study of Freud's perception of the human condition must begin with the statement noted earlier by Nancy Murdock, that "Freud was a pessimist, and thus psychoanalysis presents a rather gloomy view of the human nature." This view alone draws the clear distinction between a fallen world and the Christian view of redemption for those whose faith is firmly rooted in the finished work of Christ on the cross.

A Christian who fully understands the biblical view of man's fallen nature, due to original sin, will naturally have difficulty accepting Freud's pessimistic theory of human psychological development. Freud, having been greatly influenced by Darwin, seems to understand the internal conflict of the physical world and the spiritual world, but seems determined to find a rational alternative to the biblical view of all that God accomplished in his Son's redemptive action.

Certainly the concept of evil drives many intellectuals into what they feel to be reasonable explanations for man's natural bent toward destructive behavior, but they largely make this leap apart from the concept of original sin.

Freud's view that motivation is a force largely driven by unconscious powers and instinctual urges can, on the surface, appear reasonable. Ultimately, however, one must take the issue to the next level and honestly ask, "What drives those unconscious powers and instinctual urges? "

Carl Jung

Modern psychology has its protagonists and antagonists, especially when efforts are made to attempt to unite the scientific and the spiritual views. Carl Jung aspired to reconcile the two and met with great resistance at every turn. Jung was often classified with one end of the spectrum or the other, but was persistent in his efforts. As Sonu Shamdasani writes, "Occultist, Scientist, Prophet, Charlatan, Philosopher, Racist, Guru, Anti-Semite, Liberator of Women, Misogynist, Freudian Apostate, Gnostic, Post-Modernist, Polygamist, Healer, Poet, Con-Artist, Psychiatrist and Anti-Psychiatrist—what has C.G. Jung not been called? Mention him to someone, and you are likely to receive one of these images.... He has become a figure upon whom an endless succession of myths, legends, fantasies, and fictions continues to be draped."[18]

Jung will always be tied closely to Freud, and it is difficult to consider one without the other.

Carl Gustav Jung was a Swiss psychiatrist and a primary founder of analytical psychology. The Wikipedia website provides some background on his early life: "His father pastored a small rural Swiss Reformed church. His mother came from a wealthy family but spent much of her time isolated and depressed. Young Carl would later confess that his mother's depression led to his view of women as unreliable. Although Jung expressed his belief in evil, he was drawn to many views of religion to include studies in Christianity, Hinduism, Buddhism, Gnosticism, and Taoism. Unlike Freud, he felt spiritual experience was vital to a person's well-being. Although Jung and Freud were close for a number of years, they eventually came to disagreement and a parting of ways over the unconscious. Jung saw Freud's view as inadequate and negative."[19]

Shamdasani notes that Jung had a key role in the development of the psychoanalytic view. "As a psychiatrist, he played a pivotal role in the formation of the modern concept of schizophrenia, and the idea that the psychoses were of psychological origin and hence amenable to psychotherapy. During his association with Freud, he was the principal architect of the psychoanalytic movement."[20]

Jung's development of analytical psychology was in many ways his method of extending the views of both Freud and Adler. Jung's view of the psyche encompassed the conscious and unconscious elements combining what he termed spirit, soul and idea. He also held firmly to the belief that what a person perceives is largely determined by who they are. Like Freud, Jung often tied cases of disturbance to what he

Psychoanalytic Therapy

considered the root issue of sexuality, claiming that Christianity in particular had a negative effect on man's natural animal drives. Shamdasani notes, "Jung began to put forward a historical argument concerning modern man's alienation from instinct. In this, he drew from Nietzsche's historical account of the relation to instinct, and in particular, on his depiction of the negative effects of Christianity. Jung claimed that... Christianity weakened the 'animal state' so that a large amount of the force of the drives could be used for social preservation and fruitfulness. These statements introduce an important theme in Jung's work: that of the relation between humans, animals, and the 'animal within.' It is generally held that in comparison to Freud, Jung downplayed the significance of sexuality. This is misleading. In a lecture on psychoanalysis in Zurich in July 1912, he argued that... 'it is very rare to find a neurotic case where a sexual disturbance is not the root of the trouble. Modern life does not consider sexuality half enough. [T]he process of culture consists in a progressive mastery of the animal in man.' "[21]

One can find in many of Jung's views a bent toward every person's need for a spiritual connection to God. His father's early influence toward spiritual issues might have made a lasting impact on his need to include a supernatural element to his work. *The Jung Page* website notes that "In his memoir, *Memo-*

ries, Dreams, Reflections, Jung wrote that meaning comes 'when people feel they are living the symbolic life, that they are actors in the divine drama. That gives the only meaning to human life; everything else is banal and you can dismiss it. A career, producing of children, are all [illusion] compared to that one thing, that your life is meaningful.' "22

Jung seemed to have a more practical way of expressing the distinctions between the conscious and the unconscious elements in our makeup as humans. Raymond Corsini offers a helpful definition of Jung's use of the term *complexes*. Jung felt the unconscious makes itself known through these complexes—defined by Corsini as "emotionally charged associations of ideas and feelings that act as magnets to draw a net of imagery, memories, and ideas into their orbit."23

According to the *Oxford American Dictionary*, a complex as it relates to psychoanalysis is "a related group of emotionally significant ideas that are completely or partly repressed and that cause psychic conflict leading to abnormal mental states or behavior."

Freud and Adler used Jung's view of the complexes but also found that many patients attempted to control or manage a complex by projecting its contents. Corsini explains, "[A] man with a negative mother complex, for instance, may see all women in an exaggeratedly negative light. (Projection means attributing to another person something that really belongs to one's own personality.) Another way a person may try to avoid a complex is by repression. Thus, a woman with a negative mother complex may cut herself off from all that she considers feminine so as not to resemble her mother in any way. Another woman with a mother complex might perceive herself as an all-good, 'earth mother' type of woman. In more extreme cases, a complex may overpower an individual so that the person loses touch with reality, becoming psychotic."[24]

Although the Oedipus complex is related to Freud's emphasis on a child's personality development, Jung was one of the first to clarify the importance of the early mother-child relationship as a positive key in the child's personality development.

Jung ultimately worked to clarify and further develop his view of the two facets to the human psyche. One is the conscious side with a person's senses—mind, emotions and desires. The other is the unconscious side which holds forgotten or denied experiences. Corsini concludes, "According to Jungian theory, our conscious understanding of who we are comes from two sources: the first derives from encounters with social reality, such as the things people tell us about ourselves, the second from what we deduce from our observations of others. If others seem to agree with our self-assessment, we tend to think we are normal; if they disagree, we tend to see ourselves, or to be seen by others, as abnormal."[25]

Although Jung seemed to dance around the spiritual issues, he was one of the first to suggest and consider that there might be a benefit in viewing addictions through a spiritual component. The Wikipedia website explains, "Jung once treated an American patient (Rowland Hazard III) suffering from chronic alcoholism. After working with the patient [with] no significant progress,...near to hopeless, save only the possibility of a spiritual experience, Rowland took Jung's advice seriously and set about seeking a personal spiritual experience. He returned home to the United States and joined a Christian evangelical Re-Armament movement known as the *Oxford Group*. He also told other alcoholics what Jung had told him about the importance of a spiritual experience. One of the alcoholics he told was Ebby Thacher, a long-time friend and drinking buddy of Bill Wilson.... Thacher told Wilson about Jung's ideas. Wilson, who was finding it impossible to maintain sobriety, was impressed and sought out his own spiritual experience. The influence of Jung thus indirectly found its way into the formation of Alcoholics Anonymous, the original twelve-step program, and from there into the whole twelve-step recovery movement, although AA as a whole is not Jungian and Jung had no role in the formation of that approach."26

Jung is reported to have said to a patient regarding participation in the Oxford Group, "So long as you are there, you settle your affair with the Oxford Group. I can't do it better than Jesus."²⁷

The Wikipedia site relates a more contemporary version of Jung's impact on the medical world through television. "Dr. Niles Crane on the popular television sitcom Frasier is a devoted Jungian psychiatrist, while his brother Dr. Frasier Crane is a Freudian psychiatrist...from time to time forming a point of argument. One memorable scene had Niles filling in for Frasier on Frasier's call-in radio program, in which Niles introduces himself as the temporary substitute saying, '....and while my brother is a Freudian, I am a Jungian, so there's no blaming Mother today.' "²⁸

A Biblical Perspective

Let us first lay a foundation for the biblical view of man's essence and being. The component parts that cause us to be who we are can be reduced to how we believe God created us—that is, how did God create the elements that make up our humanity?

There are divergent views on this issue that should be mentioned. Some theologians feel the Bible teaches what is called the dichotomist view of man. A

basic description of the dichotomist view would conclude that man is a two-part being—spiritual and physical, or as Plato might label them, soul and body. The tendency to mix spirit and soul into one entity and to reject any clear distinction between the two becomes apparent. This view defines spirit and soul as one and the same, housed in a physical body.

We believe the Scriptures teach what is referred to as the trichotomist view(3)—that man is a spirit being who expresses himself through a soul (mind, emotions and will), both of which are housed in a body. It is our view that the soul and spirit are very different in function and significance.

We believe this view is not only confirmed in New Testament teaching, but is paralleled by the Trinity example of the Godhead and additionally is confirmed in Old Testament teaching where there are striking parallels of meaning with the component parts of the tabernacle.

The tabernacle was made up of an outer court where the animals were brought for physical sacrifice. The outer court was open for all to see—a representation of our external physical body.

The holy place was an area that many parallel to the soul. It was an area not seen by the public and it contained three elements: a lamp stand, representing the mind, bringing light to our understanding; a table of incense, representing the emotions, a sweet savor unto God; and the table of shewbread, representing the will, the area of the soul that must be formed, shaped and put under the heat of fire. Finally, there was the holy of holies. This was where God dwelt and represents how the Holy Spirit lives within the human spirit. See graphic in Appendix F-1.

There are also hints of this distinction of the human spirit in passages such as Ezekiel's foretelling God's act of redemption to come for Israel: *I will give you a new heart and put a new spirit in you; I will remove from you your heart of stone and give you a heart of flesh. And I will put my Spirit in you and move you to follow my decrees and be careful to keep my laws* (Ezekiel 36:26-27, NIV).

Notice that God will put a new spirit (small 's') in you, and then he will put his Spirit (large 'S') in you. This is a clear statement that his Spirit will indwell the spirit of his people.

Certainly there are two very clear passages in the New Testament that confirm the distinction between soul and spirit. 1 Thessalonians 5:23 says *May the God of peace, sanctify you through and through. May your whole spirit, soul and body be kept blameless at the coming of our Lord Jesus Christ.* Hebrews 4:12 says *The word of God is living and active. Sharper than any double-edged sword, it penetrates even to dividing soul and spirit, joints and marrow; it judges the thoughts and attitudes of the heart* (NIV).

In his rather exhaustive work on a study of biblical psychology Dr. John Woodward notes: "The Holy Spirit works in and through the human spirit, but this is not said of the human soul. *The Spirit itself beareth witness with our spirit (Romans 8:16)*."[29]

The Tricotomist View in Counseling

Using the tricotomist view of man helps us to better understand the basic difference between one who believes in and has placed their trust in Jesus Christ as their Lord and Savior and one who has not.

Coming into this world, we are born with a spirit (small "s") that is dead to God. However, our soul is very much alive, offering us the capability to think, feel and make choices. We are housed in a body, an "earth suit" as one counselor friend refers to our body. But we are dead to God and have no understanding of spiritual things. As 1 Corinthians 2:14 says, *The man without the Spirit does not accept the things that come from the Spirit of God, for they are foolishness to him, and he cannot understand them, because they are spiritually discerned* (NIV).

When we receive Jesus Christ as our Savior, the Scriptures tell us we are born from above, of the Spirit (capital "S") and the eyes of our understanding are opened to spiritual things.

Psychoanalytic Therapy

As we look now at our condition before God we might view it in a visual sense as three concentric circles or squares as shown in Appendix A-2. The smaller square in the center is the inner man, the spirit that is now indwelt by the Holy Spirit. The next larger square is the soul, the part of us that is unique. It makes up our personality, how we think with our mind, feel with our emotions and make choices with our will. Of course, all of this is housed in the largest square, our physical body. Where our body goes, our spirit and soul go also. Our body is our container, our visual presence, how we can be identified by sight.

The Scriptures teach that believers are spiritually complete in Christ. As a believer, we have been placed into the body of Christ and the Holy Spirit of God has been placed in us. We are now his. God is our Father. We are his child. That part is finished. We are now citizens of another kingdom because we are complete in him as spiritual beings.

Our soul (mind, emotions and will) however, still carries baggage from the old kingdom. The programming of our mind by the world and emotions is self-centered, narcissistic, greedy and covetous. These characteristics are a carry-over of our fallen nature—the way we have been programmed by the world, the flesh and the devil to think, feel and make choices. Everything revolves around us, our wants, our desires, our drives. Our free will has a natural tendency to give us what we want and need to feed those desires and drives. Our belief systems have been programmed to justify those tendencies. We believe this is what Paul was referring to in his letter to the church at Rome: *I can anticipate the response that is coming: 'I know that all God's commands are spiritual, but I'm not. Isn't this also your experience?' Yes. I'm full of myself—after all, I've spent a long time in sin's prison. What I don't understand about myself is that I decide one way, but then I act another, doing things I absolutely despise* (Romans 7:14-16, MSG).

To this degree we come into the world with the deterministic tendencies that psychoanalysis would likely consider instinct or beyond our natural control.

It is our redemption that separates us from the Freudian paradigm and gives us the understanding to see the struggle within and draw on God's indwelling power as we, like Paul, learn to overcome those tendencies. One of the major changes that takes place when one becomes a believer by faith is that our natural deterministic tendencies have now been made ineffective, and real choice through the indwelling power of the Holy Spirit is a reality. See Appendix A-3.

The Triune Connection

Freud was diligent and insightful in pointing out the

natural conflict that is inherent to all of humanity. The unbeliever faces the boundaries set within his own conscience. The believer faces the boundaries set by the indwelling Holy Spirit.

Freud describes id as the instinctual sexual drives of the body. They of course include the mind and emotions, but are physically driven and satisfied. Touch and feeling are central to these drives. They can be so strong that they cause us to yield to them at the expense of our own conscience. This desire for self-satisfaction in biblical terms is called the *flesh*. Galatians 5:17 says that *the flesh lusts against the Spirit, and the Spirit against the flesh; and these are contrary to one another, so that you do not do the things that you wish.*

Freud's super ego would parallel the Spirit who indwells the spirit of the believing Christian at the time of salvation. As Freud's super ego desires to limit the instinctual drives and desires of the id, the Holy Spirit wants to teach the believer to maintain control of those natural drives and desires and yield ourselves to the ways of God the Father. Romans 6:13 encourages us to *neither yield your members as instruments of unrighteousness unto sin: but yield yourselves unto God, as those that are alive from the dead, and your members as instruments of righteousness unto God* (KJV).

Finally, Freud's ego is the conscious self that

determines what is good for the person. This finds its parallel with our soul—our mind, emotions and will, our abilities to think, feel and choose. God has given the believer the free-will ability to make choices that will develop a life of joy, free from guilt and destructive behavior.

As Freud's super ego works to prevent the id from yielding to the overwhelming urges of the instinctual sexual drives, God's Spirit is at work to prevent the flesh from pulling us into the gratifying ways of the world, the flesh and the devil at the expense of the joy and peace that is inherent to the believer. Of course, the ability to choose to go against those "instinctual drives and desires" is what separates righteous living from unrighteous living.

The Power of the Flesh

Freud, like all unbelievers, lacked spiritual understanding in the area of the works of the flesh.

In its simplest form, what the New Testament often refers to as the flesh can best be described as those moments when the believer's soul and body willingly cooperate with the ever-present power of indwelling sin.

Freud's view of repression seems to have a similar connection. He believed it was possible for the mind to

Psychoanalytic Therapy

push certain thoughts away and repress them into the unconscious. He indicated that this repression was one of the defense mechanisms by which the ego could avoid internal conflict and pain.

The Scriptures are clear that the flesh is at war with God's Holy Spirit and the believer uses repression to resist the urgings of the Spirit and chooses to yield to the power of sin, thus avoiding the conflict between the Spirit and the flesh. Galatians 5:17 says *The desires of the flesh are opposed to the [Holy] Spirit, and the [desires of the] Spirit are opposed to the flesh (godless human nature); for these are antagonistic to each other [continually withstanding and in conflict with each other], so that you are not free but are prevented from doing what you desire to do* (AMP).

Clearly the negative behavior that Freud saw as stemming from the subconscious is what the Scriptures identify as the flesh, which is always at war with God's Spirit. The battle the flesh has with the Spirit also has a three-part makeup that combines to draw the believer away from God's ways. The world, the flesh and the devil are always at work to use the power of sin to pull us away from our trust and love for our heavenly Father.

Jung's background and early life in what we would believe was a Christian home probably helped to shape his view that a person's perception of reality is determined by who they are. This view, like so many other psychological views can be reduced to the distinctions between sinners and saints. All of humanity is under the heading of one of those two titles.

Due to the sin of Adam, all come into this world as what the Scripture refers to as sinners. We are born lost and separated from God. Our sin does not cause us to become sinners. We are sinners, by nature, and find ourselves spring-loaded toward sin. *When Adam sinned, sin entered the world. Adam's sin brought death, so death spread to everyone, for everyone sinned* (Romans 5:12, NLT). Once a person becomes a believer, that person becomes a saint in biblical terms. All believers continue to commit sins, but their identity as a child of God is that of a saint. The apostle Paul opens many of his letters to the churches—Philippians, Ephesians, Colossians—with the statement *To the saints....*

The Scriptures are clear to draw a marked contrast in the identity differences between believer and unbeliever—saint and sinner. In basic terms a saint is one who is holy, with right standing before God. Review Appendix A-1. → pg. 315

Does this distinction infer that a believer is sinless? No, but the believer is no longer a sinner by identity, he is a saint who sometimes sins.

Jung felt that being a Christian placed a negative effect on the "natural animal drives" within us. Again, one could assume this came to him through his early exposure to the demands of the law in the Scriptures. Like Freud, Jung could see and experience the conflict between his conscience and his innate desires, but that may have been as near as he got to understanding this form of conflict in a spiritual sense and in the reality of the battle going on between the kingdoms of good and evil. The early chapters of Paul's letter to the church at Rome made it clear that unbelievers were without excuse due to God's creation and their own conscience.

Faulty Belief Systems

As we consider what Freud termed instinctual drives, we are inclined to ponder what the force behind instinct is. Is instinct limited to a natural or fixed pattern of behavior? Is instinct merely a learned behavior, or is instinct itself driven by faulty belief systems, many of which are deeply influenced by powers outside ourselves?

Certainly we have all been influenced by sources outside ourselves. As children, we are deeply influenced by what we are taught, told, see and experience.

I, Roger, recall a disturbing incident from my own childhood. At the age of twelve I was nearing graduation from the eighth grade. In our small Midwestern town it was an annual occurrence to recognize the eighth grade boy who exhibited high marks in areas such as scholastics, sportsmanship, integrity and other positive character traits. The award was given by the local American Legion branch at a community-wide ceremony. I was fortunate to receive the honor and felt very proud in front of my peers, parents and neighbors. A few days later I was standing near the door of a corner hang out near the school when the father of one of my competitors for the award entered. He came directly to me, pointed his finger in my face, and said, "You may have won that award, but you'll never amount to a damned thing."

Now, more than half a century later, and with numerous successful ventures behind me, there are still occasions when that father's face, voice and words are vivid in my mind.

I have learned to see well beyond that moment, but there was a faulty belief system that sunk its roots into my soul that day that had subtle influences on my thinking, feeling and decision-making for years.

Faulty belief systems can become strongholds effecting our deepest thoughts and emotions. A stronghold is a wrong pattern of thinking built on faulty beliefs. Only truth can tear these strongholds down, and ultimate truth finds its source in the Scriptures. 2 Corinthians 10:3-5 tell us, *For though we live in the world, we do not wage war as the world does. The weapons we fight with are not the weapons of the world. On the contrary, they have divine power to demolish strongholds. We demolish arguments and every pretension that sets itself up against the knowledge of God, and we take captive every thought to make it obedient to Christ.* (TNIV).

Freedom came to me through an understanding and acceptance of God's truth in Christ.

Choices Begin with Beliefs

There are some adherents to psychoanalysis who seem to understand the importance of a person's need to go against this so-called instinct and learn to make healthy choices. In fact, Gerald Corey seems to suggest that one of the goals of psychoanalysis is to strengthen the will to override what are termed hidden motivations. But this view would seem to be in conflict with the pure Freudian view that human actions are ultimately determined by causes outside the will.

Every person's belief system is based on what they believe to be truth. For the Christian, truth begins with what God has given us in the Scriptures. A counselor friend puts it in a very simple statement: "Truth is what God says, and faith is acting like God tells the truth." This may sound simplistic, but it is a good foundation on which to begin a search for what truth is.

Throughout our childhood and early teen years, when everyone is an authority figure and peer pressures abound, our belief system imports data from a multitude of sources. Much of that data constitutes a mix of negative messages about ourselves: "I'm inadequate, inferior, unworthy, ungodly and afraid." These messages lead to negative thoughts and feelings about ourselves that are then confirmed by additional experiences and messages that add layers to those thoughts and feelings. Since we are not fully aware of the impact of truth on our deepest sense of being, we are motivated to construct layers of protection into our belief systems in order to feel good about ourselves and to assure our value as a person.

Ultimately these beliefs become what Scripture refers to as strongholds. A stronghold can become so powerful that it creates emotional and behavioral responses that could be viewed as instinctual or set patterns of response to certain external stimulation.

What Freud believed to be human nature that is deterministic should be viewed as applying only to one who is outside the body of Christ.

For the Christian, the indwelling Holy Spirit's purpose is to reveal truth to the soul, empowering the believer to make choices that can and will transcend the faulty belief systems, negate the power of wrong patterns of thinking and tear down the strongholds that perpetuate the resulting destructive behavior.

Chapter Seven

Reality Therapy

William Glasser was born in Cleveland, Ohio on May 11, 1925, to Ben and Betty Glasser. He would later characterize his childhood as uneventful but happy. In high school he played the cornet in the band and became interested in sports, something that he would follow throughout his life. He attended Case Institute of Technology, majoring in chemical engineering. While he was still a student, he married Naomi Judith Silver. He pursued a doctorate in clinical psychology, but decided to attend medical school at Western Reserve University after his dissertation was rejected in graduate school. He received his medical degree in 1953 at the age of 28, completed his psychiatric residency at UCLA in 1957 and was board certified in 1961.

While practicing psychiatry, he became disillusioned by the ineffectiveness of traditional psychoanalytic theory and began using alternative methods while working with adolescent girls at an institute in California. Three years later, he published *Reality Therapy: A New Approach to Psychiatry.*

Reality Therapy submits that we are responsible for what we choose to do. We are not victims of our past unless we choose to be and that all of our problems must be dealt with in the present, not the past. Rejecting Freudian theory, Glasser began to describe patients not as ill, but as weak. Individuals could function as healthy persons only if their abilities were strengthened.

Glasser published *Schools Without Failure* in 1969, which applied the principles of reality therapy to the school setting.

He was married to Naomi for over 40 years when she died in 1994. Before her death, she joined her husband in writing, *What Are You Doing? (1980) and Control Theory in the Practice of Reality Therapy (1989). Glasser wrote Reality Therapy In Action in 2000 and Counseling with Choice Theory* in 2001.

Philosophy

At its basis, Reality Therapy is a theory that states that we are all responsible for our choices—what we

Reality Therapy

decide to do and what we decide not to do. It is true that we may be a product of our past, but we are not victims of our past unless we choose to be.

"Reality therapists believe the underlying problem of all clients is the same: they are either involved in an unsatisfying relationship or lack what could even be called a relationship. If therapy is to be successful, the therapist must guide the client to a satisfying relationship and teach the client to behave in more effective ways than he or she is presently behaving. Few clients have any clear understanding that their problem comes from the way they choose to behave. Reality therapists recognize that clients choose their behavior as a way to deal with the frustration caused by their unsatisfying relationship. All of these behavior choices—ranging from profound psychosis to mild depression—are described in detail in the DSM-IV."[1] The DSM-IV is the *Diagnostic and Statistical Manual of Mental Disorders* that is used by those in the mental health field.

So the goal and focus for the Reality Therapist is to teach clients how to make more effective choices in dealing with those who are important to them. How do we choose appropriate friendships that will develop into a healthy relationship? How do we treat friends with dignity and respect? How do we get close in relationships while guarding our own boundaries and avoiding codependent relationships?

The therapist's first task with the client is to establish mutual respect so that the client will trust the therapist enough to deal with the choices he or she is making. Glasser believes that every human being needs involvement. The therapist must become involved with the client if growth is to take place. This involves warmth, understanding, trust, friendliness, openness, concern and acceptance.

Once this type of involvement has been established, the therapist is free to challenge the client with the reality and consequences of their behavior. "This is accomplished by leading them to evaluate what they do and, if it isn't satisfactory for them or those they care for, to help them gain more responsible behaviors. A responsible behavior is defined as one that satisfies one's needs and does not prevent others from satisfying theirs. Therapy should focus on the present and on getting people to understand that they choose essentially all their actions in an attempt to fulfill basic needs. When they are unable to do this they suffer, or cause others to suffer. The therapist's task is to lead them toward better or more responsible choices that are almost always available."[2]

Anything and everything is open for discussion in reality therapy. This includes recent vacations, television shows, work-related discussions or family relationships. According to Glasser, a client's problems may not enter into discussion during an hour of therapy. "Interesting nonproblem discussions are valuable in therapy because they develop the intellectual sharing that is important in Reality Therapy. They should be stimulating, with values, opinions, and beliefs brought out and some emotion experienced. Extensive talking about a patient's problems and his feelings about them focuses upon his self-involvement and consequently gives his failure meaning. Long discussions about the patient's problems can be a common and serious error in psychotherapy. It is tempting to listen to his complaints because they seem so urgent. Doing so may reduce his pain and make him feel better for a while as he basks in the attention he receives. If he doesn't change his behavior, however, his pain will return and he will grow disillusioned with therapy."[3]

Foundational Precepts

Glasser believes that there are five basic needs that every human being has. These are genetically encoded needs that we are born with that drive our behavior. Our brain functions in a manner that tells us whether or not we are satisfying these needs. When we are happy and satisfied, our needs are being met. When we are in emotional pain, one or more of our basic needs are not being met. Driven by the pain we feel, we do our best to determine how we can feel better.

The task of the reality therapist is to teach the client what Glasser called Choice Theory, so that the client can identify the need that is not being met. "Choice theory asserts that all we ever do from birth to death is behave and that our behavior is internally motivated and chosen. Every total behavior is always our best attempt to get what we want to satisfy our needs. Behavior is purposeful because it is designed to close the gap between what we want and what we perceive we are getting. Specific behaviors are always generated from this discrepancy. Our behaviors come from the inside, and thus we choose our destiny."[4]

The five encoded needs outlined by Glasser became his basis for understanding human behavior and the foundation that Reality Therapy was built on. Glasser's basic needs to include: 1) a need for being loved and belonging, 2) power and competence for self-esteem, 3) fun or enjoyment, 4) freedom and independence, and 5) survival.

These needs serve as sources for all behavior. The difference between what a person wants and what he perceives he is getting is what motivates the human being into specific behavior at any given time. Glasser stated that all human behaviors are composed of acting out or doing, thinking, feeling and physiology. Because human behavior originates from within the person, human beings are, and should be, responsible for their behavior. Therefore, the emphasis in therapy is always on taking responsibility for oneself. If we choose our behavior, we must be responsible for it. Glasser believes that human beings see their world through a perceptual system that functions as a set of lenses. In other words, we perceive the world around us and value it as either neutral, positive or negative. How we perceive it determines, in large part, what behavior we choose.

Reality therapy makes the assumption that every individual desires to be different. One of the initial goals in therapy is to assist the client in identifying their needs and desires that determine their uniqueness. Les Parrott addresses this assumption: "No matter where the search may go, no other person exists who thinks, looks, acts, and talks exactly as we do…. Based on this, we develop either a negative or positive identity. People with a positive self-image believe that they are worthwhile, that there is at least one other person in the world who cares about them. Negative identities are formed by individuals who do not think well of themselves and who, as a result, also have problems caring about other people. Characterized by irresponsible and self-defeating behavior that hurts themselves and others, these people engage in behavior that often denies reality. As a result, reality therapy views identity through one's behavior. Unlike behavioristic theory that focuses on a stimulus-response paradigm, reality therapy measures behavior against the objective standard of reality, with which individuals are either in consonance or dissonance. Because the reality therapist believes that a change in behavior must precede a change in identity, the focus is on changing irresponsible, self-defeating behavior. According to Glasser, 'we are what we do.' Therefore, in order to change 'who we are' (identity), we must change 'what we do' (behavior). Thus, change in identity follows a change in behavior."[5]

Role of the Therapist

Reality theory rejects the conventional concept of mental illness. Therefore, the reality therapist sees diagnoses such as depression, schizophrenia and bipolar disorder as serving no purpose other than to alienate and separate. Rather, the reality therapist sees these as chosen behaviors designed to satisfy the client's needs. Raymond Corsini writes, "None of these happen to us. Painful and ineffective as they may be, all these strategies are our attempt to control the world to satisfy our needs."[6]

Likewise, the reality therapist makes certain that symptoms are not the focus in therapy because focusing on symptoms keeps the client from facing their own destructive choices. "The pain or the symptom that clients choose is not important to the counseling process. Reality therapists spend little time on symptoms because they cannot be improved until clients' significant relationships are improved.... Glasser contends that clients will complain forever about their symptoms if the therapist will listen. Coupling this with long journeys into the past is what results in lengthy therapy."[7]

As we have noted previously, the reality therapist strives to keep therapy in the present. While conventional therapies tend to focus on the client's past behavior, the reality therapist views this as a waste of time and prefers to focus on current behaviors that are ineffective. Corsini continues, "It is the present that is the cutting edge upon which we live our lives, and the reality therapist focuses upon how we could, more effectively, control the world right now through evaluating our behaviors and choosing better ones."[8]

Unlike the psychoanalytic therapist, the reality therapist sees no place for, or validity in, the concept of transference. This concept simply puts thoughts into the client's head that serve no purpose. To the reality therapist, this is a "false and misleading concept."[9]

Also, much unlike psychoanalytic theory, the reality therapist sees little use for dream analysis or a focus into the unconscious. "Reality therapy deals with what the patient is presently aware of and then works to make the patient aware of as much as possible."[10]

One of the chief components of reality therapy

requires the client to take a serious look at his or her behavior and ascertain whether this behavior is effective in obtaining their goals. The therapist never takes a moral position, yet presses the client to evaluate the effectiveness of the behavior based on what the client has already told the therapist regarding what they want for their life.

Reality Therapy is a process that involves both the therapist's and the client's input. Reality therapists often make an effort to self-disclose in order to assist the client in evaluating the effectiveness of his behavior. This involves sharing personal struggles and experiences, as well as their own weaknesses, that are designed to help the client see that it is alright to have vulnerabilities. It is hoped that by doing this, the client will be more able to share his own failures.

At this point in therapy, the reality therapist can begin to teach the client how to more easily realize his or her goals through the behaviors they involve themselves in. The client needs to evaluate the choices they are making and determine to make wiser ones that will meet their own stated goals.

In accomplishing the task of making clients more effective in the control of their lives, reality therapists take certain steps. The first of these steps is getting involved with their client and establishing a friendship with them that will allow them to be open and honest. The client needs to feel support and encouragement from the reality therapist and to know that the therapist supports them and believes in them. The therapist's trust and support communicates to the client a sense of self-worth and self-esteem. The goal here is to assist the client in determining what they want in their life. Through this process, the client should come to see that they can control their lives with more effective behavior.

The second step is for the client to understand what they are doing now to get what they want, whether it's effective or not. Glasser writes, "No one can work to gain a successful identity or to increase personal success without being aware of his current behavior. If a person does not acknowledge his behavior or claims to be unaware of it, he won't be able to gain or to maintain a successful identity."[11]

It is then necessary for the therapist to help the client determine whether what they are doing is helpful in obtaining their goals. In other words, "How is it working for you?" The client needs to evaluate their choice of behavior as to whether it is effective in getting them what they claim they want. As Corey notes, "Now the patient must look at his behavior critically and judge it on the basis of whether or not it is his best choice. The reality therapist asks him to judge his behavior on the basis of whether he believes it is good for him and good for the people he cares about.... The reality therapist does not act as a moralist; he never tells a patient that what he is doing is wrong and that he must change. The therapist does not judge the behavior; through their involvement and by bringing the actual behavior out in the open, he leads the patient to evaluate his own behavior. [The patient] then usually sees that better choices are available."[12]

Once the client decides that what he is doing is not obtaining the desired result, and that better choices are indeed available to him, the therapist should assist the client in determining a more efficient way to obtain their goal and thus take control of their lives. An effective way of bringing this about is through constructive debate. Challenging each other's ideas and beliefs cause the client to feel that he is being taken seriously and that the reality therapist is taking stock in seeing the client take control of their lives. Through this, the client is able to plan new behaviors that will bring about the desired result.

"Once someone makes a value judgment, he or she must be helped to develop realistic plans for action to follow that judgment. Many people can examine their behavior and decide that it is not helping them, but they have no experience or background for planning a more successful life. They do not know how to plan for more responsible, competent behavior. Encouraging the person who needs the help to make most of the plan himself is part of the therapist's skill. A plan should never be made that attempts too much; it will usually fail and reinforce the already present failure. A failing person needs success, and he needs small instances of success to gain it.... The plan should be ambitious enough so that some change, small though it may be, can be seen, yet not so great that failure is likely. Plans are not final. If one does not work, successive plans can be made until a better one is found."[13]

After a plan has been made, the therapist and client must come to an agreement to carry it out. It is helpful for the therapist to motivate the client as best he can to fulfill the agreed-upon plan. Without a commitment to do so, it is unlikely that the plan will ever take root and become a reality in the life of the client. If there is any reluctance on the part of the client to carry out the plan, the plan can be modified. If the client tends to procrastinate, it is often beneficial to put the plan in writing. As the therapist puts into writing what the agreement looks like, it emphasizes the importance of the client's following through with the agreed-upon plan. While verbal agreements can be effective, a contract signed by both parties can create a commitment to follow through with the plan more readily. Once the plan has been accomplished, it can serve as a reminder to the client that he or she was able to successfully complete their goal and serve as a reinforcement in setting and completing future goals.

Absolutely no excuses should be accepted. The therapist's attitude should be one of showing no interest in why the plan was not carried out, but showing particular interest in when and how the client plans to carry it out now. This will bring the client to a place of choosing better behaviors right now and stop creating reasons for being ineffective in living their lives to the fullest measure.

"The only course of action—and it is a powerful one—open to the therapist or helping person is never to excuse the person who needs help from the responsibility of the commitment. We cannot help anyone if we admit that there are valid excuses for not fulfilling a reasonable plan. Valid or not, to become successful, the patient must fulfill the plan.... When someone does not fulfill his commitment, his failure should not be emphasized. We simply ask, 'are you still going to try to fulfill the commitment? If you say you are, then when?' We wait; time is rarely a serious obstacle. If we keep our involvement, if we keep making plans and getting commitments, eventually the patient will begin to fulfill them."[14]

This may indeed involve confrontation, which is often an important tool in the repertoire of the reality therapist. The client will need to determine whether their current behavior is the best thing for them, and confrontation may be needed to assist the client in making this determination. Therefore, the reality therapist must be comfortable with confronting the client about the need to set goals and meet them.

The therapist should never be punishing with words or action. The therapist's attitude should always be accepting of the client, even when the client is not following through with their responsibility. An attitude of punishment tears down the relationship necessary for trust to develop between client and therapist.

Finally, the therapist should never give the client the impression that they are giving up. "We believe that the therapist must literally persevere with the patient long enough so that the patient begins to understand that therapists will neither give up nor let patients control them. [T]he dogged therapist will become more and more a part of the patient's internal world, more and more seen as a helping, caring, concerned person, and more and more able to begin to become friends with the patient. A good friend does not give up easily."[15]

Types of Strategies

The reality therapist uses a number of strategies to assist the client in obtaining their stated goals during the course of therapy. *Structuring* is one of these strategies. Structuring helps the client to understand what the nature, the limits, and the goals of therapy are. Reality therapists assist the client in structuring their expectations for therapy.

"This structuring helps clients adjust their expectations and gives them a realistic hope for change. Providing clients with confidence in their therapist, it lets them know their therapist values their well-being.... Simple descriptions of the counseling process such as discussing fees or talking about the expected number of sessions may help alleviate the anxiety clients feel. By helping clients accept the responsibility for their behavior and by allowing them to face the reality of their situation, structuring encourages them to remain in therapy so that they can continue to face reality."[16]

Another important strategy used by the reality therapist includes *instruction*, which involves teaching the client desired skill sets that make it possible to achieve the desired goals set in therapy. Also important is the skillful questioning by the therapist, which is required in therapy to assist the client in seeing that change is needed. "The practitioner of reality therapy helps clients to evaluate their behavior by asking a number of direct questions, such as: Is what you are doing helping or hurting you? Is what you are doing now, what you want to be doing? Is your behavior working for you? Is what you are doing against the rules? Is what you want realistic or attainable? And...how committed are you to the therapeutic process, and to changing your life? Direct questions like these begin to highlight the importance of choice."[17]

Emphasizing choice is critical in reality therapy.

The client needs to realize that she is in complete control of her life by the choices she makes. It is the client's responsibility, and their responsibility alone, to make choices that enhance their lives.

When the client is finding it difficult to put into practice skills that are being taught by the therapist, the reality therapist may choose to use *role play*. Corey suggests "When clients are struggling to put to practice recently acquired skills, the reality therapist may turn to role playing techniques that help 'presentize' clients' behavior and then allow them to rehearse events that cause their anxiety. During a role playing activity, clients learn to prepare for the consequences of their behavior, including their feelings, while performing the activity. Difficulties in interpersonal relationships are often relieved through role playing specific situations with the reality therapist."[18]

The therapeutic use of *humor* can also benefit the therapist/client relationship if used carefully and can assist the client in learning to laugh at himself. "Humor is, and should be, a regular part of the whole therapeutic process. The ability to laugh freely is an integral part of a well-balanced self-concept and approach to life. In fact, the ability to laugh at one's own follies, one's own mistakes, and one's own accidental errors is one of the highest forms of a mentally healthy self-concept.... Laughing and humor are related to joy and happiness."[19]

Finally, the reality therapist needs to be proficient at assessing the client, especially in determining progress and when therapy should end.

"While the counselor in reality therapy makes little attempt to test, diagnose, interpret or otherwise assess clients, he or she does evaluate their progress toward desired goals. Although the basic requirement on the part of the client is responsibility, almost any constructive, responsible change in the clients' behavior is defined as a step in that direction. Termination of therapy is warranted, 'if the patient can act in increasingly responsible ways, resolve crises and adjustment problems through accepting that he is responsible for himself and his behavior, and that he can fulfill his needs without hurting himself or other people' (Glasser & Zunin, p.327)."[20]

A Biblical Perspective

Reality therapy views identity through a person's behavior. If you change the behavior, a person's identity will change. The inquisitive mind must then ask, "Does behavior produce identity, or does a person's concept of self and identity motivate certain behavior?"

We would, of course, agree with Glasser that one cannot have a positive identity without being aware of his or her behavior. But the biblical concept of identity suggests that identity itself is the foundation on which we build proper behavior. Let us consider the concept of sinners and sin. When we come into this world do we sin (behavior) to become sinners (identity), or is it the reverse—we sin (behavior) because we are sinners (identity)? The Scriptures make it clear that everyone born into the line of our original parents, Adam and Eve, are born with a sinful nature that has been passed down to all of humanity. Thus, we sin because we are sinners.

When a person is born again, receiving Jesus Christ as his Savior and Lord, that person's sins are identified with Christ's sacrificial death on the cross. *I have been crucified with Christ; it is no longer I who live, but Christ lives in me; and the life which I now live in the flesh I live by faith in the Son of God, who loved me and gave Himself for me* (Galatians 2:20).

At the exact instant that a person is born again, they are placed into the body of Christ; the Spirit of God now indwells that person's spirit. *If anyone is in Christ, he is a new creation; old things have passed away; behold, all things have become new* (2 Corinthians 5:17).

By identity, the new creation is no longer a sinner. The person is now a saint. As noted previously, most of the apostle Paul's letters to the churches address the people as *the saints at Ephesus, the saints in Christ Jesus at Philippi* and *the saints at Colosse.* There was no question to Paul that these believers had an identity change, even though they often continued living in sin.

The apostle also opened his letters to the churches with reminders of what that change in identity meant to them. Don't lose sight of the fact that *you are blessed with every spiritual blessing.... he has made us accepted in the Beloved.... he who has begun a work in you will complete it....* and.... *the Father has qualified us to be partakers of the inheritance of the saints in the light.* Only after reminding the churches of their identity did Paul then address what that meant to them as far as their behavior was concerned. It other words, in light of who you now are, this is how you should now behave. Clearly, to Paul, behavior was to be the result of identity. Identity had become the motivating force behind healthy behavior.

It is, of course, feasible that any of us can learn to force certain behaviors. I can choose to behave in a way that will be perceived by others as good and appropriate. But can that forced behavior really change the way I see my value and worth?

Remember our formula in an earlier chapter: Thoughts trigger emotions which lead to behaviors. *For as he thinks in his heart, so is he* (Proverbs 23:7).

As we think in the depths of our being, so shall we be in our feelings, actions and behaviors. We can profess to believe many things, but we will live according to what we truly believe in our heart of hearts.

The human race has always had a struggle for identity. But the very essence of God's concept of grace is based on changing our identity first as a way to change our behavior. *There are a few people that God has chosen by his grace. And if he chose them by grace, it is not for the things they have done. If they could be made God's people by what they did, God's gift of grace would not really be a gift* (Romans 11: 5-6 NCV.

By definition the state of grace in which all believers find themselves is the condition of being in God's favor, one of the elect. The old covenant dictated that my identity was based on my behavior. The new covenant ushered in a different plan for defining my identity—we are made holy and righteous in Christ, and our good works, our behavior and actions are the result of our new identity.

By definition moral strength is the grace to perform a duty.

The grace given to us as a gift of God is often referred to as *unmerited favor*. That is true, but it is more than that. Our Lord was full of grace and truth, yet he was not in need of *unmerited* favor. Grace is also power. The power to change the way we think, the way we feel, the way we behave, the way we rely on

God and truth. I am what I am by the grace of God, yet it is not I, but the power of God through his indwelling Spirit in me. God's grace is sufficient for me. His power is made perfect through my weakness.

The basic calling of God to his children is the call for each of us to learn to walk out our new identity. To walk in the ways of the Lord based on who we are. Actions follow identity. *The good man brings good things out of the good stored up in his heart. Out of the overflow of his heart his mouth speaks* (Luke 6:45, NIV).

A dear, departed saint, Ian Thomas, often stated in his conferences what it means to have Christ as our life. With his eyes lifted toward eternity, he would often state: "He gave his life for us, to give his life to us, to live his life through us." Isn't it amazing that God placed Christ in us so he might live his life through us? Following are several Scripture passages that confirm what we are saying here:

Long ago, even before He made the world, God chose us to be His very own, through what Christ would do for us; He decided to make us holy in His sight, without a single fault—we would stand before Him covered with His love (Ephesians 1:4).

Your old sin-loving nature was buried with Him by baptism when he died, and when God the Father, with glorious power, brought Him back to life again, you were given His wonderful new life to enjoy. For you have become a part of Him, and so you died with Him when he died; and now you share His new life and shall rise as He did (Romans 6:4-5).

It is from God alone that you have your life through Christ Jesus. He showed us God's plan of salvation; he was the one who made us acceptable to God; He made us pure and holy (1 Corinthians 1:30).

For He has rescued us out of the darkness of Satan's kingdom and brought us into the kingdom of His dear Son (Colossians 1:13).

Even when we were dead through our trespasses, He made us alive together with Christ and raised us up with Him, and made us sit with Him in the heavenly places in Christ Jesus (Ephesians 2:5-6).

For you have died, and your life is hid with Christ in God. When Christ, who is our life appears, then you will also appear with Him in glory (Colossians 3:3-4).

I have been crucified with Christ; it is no longer I who live, but Christ who lives in me; and the life I now live in the flesh I live by faith in the Son of God, who loves me and gave Himself for me (Galatians 2:2).

At salvation, God took us spiritually out of Adam and placed us into the body of Christ. Our old self (our old man, as Scripture calls it), with our unregenerate spirit, was nailed to the cross with Christ. We participated literally in Christ's death, resurrection, ascension and seating at the right hand of the Father. Our identity was changed forever. See Appendix G-1. Now we have a choice—we can live in our own strength and old ways or we can give up our fleshly efforts and allow Christ to live his life through us!

Chapter Eight

Adlerian Psychotherapy

Alfred Adler (1870–1937) was a physician and psychologist in Austria, noted as the founder of the *School of Individual Psychology*. Working with Freud and a group of Freud's colleagues, Adler was among the key individuals who advanced the psychoanalytic movement.

Although his early connection with Freud was compatible, their differences led him to form his own independent school of psychotherapy and personality theory. Nancy Murdock writes, "There were six children in his middle-class Jewish family. As a child, Alfred was characterized as frail and fearful, suffering from rickets and problems with his vocal chords that resulted in stuttering. [O]nce again, we can see the connections between a theorist's life and his creation: Alder's triumph over his early inferiorities seems to have set the stage for both his medical career and his theoretical ideas."[1]

Although Adler was Jewish, his exposure to protestant Christianity was considerable as a young boy and it may have had some impact on both his life and his views, although he was hesitant to discuss religion and even many of his biographers seemed in the dark as to any religious meaning in his life.

Paul E. Stepansky addressed Adler's seeming disinterest in any form of religious connection. "Despite the fact that he grew up in Jewish neighborhoods, Adler remained strikingly indifferent to the question of his religious identity. He neither made positive identification with his Jewishness nor experienced any anti-Semitism in the rural outskirts of Vienna.... Alfred attended the Synagogue during Jewish holidays, and perhaps on the Sabbath, but he developed no elective affinity for Judaism. His parents' home...was practically adjacent to the playground used only by gentile working-class children.... As a young man, Adler underwent baptism and became a Protestant. He never commented on his conversion and his biographers have been unable to provide a satisfactory explanation, given Adler's insulation from social anti-Semitism and subsequent indifference to questions of religious belief."[2]

Although Adler and Freud began their relationship with a great deal of respect toward each other, there were soon differences that neither could overlook or overcome. Their early connection became increasingly strained over the foundational beliefs that both had committed to in their theory development.

Adler found that he could never work with Freud's view of the role of sexuality in child development. And Freud grew mildly dismissive of Adler's belief that inferiority was the culprit in personality development.

Henry Stein shares how the two met and began their professional relationship. "In 1902, when Adler was one of the few who reacted favorably to his book on dream interpretations, Freud sent him a handwritten postcard suggesting he join the circle which met weekly in Freud's home to discuss newer aspects of psychopathology.... Adler had never accepted Freud's original theories that mental difficulties were caused exclusively by a sexual trauma, and he opposed the generalizations when dreams were interpreted, in each instance, as sexual wish fulfillment."3

Harold H. Mosak develops how the distance between the two men began to grow. "Adler's increasing divergence from Freud's viewpoint led to discomfort and disillusion in the Vienna Society. Adler criticized Freud's sexual stance; Freud condemned Adler's ego psychology.... Freud thought that Adler had not discovered anything new but had merely reinterpreted what psychoanalysis had already said.... In 1911...Adler resigned as president of the Vienna Society. Later that year, Freud forced the choice between Adler and himself. Several members of the circle expressed their sympathy for Adler by resigning and forming the Society for Free Psychoanalytic Research. The word 'Free' was meant to imply that this was still a psychoanalytic society, but one free of Freud."4

Nancy Murdock offers insight to the breach that was developing and how Adler clearly wanted to put a distance between himself and Freud's views. "Abraham Maslow, the well-known humanistic psychologist, reported that Adler vehemently denied being a follower of Freud, having established from the beginning of their relationship that his views differed from Freud's."5

Adler's reputation was expanding, and it was not long before he began to make his mark in the world of psychology in the United States. But fate was to limit his influence to just a few years before his death. As conditions began to deteriorate in Europe and the Nazis were flexing their muscles and demands, Adler made the decision to leave his country and go to America.

Murdock notes that Adler's wife was not willing to make that move so Adler made the move by himself. "Raissa, his wife, remained in Vienna, and according to Adler biographer Edward Hoffman, continued to work as a central figure of the Communist Party in Austria."6

"From 1932 on he held the first chair of Visiting Professor of Medical Psychology at Long Island College of Medicine.... He was in Aberdeen, Scotland, to deliver a series of lectures at the university when, on May 28, 1937, he collapsed while walking in the street and died from heart failure within a few minutes."[7]

The Driving Force of Inferiority

Adler seemed to be motivated more by the larger picture of mankind's struggle with life's issues than the intricacies of individual cause and effect. Murdock writes, "Known as a social activist, Adler believed that societal change was needed to improve the health of humankind. For example, he characterized the development of striving for power and superiority as the 'most prominent evil of our civilization.' "[8]

Murdock went on to give us additional insights to the underlying views that motivated Adler and ultimately led him to focus on the connection between man's natural search for significance and the driving forces of inferiority that drove that need. "[T]he culture in which we live gives very little information about our individual value, and hence we are constantly uncertain of our own worth. Our task is therefore to find ourselves worthy despite occasional human imperfection.

"Individual psychology teaches that human life is tied to (two basic motivations)—the striving for power, or superiority, and the need for belonging.... Individuals who are healthy are courageous and able to take responsibility for their lives. Dysfunctional individuals are discouraged...selfish...timid...and avoid challenge and responsibility. The goal of [individual psychology] therapy is to help the client understand his faulty life style."9 As Adler refined his views it became apparent that his concern for the individual took on new dimensions that allowed for greater hope than many of his colleagues and challenged the therapeutic community to enlarge their vision of treatment success. Mosak states that "Adlerian psychology...views the person holistically as a creative, responsible, 'becoming' individual moving toward fictional goals within his or her phenomenal field. It holds that one's lifestyle is sometimes self-defeating because of inferiority feelings. The individual with 'psychopathology' is discouraged rather than sick, and the therapeutic task is to encourage the person to activate his or her social interest and to develop a new life-style through relationship, analysis, and action methods."10

Stein adds that Adler's "emphasis on power dynamics is rooted in the philosophy of Nietzsche. Adler argued for holism, viewing the individual holistically rather than reductively, the latter being the dominant lens for viewing human psychology. Adler was

Adlerian Psychotherapy

also among the first in psychology to argue in favor of feminism, making the case that power dynamics between men and women are crucial to understanding human psychology."[11]

Although there is a tendency by many of the creative leaders and pioneers in the field of psychotherapy to hold firmly to their own methods and conclusions, Adler's theory attracted other innovators to openly support his views rather than dismiss them to limit his recognition. Murdock noted that Albert Ellis' view of an individual's perception of circumstances is the driving force in what they considered reality: "The influence of Adler's theory can be seen in many theoretical approaches,...including rational emotive behavioral therapy, family systems theory, and reality therapy. [It is] reported that Albert Ellis, the founder of REBT, was a member of the American Society of Adlerian Psychology.... Adler believed that an individual's perceptions, rather than some objective external criterion, determined their views of reality."[12]

Raymond Corsini seems to agree with Murdock. "The theories of Adler and Ellis exhibit many points of convergence.... Both accept the notion that emotions are actually a form of thinking and that people create or control their emotions by controlling their thinking."[13]

Looking more closely at how Adler applied his theory to what would ultimately become the foundation for the individual psychology movement, one can visualize the three foundation stones as inferiority, superiority and significance. Murdock notes how Adler's view plays out. "Humans are motivated to strive for superiority. [P]eople are seen as being 'pulled' by their goals (of superiority) rather than driven by their instincts.... Paradoxically, humans are also beset by feelings of inferiority. Adler thought that the need to belong insured survival.... Ultimately, the motivation for human behavior is how the individual reconciles the search for significance and feelings for others.... A person can only be known through his or her personal plan to achieve superiority, which carries the scheme for dealing with feelings of inferiority and a certain level of belongingness. Equally as important in psychological functioning is the interest in society, for without the support of others, humans would not survive. This 'social interest' is inherent in the human constitution, but also is the tendency to feel inferior. The ways these two influences are balanced determine the psychological world of the individual."[14]

Murdock quotes Adler: "Inferiority feelings are a normal part of life because 'to be human means to feel inferior. It seems all human culture is based upon feelings of inferiority.' Feelings of inferiority begin at a very early age, when the child realizes that he is much smaller and weaker than those around him.... 'Ridicule of children is practically criminal,' cautioned Adler, because it causes the child to feel insignificant and inferior."[15]

Early Child Development

Adler was convinced that the perception a child develops early in life becomes that firm foundation that individual psychology refers to as *life style* and is ingrained in the child's personality and consequently reflected in the child's thinking, feeling and behavior.

Murdock notes that, "According to Adler, everyone develops a plan for his life by the age of 5 or 6. This plan, which Adler called the life style, guides individuals' entire lives, including their perception of, and actions in, the world.... The life style is the child's way of adapting to the circumstances around him.... Every life style has a goal.... A person's goal arises out of the interaction of two influences, the need for significance and feelings of community, or social interest. According to Adler, the only way to truly understand another human is to understand the goal of the life style. All behavior is purposeful, oriented toward achieving the life style goal.... For Adler, the measure of the individual is the degree to which he cares about his society.... Adler was so passionate about the importance of social interest that in a chapter entitled *The Absolute Truth*, he discussed his conviction that humans can never truly find the absolute truth."

Continuing on, Murdock is thorough in her presentation of Adler's theory and how he perceived the human condition of inferiority to be pervasive in humankind, presenting its negative notions in children from their earliest stages of development: "Neurosis has its roots in childhood. [There are] three general kinds of children with high potential to be neurotic. The first is the child who experiences *organ inferiority* early in his development. The second is the *pampered*, or spoiled child. The third is the *neglected* child. Children who experience organ inferiority, become focused on their bodies and have difficulty seeing that life meaning is achieved by contributing to others. [I]f others pity, ridicule, or avoid the child, the situation becomes even more damaging. The pampered child achieves superiority by having others do everything for him. Experiencing instant gratification, he never learns how to tackle and solve life problems, and thus his feeling of inferiority is intensified. The neglected child never had the chance to learn about love and cooperation. He sees the world as hostile and ungiving because he has never found a trustworthy other."16

The development of these inferiority feelings in children is a result of untruths, partial truths or mere misperceptions of reality and the subsequent development of faulty evaluations and convictions regarding both the child's view of self and his environment. Har-

old H. Mosak divides these lifestyle convictions into four groups:
1. The *self-concept*—who I am.
2. The *self-ideal*—what I should be.
3. The *Weltbild*, or "picture of the world"—what the world demands of me.
4. The *ethical convictions*—the personal "right-wrong" code.

When there is a discrepancy between self and ideal-self convictions...*inferiority feelings* ensue.... Lack of congruence between convictions in the self-concept and those in the *Weltbild*...also results in inferiority feelings. Discrepancies between self-concept and ethical convictions...lead to *inferiority feelings* in the moral realm.... To oversimplify, the inferiority feeling is universal and 'normal,' although it may leave us uncomfortable.

"A common patient expression in treatment might be 'If only I could....' As a therapist response he notes, 'Adlerian therapists often request that for the next week the patient act *as if*. The patient may protest that it would only be an act and therefore phony. We explain that all acting is not phony pretense, that one can try on a role as one might try on a suit. It does not change the person wearing the suit, but sometimes with a handsome suit of clothes, one may feel differently and perhaps behave differently, thus becoming a different person."[17]

Differences with Freud

Raymond Corsini's book on current psychotherapies presents in considerable detail the significant differences between Adler and Freud as their personal discovery became more meaningful and their work developed toward their ultimate view of a practical psychology as related to the human condition. The chapter on Adlerian psychotherapy in Corsini's work does a masterful task of presenting Adler's basic assumptions. An abbreviated account follows:

1. All behavior occurs in a social context.
2. Individual psychology is an interpersonal psychology.... Transcending interpersonal transactions is the development of the feeling of being a part of the larger social whole or social interest.
3. Adlerian psychology rejects reductionism in favor of holism. People behave as *if* the conscious mind moves in one direction while the unconscious mind moves in another.
4. *Conscious* and unconscious are both in the service of the individual, who uses them to further personal goals. Adler felt that humans know more than they understand.

5. Understanding the individual requires understanding his or her cognitive organization and lifestyle. A life-style is neither right nor wrong, normal nor abnormal, but merely the 'spectacles' through which people view themselves in relationship to the way in which they perceive life.
6. Behavior may change throughout a person's lifespan in accordance with both the immediate demands of the situation and the long-range goals inherent in the lifestyle.
7. People are not pushed by causes; that is, they are not determined by heredity and environment. People move toward self-selected goals that they feel will give them a place in the world, will provide them with security and will preserve their self-esteem. Life is a dynamic striving. 'The life of the human soul is not a *being* but a *becoming*. (Adler, 1963).
8. The central striving of human beings has been variously described as completion, perfection, superiority, self-realization, self-actualization, competence and mastery. If strivings are

solely for the individuals' greater glory, Adler considers them socially useless and, in extreme conditions, characteristic of mental problems. On the other hand, if the strivings are for the purpose of overcoming life's problems, the individual is engaged in the striving for self-realization, in contribution to humanity and in making the world a better place to live.

9. Individuals may select socially useful goals or they may devote themselves to the useless side of life.

10. The freedom to choose introduces the concepts of *value* and *meaning* into psychology. Even in severe psychopathology, total extension of social interest does not occur. Even the psychotic retains some commonality with normal people.

11. Differential diagnosis between functional and organic disorder often does present a problem. Because all behavior is purposeful, a *psychogenic* symptom will have a psychological or social purpose and an *organic* symptom will have a somatic purpose.

12. Life presents challenges in the form of

life tasks. The original three tasks were those of society, work and sex.

13. Because life constantly provides challenges, living demands *courage*. Courage refers to the *willingness* to engage in risk-taking behavior when one either does not know the consequences or when the consequences might be adverse. The question we must each answer is whether we have the courage to live despite the knowledge of our imperfections.

14. Life has no intrinsic meaning. The meaning we attribute to life will 'determine' our behavior. We will behave as *if* life were really in accord with our perceptions, and therefore, certain meanings will have greater practical utility than others.[18]

The Spoiled Child

Rudolf Dreikurs, a psychiatrist who lectured on Adlerian psychology and its application to children, addressed the Adlerian theory as it relates to the spoiled child: "From the very first day of his life the human child has a place in a group with which he has to make contact in order that the necessities of his life may be satisfied. His first way of communicating with his surroundings is by crying.... From the very outset the infant has certain social functions to perform.

Dreikurs suggested that the older the child becomes, the more difficulty there is in helping him participate in his social environment. "Each day strengthens his resistance to any change, once he has grown accustomed to having his own way.... The child thus makes his first important discovery—that he can get his own way by screaming.... He need not submit to the rules.... He need not earn recognition by any achievements of his own.... He never learns to put up with anything he does not like.

Dreikurs believed that it was in this area where Freud and Adler came to one of their many divergent views. "Freudians make the fatal mistake of regarding the child and the whole of mankind as obedient to the 'pleasure principle,' so that every frustration must be the counterpart of a 'pleasure ideal.' They forget that this applies only to people who have not become happy members of society. Pleasure may be derived even from order, if it appears reasonable, and after all, pleasure simply expresses acceptance."[19]

Dreikurs was pure Adlerian however, in his views on inferiority and the human need for significance. "Whether a child is spoiled or neglected, he always develops a feeling of his own relative inferiority, which causes him to resist the rules of the group and to adopt a hostile attitude toward it.... A spoiled child in particular quickly succeeds in converting his feeling of inferiority into a strong desire for significance.... He is most afraid of not being noticed, because he thinks this means he is no longer important."[20]

Adler and Dreikurs were consistent in their view that the inferiority issue was a matter that was woven through the psychological makeup of all humanity from birth to death. "The human race is conditioned to inferiority feelings. Mankind suffers from a realization of the biological inferiority of the human race.... As man's intellect grew he was confronted by another inferiority feeling. He realized his smallness in the universe, his inevitable death and destruction and the limitations of his earthly existence.... Any person who labors under a sense of inferiority always tries to obtain power of some kind in order to cancel the supposed superiority of other people. His feeling of inferiority impels him to strive for significance."[21]

Adler's use of inferiority led to the term *inferiority complex*, which was seen as the result of recognized efforts by adult individuals to assume a level of inadequacy in an attempt to protect their self esteem. Dreikurs explains that "Many people pretend to suffer from an inadequacy in order to avoid exposing themselves to obvious failure. [W]e know that the inferiority feeling is the driving force which produces most various forms of antisocial conduct, because all impulses directed against the community vanish in proportion as the inferiority feeling diminishes and the individual learns to estimate his own value more correctly. Once a human being declares war on the community, peace cannot be restored until he has found a correct standard of values."[22]

Adler saw a progression in the structure of human development that would later cause his appropriation of Darwin's evolutionary theory as he attempted to connect an understanding of the human moral and mental qualities. Paul Stepansky writes, "Adler claimed that everything grouped under the rubric of 'psychical process'—soul, spirit, psyche, reason—was part of the evolutionary 'life-process.' In its adaptive design, mind, like body, served the principal evolutionary goal, 'the ceaseless effort to come to terms victoriously with the demands of the external world...to strive towards the attainment of an ideal.'"[23]

Mixed Views on Sexual Orientation

Adler focused a great deal of attention on the effects of childhood development and the inherent inferiority issues that he viewed as bound in the thinking and feeling of a child. His early views on sexual orientation were clear cut and specific as he reconciled the inferiority issue with homosexuality and lesbianism. Murdock writes, "Adler described love as 'the most intimate devotion towards a partner of the other sex, expressed in physical attraction, comradeship, and the decision to have children.... Adler sought to downplay the so-called competition between the sexes...for only heterosexual relationships were worthy; homosexuality was a reflection of fear of accepting the challenge of a male-female relationship.... He was even more specific about lesbian orientations, saying that they could result from the masculine protest or the wish to gain power by taking on the masculine role."[24]

Stein however, relates that Adler, in the 1930s, and nearing the end of his life, began to express an alteration of his view toward homosexuality. Stein writes, "In the 1930s the common attitude and medical opinion was quite unanimous, homosexuality was considered a moral failing and a mental disease. In 1973 the American Psychiatric Association de-listed homosexuality as a mental disorder in their diagnostic nomenclature (DSM).... The Journal of Individual Psychology, the flagship publication of Adlerian Psychology, released a volume in the summer of 2008 that reviews and corrects Adler's previously held beliefs on the GLBT community."[25]

Resolution of Inferiority Is Possible

Adler softened his view in later years that inferiority was likely not an infinite problem. He had adjusted his view indicating that most individuals will work to overcome the negative feelings of inferiority realizing that their struggle for greater personal power is merely a form of faulty compensation.

Dreikurs also saw the flawed side of this issue clarifying his beliefs by stating that "Inferiority may exist only in the imagination of the individual when he compares himself with others. The inferiority feeling is in the very deep sense quite independent of a man's true value, because when he compares himself with other people he gives them value. Anyone who doubts his own value always over-estimates the capacities of other people. [T]hey are founded on his own opinions. He plays the role of both prosecutor and judge at his own trial."[26]

Murdock was also impressed by Adler's larger view of the human condition and his underlying belief that even the most severe psychological issues could ultimately be understood and treated. "Unlike many counseling theorists, Adler proposed an understanding of the most difficult cases, the psychotics. Schizophrenics have the goal to be godlike in order to fend off their very deep inferiority feelings.... Adler portrayed the psychotics' withdrawing from others as the result of being badly unprepared for life...afraid that they will fail in everything. Finally they retreat so far that others cannot understand them."27

The Pros and Cons

Many of the major theorists experienced both accolades and contempt for their views on the human condition, the causes of psychological suffering, and their ultimate potential for specific applied treatment. Pioneers in every field, regardless of their viability, face both the good and the bad, learning to not take it personally and to hold true to their beliefs. Murdock notes that "Critics contend that Individual Psychology is too simple and that it is only common sense. All behavior is explained by referring to inferiority feelings, striving for power, and social interest. Of course, Adler would reply that common sense is the highest form of reasoning."28

Stein adds, "A psychotherapist generally cannot guide a client any further than he has traveled in his own development, which is why overcoming one's own lifestyle limitations must be experienced to be understood and appreciated."29

And Joost Meerloo, a Freudian, expresses his admiration for Adler with this acknowledgement: "The whole body of psychoanalysis and psychiatry is imbued with Adler's ideas, although few want to acknowledge this fact. We are all plagiarists, though we hate to confess it.... The whole body of social psychiatry would have been impossible without Adler's pioneering zest."30

A Biblical Perspective

Adler believed everyone comes into this world with a need for significance. We would concur with his basic premise, although we would differ regarding the cause of the problem.

Certainly one of the effects of original sin and the fall was man's awareness of himself, which placed him in an immediate inferiority situation with his creator God. God created man to be in intimate fellowship with himself, but the fall immediately changed that.

One might want to consider the reverse of Adler's view of cause and effect. Adler would likely believe that man has an inherent need for superiority. Thus, he is, by default, made to feel inferior even to those in his daily environment. There will always be someone in our circle who is more knowledgeable, more attractive or more successful. The biblical view would seem to turn that premise 180 degrees. Man comes into the world in a fallen condition—inferior in every way to the potential he was created to fulfill and realize. He is, by nature, dependent—but desirous of independence. He is consequently in a perfect setup for failure.

There is, however, an abundance of inferiority in the church today. Our denial systems, more often than not, tend to re-label much of it as humility, but much of it is a pretend humility—a learned behavior walked out in Christian circles and church communities. It is, in fact, a prime example of inferiority at work. Of all people on the earth who should not feel inferior it is the children of the one true God of the Bible.

Certainly there are individuals who were abused as children or are the spouse of an abuser. They have been conditioned to believe they are inferior. These are the exceptions who need help in reestablishing the positive truth of their value and worth as individuals.

In the proper perspective of Scripture, however, the Christian must learn to reject thoughts that lead to inferiority, inadequacy and insecurity. These are the three "I" views that can become strongholds to improper belief systems and mistaken perceptions of the believer's value and worth.

Adler's view that *humans can never truly find absolute truth* and *life has no intrinsic meaning* are very weak foundation stones on which to build value and worth.

David A. Seamands offers the difference between being accepted as a servant and being accepted as a son. "The servant is accepted and appreciated on the basis of what he does, the child on the basis of who he is. The servant starts the day anxious and worried. The child rests in the secure love of his family. The servant is accepted because of his workmanship, the son or daughter, because of a relationship."[31]

It is vital in the development of a sound, biblical view of self-worth, to carry an unshakeable understanding of a believer's value as a son or daughter of God our Father. Changing our view of our own value usually requires change in some of our belief systems.

Renewing Our Mind

What does it mean to renew our mind? *Do not be conformed to this world, but be transformed by the renewing of your mind, that you may prove what is that good and acceptable and perfect will of God* (Romans 12:2).

First, *Do not be conformed to this world*. Ray Stedman in his commentary on Romans wrote, "Do not be conformed to this world refers literally to the schemes of this world, the schemes men come up with to regulate and run their lives. The spirit of the age is always the same.... the advancement of self."[32]

In his excellent commentary on Romans, William

Newell addresses the renewing of our minds this way: "The word *renew* is used only by Paul. It means to 'grow up new, afresh'...like foliage in the spring...so that the whole mind and disposition and tastes of the man will become conformed to the fact that he is a new creature." The object of this renewing "includes the mind, with its thoughts; the imagination—so untamed naturally, the sensibilities or 'feelings'; the 'tastes,' or natural preferences—all which, since the fall of Adam, are naturally under the influence and power of the sinful flesh, and must be operated upon by the Holy Spirit.... The entire soul-life, in human existence, must come under the Spirit's control."[33]

This kind of understanding comes only through an entirely new way of thinking. Our belief system must change at the very foundation of what we know to be true. A change in our very identity has taken place and we are to conform our thinking to that new identity. *For [the Spirit which] you have now received [is] not a spirit of slavery to put you once more in bondage to fear, but you have received the Spirit of adoption [the Spirit producing sonship] in [the bliss of] which we cry, Abba (Father)! Father!* (Romans 8:15, AMP).

Adding to David Seamand's view of sonship, it is helpful to understand the meaning of adoption. DeVerne Fromke writes, "In the West, adoption is the taking of a child from one family and making it a member of another. The Greek or Roman father, however, adopted none as a son but his own child. Birth made him a child, adoption gave him sonship. Between birth and adoption there was growth, education, and discipline. In childhood the Greek or Roman father brought in a teacher, a mentor to teach the child the father's ways. The purpose was to pass down the values and traditions of the father."[34]

In the biblical parallel, a child is immature and childish, a son is mature and responsible. A child is one born of God, a son is one taught of God. A child has God's nature, a son has God's character.

This view adds new meaning to the passage we hear in our churches at Christmastime as we learn of the distinction between child and son as it pertained to our Lord and Savior Jesus Christ. *Unto us a child is born, Unto us a son is given* (Isaiah 9:6).

The renewing of the mind is a critical part of the growth, maturity, stability and development of all God's children, as we learn to live as who we are, learn the ways of our Father and learn to believe what he believes.

Seamands quotes Christian counselor Dr. Maurice Wagner, "There are three essential components of a healthy self-image: 1) a sense of belongingness, of being loved; 2) a sense of worth and value. I count. I am of value, and; 3) a sense of being competent. I am able to meet life."[35]

The Christian counselor is called upon to assist in

reprogramming the damaged self-image of those without a clear understanding of who they are or of who God is. The Christian therapist will be called on to peel back the false belief systems, rebuild new and unshakeable belief systems and do so based on the truth of God's word.

In his book, *Don't Waste Your Sorrows*, Paul Billheimer makes the point that suffering makes a considerable contribution to our character and ultimately God's kingdom. Billheimer states that the church is in the school of suffering to learn love and that sometimes failure and struggle is the only way one can be decentralized. Billheimer also points out that only after a mighty breaking can some of us see our faults.

Oswald Chambers is credited with the statement that every believer's cross is the pain involved in doing the will of God.

Again, quoting Seamand's, "It is only when I surrender myself to God,.... when I put myself under His authority, when I am filled with His love [that] I possess the true self-esteem and self-love that enables me to love other people...and self is released from trying to be someone it isn't and was never intended to be. As a result you and I can become what we were meant to be."[36]

Counseling Theory and the Scriptures

Our Search for Significance

Adler's view of our inherent inferiority led to a resultant search to overcome that inferiority and possess the significance that abounds in superiority.

Although many believers search for some form of the world's view of significance, it is apparent that a biblical view never promotes striving for superiority.

As part of the believer's renewal of the mind, it is helpful to better understand the lies we believe in our striving for meaning and importance. Robert McGee, in his books and workbooks dealing with the believer's search for significance, brings the focus of our quest down to four primary beliefs. First is the false belief that in order to feel good about oneself, they must achieve certain goals. This faulty view has performance-based acceptance at its core. Adding to this setup for failure is the belief that in order to feel good about oneself, they must please certain people. In other words, one's performance matters more than one's person. Adding to these mistaken beliefs is the premise that if one fails at reaching certain standards and pleasing certain people, then they are a failure and unworthy of love. Finally, of course, the presence of a denial system that states that we are simply who we are, and real change can never occur.

Breaking the bondage of destructive belief systems is within the power of every Christian. The most powerful change agent in the universe is the person of the Holy Spirit, who indwells those who believe.

The power of God's word is the foundation on which we must build our identity, our personal value and the positive worth that is the rightful identity for a child of the living God.

- I am completely and totally acceptable, just as I am, regardless of my performance (2 Corinthians 5:21, Romans 5:1).
- I am someone very special, regardless of what I or other's think (Genesis 1:27, Exodus 19:5, Isaiah 43:7).
- I am deeply loved by God, making it okay for me to accept myself as valuable in his sight (Jeremiah 31:3, Romans 8:32).
- God is the only true measure of my worth and I do not have to be overly concerned about the disapproval of others (John 15:9-10, Romans 8).

Chapter Nine

Solution-focused Brief Therapy

Solution-focused Brief Therapy (SFBT) was originated by psychotherapist and author Steve de Shazer (1940-2005). de Shazer, along with his wife, Insoo Kim Berg (1934-2007), and other colleagues, developed their theory with an overt emphasis on a future-focused, goal-directed process that put priorities on solutions rather than the problems that caused most clients to need and seek therapy.

In 1978, de Shazer opened his Brief Family Therapy Center in Milwaukee, and over several years and hundreds of hours, observed therapy sessions, carefully analyzing client's response to certain questions as well as their emotional response and behavior during the sessions. This was applied to the ultimate outcome of the therapy and progress that could be identified.

The website for the Institute for Solution-Focused Therapy gives us additional insight. "Since that early development, SFBT has not only become one of the leading schools of brief therapy, it has become a major influence in such diverse fields as business, social policy, education, and criminal justice services, child welfare, [and] domestic violence offenders treatment. Described as a practical, goal-driven model, a hallmark of SFBT is its emphasis on clear, concise, realistic goal negotiations. The SFBT approach assumes that all clients have some knowledge of what would make their life better, even though they may need some (at times, considerable) help describing the details of their better life and that everyone who seeks help already possesses at least the minimal skills necessary to create solutions."[1]

What actually determines the length of brief therapy is a matter of opinion, as Bill O'Connell submits in his book on solution-focused therapy. "There are differences in definition as to what constitutes brief therapy. Eckert (1993) defined brief therapy as being 'any psychological intervention intended to produce change as quickly as possible whether or not a specific time limit is set in advance.'... Although there are major differences between brief therapists, there is a degree of consensus that brief therapy means fewer than 20 sessions.... Smith (1980) found that the major impact of therapy occurred in the first six to eight sessions."[2]

SFBT therapists believe that most clients have learned to solve problems through the normal experiences of their life and therefore, short of an immediate solution to their existing problem, can call on examples from the past for applicable solutions to present issues.

Pichot and Dolan, writing on the effective use of solution-focused brief therapy in an agency setting, offer excellent details on the use of the therapy. "[T]he activities and process of thinking necessary for solution building are very different from those associated with the traditional problem-solving approach. [P]roblem solving typically takes place as follows: The helping professional gathers information in order to identify the problem,.... how the problem first occurred...and the symptoms and effects associated with the problem. Then the helping professional takes some time to speculate about the underlying cause(s) of the problem. Finally, based on what is determined to be the real cause of the problem, a course of treatment is prescribed with the intention of either resolving the problem or reducing the severity of the associated symptoms."[3]

Pichot and Dolan proceed to present the contrasts that solution-focused brief therapy offers as they work with their clients on how they want their lives to be different. The authors then break their process down into three steps that are contrasted with the standard problem-solving approach. "Solution building starts with the end of the story of the clients' future success as opposed to the beginning of their problems.... In the second step...the helping professional and the client remain vigilant to instances in which the client has already experienced or is currently experiencing any aspects of the solution identified in step one, even in the smallest way.... The third step...departs even further from the traditional models by focusing intensely on empowering the client to develop an extremely detailed and vivid description of the exact desired outcome. [D]escribing the goal in great detail provides a foretaste of the rewards associated with it [and] the clients feel more motivated."4

In a practical sense many of the foundational differences that separate the problem-focused and solution-focused approach begin with how the therapist frames basic questions in the therapy session. O'Connell offers the following examples. (Note: We have varied the format and designated the writer's examples with the appropriate initials, PF for problem-focused and SF for solution-focused.)

- PF—How can I help you? vs. SF—How will you know that coming here today has been helpful?
- PF—Could you tell me about the problem? vs. SF—What would you like to change?
- PF—Is the problem a symptom of an

underlying issue? vs. SF—Can we dig deep to discover solutions?
- PF—Can you tell me more about the problem? vs. SF—Can we discover exceptions to the problem?
- PF—How are we to understand the problem in the light of the past? vs. SF—What will the future look like without the problem?
- PF—What defense mechanisms are operating? vs. SF—How can we use the skills and strengths of the client?
- PF—How many sessions will we need? vs. SF—Have we achieved enough to end [therapy]?[5]

The Miracle Question

A prime example of the solution-focused brief therapy approach to the client and the methods used to place an emphasis on the future when the client can, and will, function more satisfactorily is the *miracle question*. Many solution-focused brief therapy therapists find the miracle question particularly effective with depression. The effect is to help the client focus on what is possible rather than what is not working.

Insoon Kim Berg was one of the first to utilize the

method of intervention when a client offered, "Maybe only a miracle will help!" This led to Berg's use of a particular concept in helping clients imagine what life would be like if the problem was solved.

Although the miracle question has numerous slight variations in its presentation, Pichot and Dolan offer a direct quote from a book authored in 1998 by Insoo Kim Berg along with Peter DeJong: "I want to ask you a strange question. Suppose that while you are sleeping tonight and the entire house is quiet, a miracle happens. The miracle is that the problem which brought you here is solved. However, because you are sleeping, you don't know that the miracle has happened. So, when you wake up tomorrow morning, what will be different that will tell you a miracle has happened and the problem which brought you here is solved?" (pp.77-78).[6]

The writers go on to suggest that the therapist use the client's response to see the possible solutions through the client's eyes.

The Institute for Solution-Focused Therapy adds that the miracle question can be helpful in assisting the client to begin taking small steps toward reachable goals as soon as the next day. "The miracle question developed out of desperation with a suicidal woman with an alcoholic husband and four 'wild' children who gave her nothing but grief. She was desperate for a solution, but [felt] that she might need a 'miracle' to get her life in order. Since the development of this technique, the MQ has been tested numerous times in many different cultures."7

Pichot and Dolan note what they believe to be the five crucial elements that collectively make up the effectiveness of the miracle question: "The first element is the concept of a change occurring that is of some significance to the client and that would not occur naturally.... The second element is a basic understanding of what the miracle is,...most often defined...as 'the problem that brought you here is solved.'.... The third element...is immediacy. The miracle is described as happening tonight and in a setting that will normally occur.... The fourth element is that the client is unaware that the miracle has occurred. They are unaware...because they were asleep. Without this detail, there is nothing for the client to discover. The fifth element...is the importance of encouraging the client to methodically discover the small telltale signs which indicate that the miracle has occurred.... The miracle question and the elements contained in it are the foundation of solution-focused therapy. Without these elements, therapists are unlikely to be able to assist their clients in getting to the other side of the problem and are not capturing the essence and power of solution-focused therapy."8

Exception Questions

Exception questions are often recommended as an effective way for the therapist to assist the client in recognizing times when the problem does not exist or times when the problem is less severe. Examples of *exception questions* might include, "When does the problem cease to occur?" "What are you doing, or not doing, when the problem is lessened or non-existent?" "How can you change to achieve that result more often?" This process not only helps to identify those times, but can also be used to help the client recognize their own skills and resources to see beyond their immediate problem.

Pichot and Dolan suggest that the therapist must be aware and able to recognize the paths that lead to these exceptions. "Exceptions are scattered throughout client conversation, and it takes a well-trained ear to recognize them and to appreciate the opportunities they offer.... Once therapists understand the value of exploring these exceptions, their way of listening changes.... The change process often appears arduous, and exceptions often offer a glimmer of hope that change is underfoot and can be a reality. As exceptions come to light, clients gain hope, for they begin to see that part of their miracle is happening today."[9]

Solution-focused Brief Therapy

Scaling Techniques

Scaling is a process often used by solution-focused brief therapy therapists to help the client evaluate and track their own progress. Alasdair Macdonald's research on SFBT imparts the following: "Scaling questions...help the client to move from all-or-nothing goals toward less daunting, manageable, steps. The scale has no reality outside the negotiation with the therapist but is an instantly usable means of tracking progress. Scales also increase clarity of communication with other professionals who may be involved with the client.... People who have come to therapy only as a last resort may be able to identify goals but initially have no confidence that they can reach them. In relationship problems it is useful to ask, 'On a scale of 0-10, how confident are you that you will be together in two years' time?' Clients often learn from their own replies, whether the partner is present or not.... If one says 2 and the other says 10, then they have learned something about how they are communicating with each other."[10]

Scaling techniques can be helpful when a client finds difficulty in identifying exceptions since the scaling process is not limited by language and expression barriers.

O'Connell suggests there are specific assumptions that should guide the solution-focused brief therapist.

Primary to those assumptions is the view that *If it isn't broken, don't fix it.* "This principle is a warning to practitioners to be careful about expanding the 'problem' by looking for more and more aspects of the client's life to fix.... SFBT does not see clients as being emotionally or psychologically sick (and therefore in need of a cure) or damaged (and therefore in need of repair), but as temporarily unable to overcome a life difficulty because they have not yet found a way out of or around it. Instead of focusing on pathology (the answer doesn't lie there), it seeks out and builds on what is healthy and functioning in people's lives.... Building on what is right, rather than fixing what is wrong...also helps to limit the agenda and keep therapy brief."[11]

A Biblical Perspective

It is reasonable to expect that most Christian counselors, through their personal faith alone, have come to a greater understanding of mercy, grace and compassion. By the very nature of their calling to such a field of service it would seem reasonable that a future-focused, goal-directed process, putting priorities on solutions rather than problems, would be a vital part of their goal as a therapist.

The Scriptures often implore us to look to the future rather than dwelling on the past. *Since you have been raised to new life with Christ, set your sights on the realities of heaven, where Christ sits in the place of honor at God's right hand. Think about the things of heaven, not the things of earth. For you died to this life, and your real life is hidden with Christ in God. And when Christ, who is your life, is revealed to the whole world, you will share in all his glory* (Colossians 3:1-4, NLT).

Counselors who have worked with couples going through marital issues often find the need to help the couple work through a forgiveness phase to begin the healing process. Once that has been clearly addressed, it is sometimes the greater work to help the clients learn to live in the *present/future* rather than the *present/past*.

We would agree with the Solution-focused Brief Therapy view that "all clients have some knowledge of what would make their life better and the minimal skills necessary to create solutions." Solution-focused therapy presents a practical view in focusing on what is healthy and functioning and building on that instead of working to correct what is wrong and how the client got to their current status. This is where the issues get more difficult for the Christian counselor.

Since the Bible and faith are largely structured on cognitive thinking we can never lose sight of the damage that destructive belief systems can do to our lives and relationships, and the importance of using truth to tear down the strongholds that have been built in our thinking and judgment. This often requires that valuable time be spent looking at the data that a client has received over the years, especially damaging messages that has led to the destructive strongholds in their thinking, as noted in an earlier chapter.

The Christian counselor is wise to help the client consider the areas of the problem where God may be working that will be in direct conflict with the solution the client has in mind. Often when the flesh is in control of a person's thinking, there is a tendency to find solutions that will not be painful. On the contrary, God will often allow problems to come into our lives that are painful for the very purpose of directing our path toward his solution. Only his solution will resolve many of the issues the client has been in denial about for years. *Dear friends, do not be surprised at the painful trial you are suffering, as though something strange were happening to you. But rejoice that you participate in the sufferings of Christ, so that you may be overjoyed when his glory is revealed* (1 Peter 4:12-13, NIV). Paul reminds the believers in Rome, *We can rejoice too, when we run into problems and trials, for we know that they help us develop endurance* (Romans 5:3, NLT).

Quick solutions can often work in contradiction to how the Lord is working in a life. It is difficult for many Christians to come to the reality that God is as interested in doing something *in* us as he is in doing something *through* us. We must never lose sight of the fact that God may see problems and pain, whether good or bad, from a different perspective than we do. As C.S. Lewis wrote, "If God is wiser than we, His judgment must differ from ours on many things, and not least on good and evil. What seems to us good may therefore not be good in His eyes, and what seems to us evil may not be evil.... We want, in fact, not so much a Father in Heaven as a grandfather in heaven—[with] a senile benevolence,...whose plan...at the end of each day [is], 'a good time was had by all.' "[12]

If we are truly to trust in and rely on the Scriptures, then we must broaden our view of painful and difficult circumstances in the light of the apostle Paul's challenge to believe that *all things work together for good to those who love God, to those who are the called according to His purpose* (Romans 8:28). This verse is difficult to reconcile with tragic events and the agony of many diseases. Events like these seem to contradict the apostle's call to trust God in all things. But these times are often used by God to show us his solution-focused ways.

The appropriate attitude in difficult situations is always one that commands hope and patience. The internal working of the Holy Spirit in the life of God's children is always at work to conform us to the image of his Son. This requires molding, shaping and the painful reaping of what we have sown in our past. Change can be painful. Turning from sin can bring anger and bitterness to the surface. Seeking and giving forgiveness can sometimes bring with it a sadness.

As we learn to do things God's way and line up our thinking with his ways, we will come face to face with the seemingly endless battle between the flesh and the Spirit. But we are to pick up our cross and follow him. *If anyone wishes to come after Me, he must deny himself, and take up his cross daily and follow Me* (Luke 9:23, NASB).

To paraphrase a statement made by Oswald Chambers, *The cross for every believer is doing the will of God!* This denial of the self is sometimes referred to as brokenness. As we noted in another chapter, God placed his Son in us so that he might live his life through us. He will do so if we will simply get out of the way. The process that God uses in getting me out of the way so that Christ can live his life through me is a process of brokenness. His strength is made perfect in our weakness.

Brokenness can stem from my realization that God has a better plan than I do and I must choose to allow him to work that plan out in my life. This involves surrendering my rights, giving up my control, being willing to risk failure, allowing myself to be weak, being prepared to be rejected, being willing to allow others to receive credit, allowing myself to be teachable and discontinuing my performance for God's approval and allowing Christ to perform his will in and through me. This can be difficult, but not as difficult as the alternative.

The alternative way is for God to allow me to experience the pain that naturally occurs in my life to teach me that his way works best. C.S. Lewis noted that, "Pain is God's megaphone." Indeed it is. God uses our pain, according to Lewis, to get our attention, as though he were speaking to us through a megaphone so that we can hear him loudly and clearly. God's purpose in this is to reveal *the insufficiency of self-sufficiency*, so that we turn to him.

In 2 Corinthians 1:8-10, Paul says that he learned this lesson first-hand. *I think you ought to know, dear brothers, about the hard time we went through in Asia. We were really crushed, and overwhelmed, and feared we would never live through it. We felt we were doomed to die and saw how powerless we were to help ourselves; but that was good, for then we put everything into the hands of God, who alone could save us, for He can even raise the dead. And He did help us, and saved us from a terrible death; yes, and we expect Him to do it again and again* (NLT).

God wants us to know about our inadequacy apart

from himself. Someone has said that God uses our life as a training program to teach us that we are inadequate without him. Men and women throughout Scripture have borne out this testimony in their own lives, learning that they were complete and total failures apart from him.

Ian Thomas said, "Moses began by being a failure.... Abraham began by being a failure. Jacob was a hopeless failure. David was a hopeless failure. Elijah was a hopeless failure. Isaiah was a hopeless failure and a man of unclean lips, but it is in the school of destitution—the bitter school of self-discovery—that finally you graduate into usefulness, when at last you discover the total bankruptcy of what you are apart from what God is. These men made this discovery, and were blessed!"[13]

Dwight L. Moody, the noted evangelist and founder of Moody Bible Institute, was said to have related the following in reference to God's breaking of Moses: "Moses spent forty years in Pharaoh's palace as a prince trying to be somebody. He spent another forty years in the desert finding out that he was a nobody. Then it took another forty years to discover what God can do with a nobody." Indeed, God's process is that of bringing our independence to a state of brokenness.

God's desire is that we come to understand who we truly are—that we have been made righteous and holy in Christ. This is made possible by having his life at work in and through us. His life and his life alone is what makes us adequate.

Chapter Ten

Existential Psychotherapy

Existentialism began as a philosophical concept that was first recognized in the work of several nineteenth and twentieth century philosophers who viewed the human being not solely as a thinking being, but as a being that behaves, feels or emotes, and lives in his environment. These philosophers, although in considerable disagreement regarding philosophy and doctrine, took this acting, feeling and living human being as a beginning point for philosophical thought.

Encyclopedia.com defines existentialism as, *any of several philosophic systems, all centered on the individual and his relationship to the universe or to God.*

The best-known philosophers from the nineteenth century are Soren Kierkegaard from Denmark and Friedrich Nietzsche from Germany. These men came to be seen as the forerunners of existential thought, although neither actually used the term existentialism in their writings. Kierkegaard came to be considered the first existentialist and has been called the "Father of Existentialism." During the twentieth century, Martin Heidegger, a German philosopher, greatly influenced the work of other existential philosophers such as Sartre, Simone de Beauvoir and Albert Camus. Although there are certainly common themes among the writings of these philosophers, there are major differences between them as well. Not all of them even accepted the validity of the term existentialism as applied to their own work.

"It can be said that existentialism doesn't exist but existentialists do. How else can you explain the varied camp that houses Sartre, the founder of the nausea school of French philosophy, Kierkegaard, the pious Protestant cleric, Marcel the Catholic, Buber the Jewish philosopher and Nietzsche, who declared God dead? The litany of differences also includes Dostoevski, the Russian author, Unamuno, the Spanish poet, the German philosophers Jaspers, Husserl and Heidegger, and a whole series of therapists including the psychoanalytic Boss and Binswanger, the Gestaltist Perls, client-centered Rogers, and May, Frankl, Moustakas, van Kaam and Laing.... Existentialists are a mixed breed which may include atheists, theists, philosophers, literary figures and men of practical and applied fields such as medicine, psychotherapy, and education."[1]

History

The term existentialism was first used by the French philosopher Gabriel Marcel during the mid-1940s. The term would later be applied in a lecture presented by Jean-Paul Sartre in 1945. The lecture was published as a short book which did much to popularize existential thought.

While a large number of individuals shaped the early existential movement, they are too numerous to discuss here. For the sake of brevity, we will discuss three primary leaders of the twentieth century who helped shape what is commonly known today as *Existential Psychotherapy*. These theorists are Rollo May, James Bugental and Viktor Frankl.

Rollo May

May lived from 1909 to 1994, growing up in Ohio and Michigan. As a young man, he spent a great deal of time studying Greek civilization, which he would later say gave him a perspective on human nature. He traveled to Vienna and studied with Alfred Adler. While working on his doctoral degree, he was diagnosed with tuberculosis. He spent two years in a sanitarium studying and learning about the essential characteristics and qualities of anxiety. His doctoral thesis was eventually published in 1950 under the title *The Meaning of Anxiety*. In this work, he made a number of distinctions regarding anxiety, including the distinction between what he called neurotic anxiety and existential anxiety. His claim was that anxiety is a natural and integral function of the human being.

May would write of the influences on his life, which included Ernest Angel and Henri Ellenberger. In fact, he coauthored a book with these two men titled *Existence*, which is believed to be the formal beginning of the existential movement in American psychology. Also of importance in May's life was the influence of Paul Tillich, who was an important existential theologian who applied existential concepts to Christian theology. Due to this influence, much of May's writings focus on the nature of human experience, such as recognizing and dealing with power, accepting freedom and responsibility and discovering one's own identity.

May became the principal American spokesman of European existential thinking in the years that followed. Gerald Corey noted that "May was one of the main proponents of humanistic approaches to psychotherapy, and he was the principal American spokesman of European existential thinking as it is applied to psychotherapy. His view is that psychotherapy should be aimed at helping people discover the meaning of their lives and should be concerned with the problems of *being* rather than with problem solving. Questions of being include learning to deal with issues such as sex and intimacy, growing old, and facing death.... According to May, it takes courage to 'be,' and our choices determine the kind of person we become. There is a constant struggle within us. Although we want to grow toward maturity and independence, we realize that expansion is often a painful process."[2]

Rollo May published many books during his lifetime, including *The Art of Counseling, The Courage To Create, Freedom and Destiny, The Discovery of Being, Love and Will, They Cry for Myth* and *Paulus*.

James Bugental

Bugental's influence is not as well recognized as that of Rollo May, but he made a significant impact on existential thinking. He was, in fact, greatly influenced by May in his thinking and writing.

Bugental was born in December, 1915 and died in September, 2008. He was a predominant theorist and advocate of existential-humanism. He was not only a psychologist, but he taught and wrote extensively as well. He received his doctorate from The Ohio State

University and was the first recipient of the American Psychological Association's Division of Humanistic Psychology's *Rollo May Award*.

His writings include *The Search for Authenticity, The Search for Existential Identity, Psychotherapy and Process, The Art of the Psychotherapist* and *Psychotherapy Isn't What You Think*.

Bugental's summary of humanistic-psychology is found in his book *The Search for Authenticity*. Bugental explains that as humans, we have choices and responsibilities that we must be aware of in our search for meaning, value and creativity. We have a conscious awareness of ourselves in our relationship to others, which gives us a uniquely human context. As humans, we cannot be reduced to simple components. "In his work, *The Art of the Psychotherapist*, Bugental outlines the role of the therapist in his or her relationship with the client: He views therapy as a journey taken by the therapist and the client that delves deeply into the client's subjective world. He emphasizes that this quest demands the willingness of the therapist to be in contact with his or her own phenomenological world. According to Bugental, the central concern of therapy is to help clients examine how they have answered life's existential questions and to challenge them to revise their answers to begin living authentically."[3]

Viktor Frankl

Frankl was born in March of 1905, in Vienna, Austria, and died there in 1997. As a child, he was involved in socialist youth organizations and became interested in psychology at an early age. He began writing Sigmund Freud at age sixteen, and actually sent him one of his writings, which was published three years later. He earned a medical degree from the University of Vienna in 1930. He was married in 1942 and he and his wife and parents were deported after Germany invaded Austria. He would spend the next several years in four concentration camps, including the Theresienstadt camp near Prague and Auschwitz. Frankl survived the Holocaust, but his wife and parents did not.

When Germany was defeated in 1945, Frankl returned to Vienna and began writing. He published a book outlining his thoughts regarding what he called Logotherapy. He would later title this work *The Doctor and the Soul: An Introduction to Logotherapy.* The term logotherapy essentially translates into the word *meaning*, which is derived from the prefix *logo*. "Logotherapy is mostly concerned with an inherent need for meaning and values in the human life. Having personally suffered and survived the concentration camps and the loss of his family, his conviction that humans can affirm life in spite of suffering and loss of everything and everyone, deserves respect. Existentialism's call for freedom despite circumstance often seems applicable only to fortunate people. Frankl disproves that, and is able to aid the patient to find meaning and value."4

Frankl believed that human suffering could and should be turned into achievement and accomplishment and that guilt can be an opportunity to change oneself for the better. He believed that life does not owe a person happiness, but that it offers us meaning—a meaning that transcends human circumstances. This search for meaning should become our motivation for living.

He further believed that human beings are unique and consist of body, mind and spirit. In fact, he believed that one of the goals of therapy was to assist the client in becoming aware of their spiritual resources and to use *defiant power to the human spirit* to stand against adversity. His view of salvation was that it came by way of love. To him, love was the highest goal to which humans can aspire, and our salvation comes through our love for others.

Frankl was honored by receiving the prestigious *Oskar Pfister Award* in 1985 and was recognized by The American Medical Society, The American Psychiatric Association and The American Psychological Association. He taught extensively at many universities and was the recipient of twenty-nine honorary doctorates from universities around the world.

His writings include *Psychotherapy and Existentialism, The Doctor and the Soul: An Introduction to Logotherapy, On the Theory and Therapy of Mental Disorders: An Introduction to Logotherapy and Existential Analysis, Man's Search for Meaning, The Unheard Cry for Meaning: Psychotherapy and Humanism, The Will to Meaning: The Foundations and Applications of Logotherapy, Man's Search for Ultimate Meaning, Viktor Frankl—Recollections* and *The Unconscious God.*

Philosophy

Existentialists believe that human beings are bound in their existence to the world and the world is bound to its existence to human beings. One does not exist without the other—they are mutually exclusive. This bond is incapable of being broken or disintegrated. It is a binding relationship. "According to the Existential approach, human existence reveals the total, indissoluble unity or interrelationship of the individual and his or her world.... In the truest sense, the person is viewed as having no existence apart from the world and the world as having no existence apart from persons."[5]

Existentialism tends to focus on one's self-awareness, which allows an individual to make choices for him or herself. When we expand our awareness, we increase our ability to live fully. We increasingly become aware that "we are finite, and we do not have an unlimited time to do what we want with our lives."[6]

Existentialism has a great deal to say about a person's freedom to choose alternatives for their lives and then take responsibility for those choices and alternatives.

"We have the potential to take action or not to act; inaction is a decision. We choose our actions and therefore we can partially create our own destiny."[7]

In regard to freedom, the existentialist would say that humans live in a world without meaning and without rules, yet are still forced to make decisions regularly. "In particular, [existentialism] denies the existence of natural law, an unchanging human nature, or indeed any objective rules. Each individual is cursed with freedom and must make his or her own way in the world, although many people resort to devices to hide this from themselves. Life is without ultimate meaning, but we are forced to make choices all the time. [M]en and women are free to make of themselves the kind of people they want to be and, to some extent, to make for themselves the kind of world they want to live in…. Our being-in-the-world [alone] is bound up with our being-with-others, and in this sense Existentialism has an overriding moral dimension, even if it eschews any notion of moral rules or absolutes."[8]

Existentialism focuses on an individual's deep need for creating an identity for themselves and our deep-rooted desire to connect ourselves with others. We all have a deep-rooted need for meaning, significance and purpose. Corey writes that "Meaning is not automatically bestowed on us but is the product of our searching and our discovering a unique purpose."[9]

Existentialists note that human beings tend to be anxious in the process of achieving purpose and in their search for self-awareness and survival. This anxiety is seen as a normal and inevitable human condition that arises due to this search, and can be a condition that causes growth in the person if anxiety is not allowed to become what the existentialist refers to as *neurotic anxiety*. "Existential anxiety, which is basically a consciousness of our own freedom, is an essential part of living; as we increase our awareness of the choices available to us, we also increase our sense of responsibility for the consequences of these choices."[10]

Finally, existentialism makes death a primary theme—this is a death that is not seen in a negative light, but a death that makes living significant. "We are basically alone, yet we have an opportunity to relate to other beings. We are subject to loneliness, meaninglessness, emptiness, guilt, and isolation.... Death and life are interdependent, and though physical death destroys us, the idea of death saves us."[11]

To the existentialist, it is necessary to think about

death if we are to think significantly about life. The boundary situation that death defines for us can cause us to either excel in life or create what the existentialist calls *existential despair*. "If we realize that we are mortal, we know that we do not have an eternity to complete our projects and that each present moment is crucial. Our awareness of death is the source of zest for life and creativity."[12]

Foundational Precepts

There are quite a number of terms used in existential psychotherapy that describe the concepts employed in explaining the theory. Following are the primary precepts applied throughout the theory that the serious student of existentialism will need to understand.

<u>Existence Precedes Essence</u>—This precept, coined by Sartre, simply means that the life of a person is what defines his or her essence or what it means to be human. The idea is that what defines a person is based not on one's nature or culture, but on who that person becomes or what that person makes of him or herself. In other words, an individual is defined by his or her actions and is subsequently responsible for their own actions or behaviors. As Sartre

explained in his writings on humanism, "Man first of all exists, encounters himself, surges up in the world, and defines himself afterwards." If *essence* defines what something is, and *existence* defines that it is, then it follows that what can be thought or said about any given thing belongs to its essence. "[The] fundamental premise, that 'existence precedes essence,' implies that we as human beings have no given essence or nature but must forge our own values and meanings in an inherently meaningless...world of existence."[13]

Facticity—If someone were to conduct a psychological evaluation on an individual, the information that would be gained by the evaluation would fall into the category of facticity. This includes items such as a person's weight, height, eye and hair color, race, family history, marital status and other historical facts. If one uses this type of facticity to define themselves, then these characteristics and facts become their identity—how the person defines him or herself. From an existential perspective, however, this would be in error, since the type of being that one is cannot be defined in factual or third-person terms. Although one's facticity is set and will not change, it cannot determine or define who a person is.

Transcendence—Since facticity cannot be both who a person is and, at the same time, merely a matter of fact, the kind of being one is must be considered in terms of the stance that person takes toward their facticity. This is what existentialists call transcendence. Transcendence refers to how one sees themselves in the first-person and is characteristic of one's relationship to the world around them. Based on one's choice and one's decision making, transcendence takes the person's self-definition past what is and into what could be, based upon one's projects. Because one's projects define who they are, the world, in a sense, can reveal to a person who he or she actually is.

Alienation—The term alienation indicates a dual estrangement of the self from both the world and oneself. Because of transcendence, one's projects cause the world to take on meaning, but the world itself is not brought into being through one's projects. In this regard, Heidegger would say that the world retains its otherness and thus can come forth as utterly alien at times. The strangeness of the world becomes one in which a person does not feel at home.

Also of importance is the fact that one's world includes other people, and because of this, a person is not exclusively the discloser of the world, but one who is revealed in the projects of others. Thus, one is not merely a function of their own projects, but has other's projects to consider. Sartre called this *the look*, meaning that when one becomes aware of being looked at by another, that person becomes aware of his or her nature or character and becomes aware of being or doing something that is visible to others. One can take a third-person perspective on oneself precisely because there are others in the world. This reveals to a person the extent to which they are alienated from themselves or the world. Who one is can be revealed only by the other.

The Other and the Look—The experience of the other is the experience of another individual who lives in the same world as oneself. When one experiences someone else in this world, but experiences this other person from afar, or what existentialism calls *over there*, the world is seen by both individuals as objective, in that it is identical for both subjects. That is, you experience the other person as experiencing the same as you. This experience is what existentialist's term *the look*, which objectifies what it sees and is characterized as limiting one's freedom. As such, when one experiences oneself in the look, one does not experience oneself as nothing, but as something.

Authenticity and Inauthenticity—Existentialism defines authenticity as a person acting as oneself—not according to how others might expect them to act or how norms would dictate they should act. The authentic act, then, is in compliance with one's freedom. Although facticity cannot determine one's choices, as in blaming one's childhood for the choice one made, facticity is a condition of freedom. This is to say, one's values are indeed emphasized when one makes a choice. This interaction between authenticity and facticity causes one to take responsibility for one's choices and become more transparent. One begins to understand that they are an individual who can be responsible and have integrity.

In contrast, inauthenticity would define the life of a person living without integrity or responsibility, or in accordance with one's freedom. While the authentic person commits himself to a certain course of action and a certain way of being in the world, the inauthentic person occupies such a role with vacillation and a lack of commitment. For this individual, how one should act is based on a preconceived notion of how a person in a certain position, such as a physician, should act. The inauthentic person acts according to social norm or according to one's perception of how they can be more widely accepted by others.

Freedom—Values are learned as one develops in life and maturity, and over time become a part of us—a belief system. Subsequently, one's values become a filter through which one makes choices. When a person fails or chooses not to evaluate differing value systems when making a choice, he or she is basically choosing to not make a choice at all. Essentially, that person is refusing to live out of his or her freedom, which is considered to be an inauthentic existence by the existentialist.

According to Murdock, "An essential aspect of human existence is freedom—the notion, according to Yalom that 'the individual is entirely responsible for—that is, the author of—his or her own world, life design, choices, and actions.' May and Yalom point out the terrifying consequences of accepting one's freedom: if we are totally free to choose and act, then we must recognize that 'there is no ground beneath us: there is only an abyss, a void, nothingness.' Ultimately, freedom implies responsibility for ourselves; our actions, but also our failures to act. Awareness of our freedom implies responsibility to choose. Even if we are not aware of it, we are constantly making choices and our actions reflect these. The reality of freedom, choice and responsibility brings to us the notion of *existential guilt*: guilt that we experience about possibilities unfulfilled. Existential guilt is unavoidable, because every time we make a choice we are discarding other possibilities."[14]

The choices one makes, over time, become one's values. As one matures, he or she evaluates their values and may or may not change them over time. This change in values would reinforce the notion that one is ultimately responsible for his or her values and choices and for one's subsequent behavior or action. The relationship between freedom and responsibility is mutually exclusive. The amount of responsibility one exhibits is a result of one's freedom.

Angst and Anxiety—Fear is produced in an individual when something is present that is fear producing, such as a snake or someone pointing a gun in one's direction. Angst or anxiety, terms that are often used interchangeably by the existentialist, are present in every individual, and arise when one realizes that they have freedom and are responsible for making choices. They come to realize that there is no ground beneath them—they are in a state of *nothingness*. In other words, angst and anxiety are a result of one experiencing freedom and responsibility. Angst and anxiety are set apart from fear because they have no object. They are something that takes place in an individual when that person realizes that they cannot blame someone or something else if they fail.

Existential anxiety is considered to be perfectly normal in most individuals, and is not something that, by definition, is to be dreaded or to be found negative. It is a sign that one needs to attend to something or take care of the thing that is causing it. One is to utilize his or her anxiety and use it constructively. Instead of suppressing it, one is to use it as grounds for change in order to reach one's full potential.

Death, Despair and Nothingness—For the existentialist, death looms as the end of existence. The realization of this inevitable death, along with the recognition of one's responsibility for one's actions, can lead to an existential despair that overwhelms the individual. When this takes place, one finds him or herself continually confronting the nothingness of existence. This causes a breakdown in one's identity, leading to even more despair and feelings of hopelessness.

Meaninglessness—Once a person is faced with his/her inevitable death, feelings of meaninglessness often begin to take place. "When the world they live in seems meaningless, clients may wonder whether it is worth it to continue struggling or even living. Faced with the prospect of our mortality, we might ask: 'Is there any point to what I do now, since I will eventually die? Will what I do be forgotten once I am gone? Given the fact of mortality, why should I busy myself with anything?' For Frankl such a feeling of meaninglessness is the major existential neurosis of modern life. Meaninglessness in life leads to emptiness and hollowness, or a condition that Frankl called the *existential vacuum*. Because there is no preordained design for living, people are faced with the task of creating their own meaning. At times people who feel trapped by the emptiness of life withdraw from the struggle of creating a life with purpose."[15]

Isolation—With increasing amounts of meaninglessness in one's life, isolation begins to take place. "We are always and ultimately alone, according to existential theorists. If one accepts one's mortality, freedom, and responsibility to create meaning, the realization of our isolation is unavoidable. People deal with aloneness in many ways, but it presents quite a dilemma, for 'trying too hard to achieve security through merger may result in damage to the self; still, abandoning the effort to connect at all leads to emptiness' (Randall, 2001)."[16]

The Absurd—When one is living in a world of nothingness, meaninglessness and isolation, life begins to appear absurd. We use the term *appear* because, for the existentialist, life that is connected and engaged is only in appearance. Over time, anxiety and angst undermine the normalcy of life, and it becomes *absurd* in appearance. The term absurd indicates that there is no meaning to be found in the world except for the meaning we give it.

Therapeutic Interventions

Existential therapy is best seen as a philosophical view of the world that influences a therapist's outlook regarding how therapy is to be carried out. It is not, therefore, a therapeutic model, nor a model using specific techniques, but emphasizes one's freedom to choose what to make of one's circumstances. "This approach is grounded on the assumption that we are free and therefore responsible for our choices and actions. We are the authors of our lives, and we draw up the blueprints for their design.... A basic existential premise is that we are not victims of circumstance, because to a large extent we are what we choose to be. A major aim of therapy is to encourage clients to reflect on life, to recognize their range of alternatives, and to decide among them. Once clients begin the process of recognizing the ways in which they have passively accepted circumstances and surrendered control, they can start on a path of consciously shaping their own lives.... Existential counseling is not designed to 'cure' people in the tradition of the medical model. Rather, clients are viewed as being sick of life or awkward at living. They need help in surveying the terrain and in deciding on the best route to take, so that they can ultimately discover their own way. Existential therapy is a process of searching for the value and meaning in life. The therapist's basic task is to encourage clients to explore their options for creating a meaningful existence. We can begin by recognizing that we do not have to remain passive victims of our circumstances but instead can consciously become the architect of our life.... The existential movement stands for respect for the person, for exploring new aspects of human behavior, and for divergent methods of understanding people. It uses numerous approaches to therapy based on its assumptions about human nature.... The existential view of human nature is captured, in part, by the notion that the significance of our existence is never fixed once and for all; rather, we continually re-create ourselves through our projects. Humans are in a constant state of transition, emerging, evolving, and becoming. Being a person implies that we are discovering and making sense of our existence.... The basic dimensions of the human condition, according to the existential approach, include (1) the capacity for self-awareness; (2) freedom and responsibility; (3) creating one's identity and establishing meaningful relationships with others; (4) the search for meaning, purpose, values, and goals; (5) anxiety as a condition of living; and (6) awareness of death and nonbeing."[17]

Increasing Self-Awarenes—According to Corey, one's capacity to live fully is determined by one's expansion of their self-awareness. The decision to expand one's self-awareness is fundamental to human growth, because without it other human capacities will not be developed. "Increasing self-awareness, which includes awareness of alternatives, motivations and factors influencing the person, and personal goals, is an aim of all counseling. It is the therapist's task to indicate to the client that a price must be paid for increased awareness. As we open the doors in our world, we can expect more struggle as well as the potential for more fulfillment."[18]

Freedom and Responsibility—One of the primary tasks of the existential therapist is to help the client to determine exactly how they are avoiding freedom in their lives and encourage them to be open to taking advantage of the freedom that is theirs. The therapist must assist the client in helping them accept that they have choices and are responsible for making those choices. "Two central tasks of the therapist are inviting clients to recognize how they have allowed others to decide for them and encouraging them to take steps toward autonomy."[19]

Striving for Identity and Relationship to Others—A great number of those entering therapy have lost their identity by allowing others to make decisions for them. These people have become so dependent on the opinions of others that they cannot make a decision for themselves. Rather than trusting in themselves to make a reasonable decision, they become what important others expect of them, giving up their identity. "One of the greatest fears of clients is that they will discover that there is no core, no self, no substance and that they are merely reflections of everyone's expectations of them.... Perhaps one of the functions of therapy is to help clients distinguish between a neurotically dependent attachment to another and a life-affirming relationship in which both persons are enhanced. The therapist can challenge clients to examine what they get from their relationships, how they avoid intimate contact, how they prevent themselves from having equal relationships, and how they might create therapeutic, healthy, and mature human relationships.... Existential therapists are especially concerned about clients avoiding responsibility; they invite clients to accept personal responsibility. When clients complain about the predicaments they are in and blame others, the therapist is likely to ask them how they contributed to the situation.... Thus, the purpose of psychotherapy is not to 'cure' the clients in the conventional sense, but to help them become aware of what they are doing and to get them out of the victim role."[20]

The Search for Meaning—If a client has little or no self-awareness, is not in touch with their own freedom to make choices, does not take responsibility for those choices and has lost their identity, purpose and significance, they are likely to have lost all meaning in their lives as well. "Existential therapy can provide the conceptual framework for helping clients challenge the meaning in their lives. Questions the therapist might ask are, 'Do you like the direction of your life? Are you pleased with what you now are and what you are becoming? If you are confused about who you are and what you want for yourself, what are you doing to get some clarity?' Perhaps the task of the therapeutic process is to help clients create a value system based on a way of living that is consistent with their way of being.... The therapist's job might well be to trust the capacity of clients to eventually discover an internally derived value system that does provide a meaningful life.... The therapist's trust is important in teaching clients to trust their own capacity to discover a new source of values."[21]

Anxiety as a Condition of Living—As we have noted, existentialism differentiates between neurotic and existential anxiety, the latter being a potential source for growth to take place. According to May, life cannot be lived, nor can death be faced, without anxiety. "Existential anxiety is a constructive form of normal anxiety and can be a stimulus for growth. We experience this anxiety as we become increasingly aware of our freedom and the consequences of accepting or rejecting that freedom. According to May (1981), freedom and anxiety are two sides of the same coin; anxiety is associated with the excitement accompanying the birth of a new idea. Thus, we experience anxiety when we use our freedom to move out of the known into the realm of the unknown.... Existential therapy helps clients come to terms with the paradoxes of existence—life and death, success and failure, freedom and limitations, and certainty and doubt.... Counselors have the task of encouraging clients to develop the courage to face life squarely, largely by taking a stance, performing an action, or making a decision.... The existential therapist can help clients recognize that learning how to tolerate ambiguity and uncertainty and how to live without props can be a necessary phase in the journey from dependence to autonomy. The therapist and client can explore the possibility that although breaking away from crippling patterns and building new lifestyles will be fraught with anxiety for a while, anxiety will diminish as the client experiences more satisfaction with newer ways of being. When a client becomes more self-confident, the anxiety that results from an expectation of catastrophe will decrease."[22]

<u>Awareness of Death and Nonbeing</u>—We have previously focused on how important the topic of death is to the existentialist. This topic plays an important role in therapy as the client deals with his or her feeling and fears associated with their own eventual death. "It can be the factor that helps us transform a stale mode of living into a more authentic one (Yalom, 1980). Thus, one focus in existential therapy is on exploring the degree to which clients are doing the things they value. Without being

morbidly preoccupied by the ever-present threat of nonbeing, clients can develop a healthy awareness of death as a way to evaluate how well they are living and what changes they want to make in their lives. Those who fear death also fear life. If we affirm life and live in the present as fully as possible, however, we will not be obsessed with the end of life."[23]

The client being seen by the existential therapist is regarded as one with whom the therapist must engage in an understanding, honest and empathetic manner. The existentialist sees therapy as relationship driven rather than theory driven, making it necessary to be authentic and trusting.

"Existential therapists do not attempt to give clients solutions to their problems. In fact, they are more likely to challenge clients, encouraging them to have the courage to face their ultimate concerns. [These therapists] have been described as consultants who have a very real, deep caring for the client. The therapist also attempts to demystify the counseling process and relate authentically to the client,...emphasizing that the client and counselor have a mutual investment and risk in the therapeutic encounter."[24]

There are several particular *techniques* outlined by Murdock that are used by existential therapists.

Attention to Nonverbal Behavior—"Because the emphasis in existential psychotherapy (ET) is on awareness of one's being, ET counselors are very interested in observing the client's nonverbal expression and calling their attention to it (Cooper, 2003)."[25]

Self-Disclosure—"It is quite common for ET practitioners to share their personal reactions with their clients. Stemming from the ET value that the counselor must be authentic and present, self-disclosure is seen as deepening the therapeutic encounter. The counselor can disclose in one of two ways: about the process of therapy (i.e., the client-counselor relationship) or about the therapist's own existential struggles (Colledge, 2002)."[26]

Paradoxical Intention—"One of the best known ET techniques, paradoxical intention, originated with Frankl (1984). Used mainly for what Frankl terms neurotic fear (as compared to the realistic fear of unbeing), it involves encouraging the client to 'go with' a troublesome symptom or problem and experience it deliberately (Cooper, 2003). By facing and experiencing whatever it is we greatly fear allows us to engage the unique human capacity to laugh at ourselves and thereby gain distance from our symptoms."27

Dereflection—"Another strategy offered by Frankl, dereflection, consists of directing the client to turn her attention out to the world. It is meant to combat the tendency that Frankl saw in some distressed individuals to focus too intently on internal processes (Cooper, 2003)."28

Dream Analysis—"Yalom (1980) is a big fan of dream analysis. Rather than looking for unconscious conflicts between psychic entities as a psychoanalytic therapist would, the ET therapist is looking for manifestations of the client's issues."29

Bracketing—"The ET counselor must learn to suspend her own beliefs and biases in favor of fully understanding the client's world (Strasser & Strasser, 1997). This process is called bracketing."30

Guided Fantasy—"Yalom describes using imagery to increase death awareness (1980, p. 175). The client is asked to meditate on her death in some way; picturing her funeral, write her obituary, speculate on where, how, when."31

A Biblical Perspective

The centerpiece of existentialism is wrapped in the age-old quest for meaning and value. Many Christians are in search of satisfaction in those same areas. One cannot study the views of existentialism without realizing that they are searching for what the true believing Christian already is and already has.

When it comes to the issue of meaning we stress that unbelievers, as well as many believers, agonize over two basic issues regarding God. They may acknowledge the existence of God, but looking at the world around them and their own circumstances, the question in the recesses of their mind is the nagging question, "Does God really care?" With all of the pain and misery in the world, in light of their personal pain right now, is God really involved with people personally? Regardless of how they feel about that question, there is then a deeper, more profound issue with God. If perchance he does care and is a loving God, then, "Is God really all powerful?" If he is truly omnipotent, why isn't he doing something about all of the misery we see, including my dilemma, my pain, my problems?

When reasonable people try to intellectualize and explain God's seeming lack of involvement in his creation, we find ourselves in a dark box in need of greater light. For the believing Christian, who God is and what God says is absolute truth. The only vehicle he left us to move beyond the inadequacy of our own reasoning and understanding is faith. *The just shall live by faith; But if anyone draws back, My soul has no pleasure in him* (Hebrews 10:38). *We walk by faith, not by sight* (2 Corinthians 5:7).

So—Who Am I?

While the existentialist asks "Who am I?" the believer in God comes to grips with the only sure answer to the questions of meaning and value—those given to us through God's absolute and faithful messages in the Scriptures.

As believers in the sacrificial death of Jesus Christ for our sins, we no longer live in the shadow of guilt, shame and inadequacy. We are redeemed by the blood of the Lamb. We have been raised from the deadness of a life apart from God and given a place as a part of the bride in the most magnificent wedding that will take place before all of the created universe. This is who we are.

We have been placed into the body of Christ. The Holy Spirit has been given to us as a seal assuring us our place. Who am I? is no longer part of our vocabulary. We are his! We are the only light this dark world has. The very favor of God rests upon us. As the Reformers acknowledged: We are saved by grace alone, in Christ alone, through faith alone.

John, the apostle, avoided the use of the word "faith," but instructed us with the action word "believe" nearly one hundred times. Believe it. Rely on it. Trust it.

Identity Determines Choices

The existentialist urges that it takes courage to *be*. Indeed, for the Christian it takes a humble courage to *believe*—to recognize and accept our weaknesses, for in our weakness God is made strong. It takes courage to believe in God's sovereignty. It takes courage to dig into, accept and begin to live in the fullness of God's grace and freedom. It takes courage to rely on the fact that the truth has given us a freedom the unbeliever can never understand. *The man without the Spirit does not accept the things that come from the Spirit of God, for they are foolishness to him, and he cannot understand them, because they are spiritually discerned* (1 Corinthians 2:14, NIV).

Just as reality therapy believes that behavior produces identity, the existentialist believes that choices determine the kind of person we become. Those views appear to be one and the same in how they influence the realization of meaning in life.

Contrary to that view, the Christian believes the kind of person we have become, through the new birth, God's forgiveness, and his infinite grace, clearly lay forth the kind of choices we will now make because of who we already are, by identity.

The call by the existentialist to live authentically is, for the Christian, a call to live a life based on who we are, not who we will one day become. Our challenge is to live according to the identity and value we have been given by our God who loved us and gave his life for us.

The existentialist view that we must live authentically is valid for all. It is all too common in contemporary local churches for many Christians *to act upon a preconceived notion of how a person in a certain position...should act.* We tend to act according to the Christian social norms and perceptions of how a Christian should act and talk. More often than not we, like the existentialist, get caught up in what they term inauthenticity. More to the point—phony! The most commonly misused four letter word for church members today is *fine*, when we are living in the pain of life's exhausting demands.

The existential view of human nature that the significance of our existence is never established and that we continually re-create ourselves through our projects is clearly based on the faulty view that "doing" is the vehicle to "being." A view contrary to Scripture.

And What of Death?

The existential view that death is something that destroys us is of particular interest to those who live life with a Christian perspective.

In its most basic form, the existentialist's search for meaning and value is empowered by their view of death. One drives the other. If death is the limit of our existence, then meaning and value also have great limitations. If whatever meaning I generate in life is ultimately and totally destroyed except for its place in memory, then what is the true value of a life?

If one is left to couple the pain and tragedy that abounds on this earth with the finality of the belief that *death is destruction*—one is, by default, left with an infinite and empty search for meaning and value. For the believer, however, death is not the end of life. As believers, we are either here on this earth or we are with Christ. When we die, we go immediately to be with the Father. Review Appendix G-1 again.

If we were to ask you to reduce the Scriptures down to one word—what would you propose?

Contemplate the question for a moment.

Although God, Jesus Christ, forgiveness, redemption and other words would be valid responses, it's our view that God's word is about...*Life*! *God so loved the world that He gave His only begotten Son, that whoever believes in Him should not perish but have everlasting Life* (John 3:16).

I have come that they may have life, and that they may have it more abundantly (John 10:10).

Blessed are those who do His commandments, that they may have the right to the tree of life, and may enter through the gates into the city (Revelation 22:14).

These are written that you may believe that Jesus is the Christ, the Son of God, and that believing you may have life in His name (John 20:31).

But an angel of the Lord during the night opened the gates of the prison, and taking them out he said, "go your way, stand and speak to the people in the temple, the whole message of this Life." (Acts 5:19-20 NCV).

Epilogue

In total candidness, we have experienced a vast number of mixed thoughts and feelings as we researched this book. The body of Christ needs competent psychologists and therapists who can assist their clients in finding direction in dealing with the problems they face. Certainly many of the theorists we looked at in this volume have given us numerous useful tools that can assist us in accomplishing this goal.

Often however, it seems the influence of Christian thought was nearing a breakthrough in a particular theorist's rationale, but *reasoning* took its toll and the concept was reduced to an intellectual understanding that does not stand in the light of God's unshakable truth.

We firmly believe that a worldview that does not accept and build on the truth of the Scriptures regarding what God has said about the human condition can only fall short in the development of comprehensive, effective solutions.

The call of God for men, women and children to receive and trust in his purpose and plan for our lives requires a childlike step of faith and a willingness to embrace

- a personal creator God
- original sin through Adam and Eve
- the effect of sin on all humanity
- God's just and loving solution
- the deity of Jesus Christ
- one sacrificial death for sin
- a stunning resurrection
- our need to be born from above
- the forgiveness of sins
- the indwelling Holy Spirit
- a new identity
- the power of faith

A close study of the theorists covered in this volume indicates many of them had a gnawing desire to embrace the truths behind Christian thought and beliefs. More often than not, however, they could not allow these simple realities into their complex reasoning.

In their writing on various theorists, Stanton L. Jones and Richard E. Butman noted that "There is some compatibility between Christianity and any system that places a high premium on human rationality. Cognitive therapy would say that what we believe has tremendous implications for our personal well-being.

Epilogue

[T]houghts have implications for the quality of our lives.... We see this especially in the area of suffering. When we view our temporal lives as primary and have as our highest goals comfort and prosperity, then suffering will be a misery-producing and faith-undermining experience. But if suffering is viewed as an opportunity for testimony for the gospel, as a means for fellowship with Christ in his sufferings, as preparation for eternal glory through learning to loosen our ties to this life, and as an opportunity to learn to better comfort others, suffering can be transformed into a meaningful path that one treads for the sake of God's love (Kreeft, 1986)."[1]

Dinesh D'Souza, writing in the Hillsdale College publication *Imprimis*, made reference to comments made by German philosopher Friedrich Nietzsche, who was known for his atheistic views: "The ideas that define Western civilization, Nietzsche said, are based on Christianity. Because some of these ideas seem to have taken on a life of their own, we might have the illusion that we can abandon Christianity while retaining them. This illusion, Nietzsche warns us, is just that. Remove Christianity and the ideas fall too. Consider the example of Europe, where secularization has been occurring for well over a century. For a while it seemed that secularization would have no effect on European morality or social institutions. Yet increasingly today there is evidence of the decline of the nuclear family. Overall birthrates have plummeted, while rates of divorce and out-of-wedlock births are up. Nietzsche also warned that, with the decline of Christianity, new and opposing ideas would arise. We see these today in demands for the radical redefinition of the family, the revival of eugenic theories, and even arguments for infanticide. In sum, the eradication of Christianity—and of organized religion in general—would also mean the gradual extinction of the principles of human dignity."[2]

As a final thought, we must ask ourselves, "Are there benefits to psychiatry and psychology?" Yes! We need competent psychiatrists because modern medications can be very helpful in controlling the lingering effects of severe depression, bipolar disorder and difficult mental illnesses like schizophrenia and borderline personality disorder.

We would also be remiss in failing to recognize the research that has been done in the fields of marriage and family counseling, as well as childhood and teenage development. Many of the studies done in recent decades have been helpful to both secular and Christian counselors. We can better understand the impact and effect that the disintegration of our cultural mores have had on Western civilization as we watch the societal movement away from its Christian underpinnings.

As fellow sojourners who know that we are just passing through on our journey to our eternal home,

Epilogue

we commend you for answering God's call on your life to work in the one or more of the many areas we refer to as Christian counseling and/or discipleship. It is a noble field, a demanding field, an accomplished and satisfying field of endeavor and ministry to others.

Bless you, as you put your future and the well-being of those who come to you in God's capable and loving hands.

I have been crucified with Christ;

it is no longer I who live,

but Christ lives in me;

and the life which I now live in the flesh

I live by faith in the Son of God,

who loved me and gave Himself for me.

(Galatians 2:20)

Appendices

Appendix A - 1

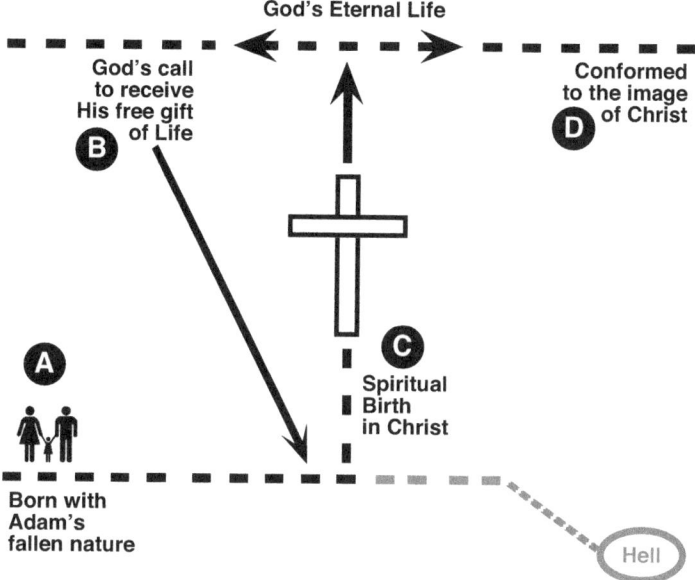

A - Romans 5:12: *Just as through one man sin entered the world, and death through sin, and thus death spread to all men, because all sinned.*

B - John 1:12: *But as many as received Him, to them He gave the right to become children of God, to those who believe in His name.*

C - Romans 8:30: *And those whom He thus foreordained, He also called; and those whom He called, He also justified (acquitted, made righteous, putting them into right standing with Himself). And those whom He justified, He also glorified [raising them to a heavenly dignity and condition or state of being].* AMP

D - Romans 8:29: *For whom He foreknew, He also predestined to be conformed to the image of His Son.*

Taken from *Breaking the Self-centered Life – Revised Edition,* by Roger Alliman, 2010.

Appendix A - 2

Trichotomist View of Man

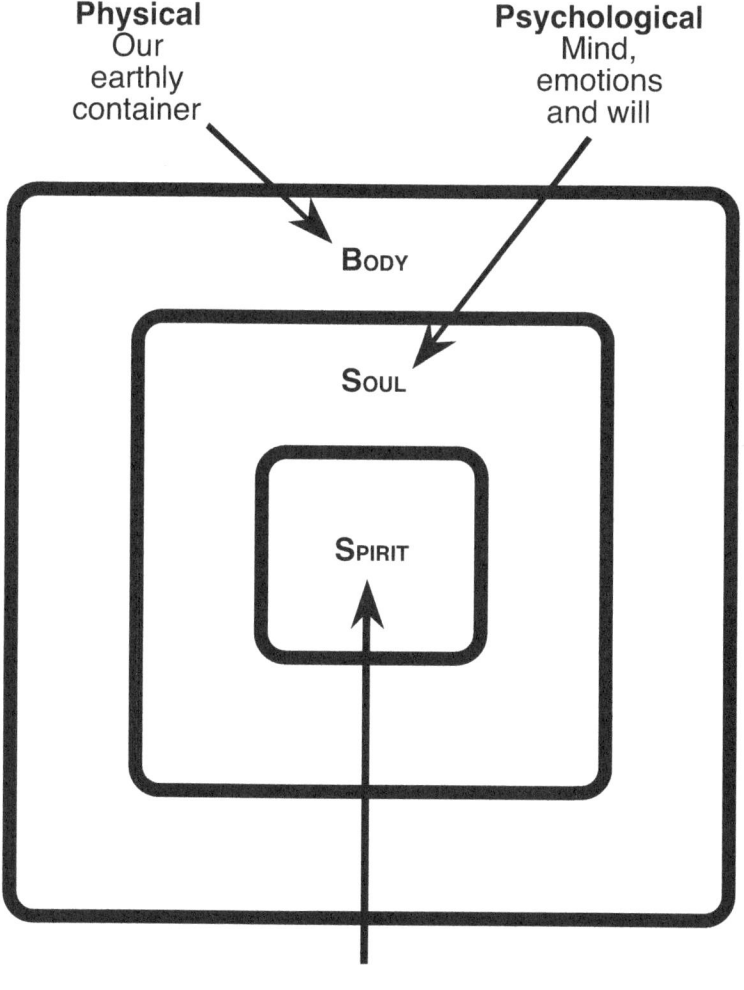

Appendix A - 3

Life in the Spirit

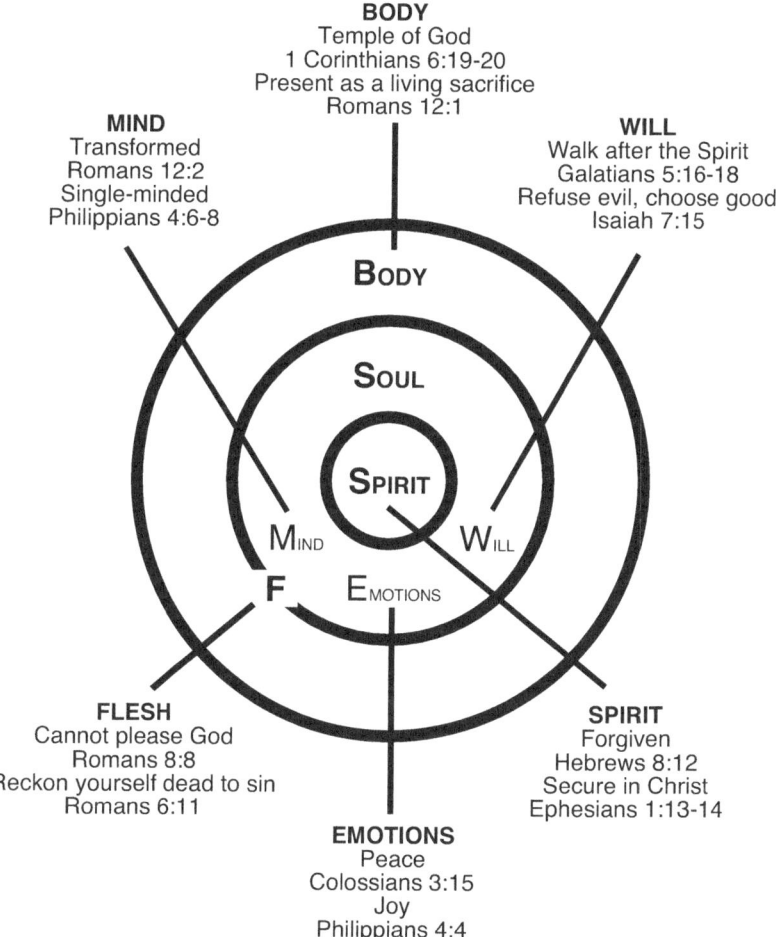

BODY
Temple of God
1 Corinthians 6:19-20
Present as a living sacrifice
Romans 12:1

MIND
Transformed
Romans 12:2
Single-minded
Philippians 4:6-8

WILL
Walk after the Spirit
Galatians 5:16-18
Refuse evil, choose good
Isaiah 7:15

FLESH
Cannot please God
Romans 8:8
Reckon yourself dead to sin
Romans 6:11

EMOTIONS
Peace
Colossians 3:15
Joy
Philippians 4:4

SPIRIT
Forgiven
Hebrews 8:12
Secure in Christ
Ephesians 1:13-14

Appendix A - 4
Man as Spirit, Soul and Body

Generally speaking, there are three theological models that define who man is. These are known as monism—the belief that man is comprised of only one part—the dichotomous view, stating that man is comprised of two parts and the trichotomist view, which sees man as comprised of three distinct parts.

The monistic view of man is popular today and is emphasized in present psychological thought to describe the fundamental wholeness of man's being. Man is viewed monistically simply as a self, with no distinguishable parts. In this view, the belief that man is comprised of body, soul and spirit is considered outdated. Contemporary preference by social scientists, anthropologists and psychologists abandons the concept of soul and spirit largely because they cannot be studied scientifically.

The dichotomous view sees man as two constituent elements comprised of the physical (i.e. the body) and the spiritual (the soul and spirit). Here, spirit and soul are seen as being interrelated, being indistinguishable, one from the other. Under this view, man has a two-fold nature—on the one hand material (body), on the other, immaterial (soul and spirit).

The trichotomist view sees man as having three

distinguishable parts, consisting of body, soul and spirit.

Just as God is a Trinity, man is also a trinity, being created in his likeness. According to the trichotomist, the human soul and spirit are not identical as shown by several scriptures.

Scripture tells us, for instance, that the soul and spirit are indeed divisible as described by the writer of Hebrews, *The word of God is living and powerful, and sharper than any two-edged sword, piercing even to the division of soul and spirit* (Hebrews 4:12). In the words of Mary, mother of Jesus, *My soul magnifies the Lord, and my spirit has rejoiced in God my Savior* (Luke 1:46-47). These Scriptures absolutely distinguish between the soul and the spirit.

We find the same distinction when Paul states, "*May the God of peace himself sanctify you completely; and may your spirit and soul and body be kept sound and blameless at the coming of our Lord Jesus Christ* (1 Thessalonians 5:23, Holman). This clearly indicates that man is a tri-part being.

David makes the distinction when he says to God, *Into your hands I commit my spirit; redeem me, O LORD, the God of truth. I will be glad and rejoice in your love, for you saw my affliction and knew the anguish of my soul. Be merciful to me, O LORD, for I am in distress; my eyes grow weak with sorrow, my soul and my body with grief* (Psalm 31:5,7,9). Mary, King

Appendix

David, the apostle Paul and the writer of Hebrews all make a distinction between the human spirit, soul and body.

These distinctions are also made in the Greek language. In Greek, the term for body is *sarx*, referring to a dwelling place that distinguishes man's material body from his immaterial self. Our body has a world consciousness that relates to our environment. The term soul is translated as *psuche* in Greek and is the same root word from which we get the term *psychology*. It is the part of the human that makes up our personality and causes us to have a self-consciousness, that enables us to relate to others. The soul is comprised of our mind or thinking ability, our emotions or feeling ability and our will or decision making ability. *Psuche* refers to man's inner self, which includes our emotions, the will and desire and the mind, including our perception. It is equivalent to the ego, person or personality in Greek and is a distinct and separable part of man. And finally, the term *spirit* is translated as *pneuma* in Greek and refers to the immaterial part of our being. This is the part of us that relates to God and gives us a God-consciousness. Our spirit determines our identity. Man, therefore, is a spirit being that has a soul housed in a body.

We come into this world born in sin. Some writers have called this man's birth defect, meaning that we are born separated from God, dead spiritually and without life. *It's your sins that have cut you off from God. Because of your sins, He has turned away and will not listen anymore* (Isaiah 59:2 NLT). *In the past you were spiritually dead because of your sins and the things you did against God. Yes, in the past you lived the way the world lives, following the ruler of the evil powers that are above the earth. That same spirit is now working in those who refuse to obey God. In the past all of us lived like them, trying to please our sinful selves and doing all the things our bodies and minds wanted. We should have suffered God's anger because we were sinful by nature. We were the same as all other people* (Ephesians 2:1-3, NCV).

We are born in sin separated from God and born with a spirit that was dead to God. But God gives us a new spirit and indwells it with his Spirit when we are born again! *I will give you a new heart and put a new spirit within you; I will take the heart of stone out of your flesh and give you a heart of flesh. I will put my Spirit within you and cause you to walk in my statutes, and you will keep My judgments and do them* (Ezekiel 36:26-27). We have new life in, from, and through him. Paul describes it this way: *I have been crucified with Christ; it is no longer I who live but Christ lives in me; and the life which I now live in the flesh, I live by faith in the Son of God, who loved me and gave his life for me* (Galatians 2:20). God gave his life for us, to give his life to us, so that he might live his life through us!

In regard to the trichotomist view, Oswald Chambers stated in *Biblical Psychology* that, "the spirit is the essential foundation of man; the soul his peculiar essential form; the body his essential manifestation. Remember, the whole meaning of the soul is to express the spirit, and the struggle of the spirit is to get itself expressed in the soul". This is what the Bible refers to as *walking after the Spirit.*

Watchman Nee expressed the doctrine of trichotomy in his three-volume work *The Spiritual Man.* Speaking of the importance of identifying the spirit, he wrote, "It is imperative that believers recognize a spirit exists within them, something extra to thought, knowledge and imagination of the mind, something beyond affection, sensation and pleasure of the emotion, something additional to desire, decision and action of the will. This component is far more profound than these faculties. God's people not only must know they possess a spirit; they also must understand how this organ operates—its sensitivity, its work, its power, its laws. Only in this way can they walk according to their spirit and not the soul or body of their flesh."

In his *Reference Bible,* C.I. Scofield defined the human soul as the "seat of the affections, desires, emotions, and will—the self." T. Austin-Sparks in *What Is Man?,* states that, "[The soul is] the plane and organ of human life and communication. Thus, what is received by the spirit alone with its peculiar faculties is translated for practical purposes, firstly to the recipient himself, and then to other humans, by means of the soul. This may be an enlightened mind for truth (reason); a filled heart, with joy or love, for comfort and uplift (emotion); or energized will for action or execution (volition). Soul, or self-consciousness as the union point between spirit and body, was created free to choose to which of these two opposite poles [the flesh or the spirit] it would be attracted."

Finally, Jessie Penn-Lewis quoted Tertullian, Pember and Andrew Murray in support of trichotomy. In her work titled *Soul and Spirit,* she summarized the functions of the soul: "We see that all these writers practically define the 'soul' as the seat of the personality, consisting of the will and the intellect or mind; a personal entity standing between the 'spirit'... and the 'body' — open to the outer world of nature and sense; the soul having power of choice as to which world shall dominate the entire man."

Portions taken from
*Man as Spirit, Soul, and Body:
A Study of Biblical Psychology,*
by John B. Woodward, PhD

Appendix B - 1
Gestalt
Principles of Perception

You have probably seen illustrations of the principles the Gestaltists derived. For example, the principle of proximity says that when stimuli are close together, they tend to form one perceptual unit. You are likely to perceive this figure as six sets of paired slashes rather than as twelve slashes.

// // // // // //

The principle of closure says that when incomplete figures are perceived, the mind usually completes the figure:

Here you are likely to perceive a triangle rather than two rows of typed slashes and an underline.

Susan X. Day, *Theory and Design in Counseling and Psychotherapy* (Boston, MA, Houghton Mifflin Company, 2004).

Appendix B - 2

The drawing below portrays either a young woman or an old woman, depending on how you see it. Perls seized upon these and other ideas from the German Gestalt psychologists and applied them to all kinds of human experience, not just perception.

Susan X. Day, *Theory and Design in Counseling and Psychotherapy* (Boston, MA, Houghton Mifflin Company, 2004).

Appendix B - 3
A Boundaries Overview

A boundary is the emotional and physical space between you and another person. Personal boundaries help us enjoy healthy relationships and attract people who are positive forces in our life. To maintain healthy intimacy in relationships, we need to first establish healthy intellectual, emotional and physical boundaries. Personal boundaries factor into creating rich, fulfilling relationships that are necessary in keeping us in balance on our personal journey through life.

Here are five important points to keep in mind as you establish personal boundaries:

1 - *Saying No.* Knowing when to say no and not feeling guilty about it is imperative. You are not expected to do everything anyone asks of you.

2 - *Values.* Healthy personal boundaries are based on strong moral beliefs. Going against your values for another person means you may want to reassess your relationship.

3 - *Identity.* Boundaries help form your integrity. They force you to evaluate what you want and what you don't want in your life.

4 - *Speak Up.* When others cross your personal boundaries, tell them assertively. It is not wrong to let others know where you stand. Calmly talking about your boundaries enforces your sense of personhood and purpose.

5 - *Trust.* Don't let others tell you that your personal boundaries are unacceptable. You know what you need better than anyone. Trust your gut.

The following is taken from *Boundaries* by Drs. Henry Cloud and John Townsend, (Grand Rapids, MI: Zondervan Publishing, 1992).

> *The Law of Responsibility* — People who set limits exhibit self-control and show responsibility for themselves. Setting limits is an act of love; by binding and limiting the harmful actions, they protect the good.
>
> *The Law of Power* — We must acknowledge our basic inability to change other people. You only have power over yourself. Give up trying to have control and power over someone else.
>
> *The Law of Evaluation* — When you set boundaries, be lovingly responsible to the person in pain. How do you think [others] will react when you start setting boundaries? How will you respond to their reaction?
>
> *The Law of Exposure* — Passive boundaries, such as withdrawal, triangulation, pouting, affairs and passive-aggressive behavior, are extremely destructive to a relationship. Boundaries need to be communicated first verbally and then with actions.
>
> *And What About Marriage* — Whenever there is talk about setting boundaries in a marriage, there is the question of submission. Does the wife have free choice or is she "under the law" and feeling wrath, guilt, insecurity and alienation, feelings that the Bible promises the law will bring? Does the husband offer the wife unconditional love?
>
> *Balance* — Many dimensions need to be balanced in a relationship. Problems come when the balance is not mutual. If one controls togetherness, and the other controls separateness, there is imbalance. Setting boundaries may correct this imbalance.

Appendix B - 4
What Is Biblical Salvation?

1. *Belief*—An activity of the mind. We must believe in order to be saved, but belief will never save us. Believing is simply a prerequisite for salvation. Our salvation is not based on what we do — it is based on what God has done *for* us and *in* us.

> • *Whoever would draw near to God must believe that he exists and that he rewards those who seek him* (Hebrews 11:6, ESV).
>
> • *No one can come to me unless the Father who sent me draws him. And I will raise him up on the last day* (John 6:44, ESV).
>
> • *Are there still some among you who hold that only believing is enough? Believing in one God? Well, remember that the devils believe this too— so strongly that they tremble in terror* (James 2:19 ESV).

2. *Faith*—An activity of the will. We must have faith to be saved, but even that faith is a gift from God. We are sanctified (set apart) by our faith. We are saved by grace alone, through faith alone, in Christ alone.

> • *That they may receive forgiveness of sins and a place among those who are sanctified by faith in me* (Acts 26:18, NIV).

3. *Christ's death for me* — Without his sacrificial death we could not have been saved. But his death did not save us — it made possible our reconciliation with God. Our sins made us an enemy of God; reconciliation made peace with God possible.

> • *Christ reconciled you to God in the body of his flesh through death, in order to present you holy and faultless and irreproachable in his Father's presence* (Colossians 1:22).

4. *Confession and Forgiveness* — Must we confess every known sin in order to be forgiven? What if we miss one? What if we die without having confessed a particular sin? Confession and forgiveness do not save us. Our sins — past, present and future — are forever forgiven. He has forgiven us of our sins so that he can indwell us and live his life through us!

> • *I have been crucified with Christ; it is no longer I who live, but Christ lives in me; and the life I now live in the flesh I live by faith in the Son of God, who loved me and gave himself for me* (Galatians 2:20).

5. *The Blood of Christ*—The life is in the blood, but Christ's life is in the Spirit! His blood does not save us. His blood cleanses us of our sins, justifying us and bringing us peace with God.

Appendix

- *Christ's death on the cross has made peace with God for all by his blood* (Colossians 1:20).
- *Since, therefore, we have been justified by his blood, much more shall we be saved by him from the wrath of God* (Romans 5:9 ESV).

6. *Baptism*—Baptism does not bring us salvation. It is a sign to others that we have died with Christ and risen with him in newness of life.

- *In baptism you see how your old evil nature died with him and was buried with him; and then you came up out of death with him into a new life, because you trusted the Word of the mighty God who raised Christ from the dead* (Colossians 2:12). Also see 1 Corinthians 1:17.

7. *His Life?*—He came that we might have life, and have it abundantly! His life in us is eternal life.

- *This is how God showed His love to us: He sent His one and only Son into the world so we could have life through Him* (1 John 4:9).
- *For if while we were enemies we were reconciled to God by the death of his Son, much more, now that we are reconciled, shall we be saved by his life* (Romans 5:10 ESV).
- *He who has the Son has life; he who does not have the Son of God does not have life* (1 John 5:12).

Appendix C - 1

From Bondage to Freedom

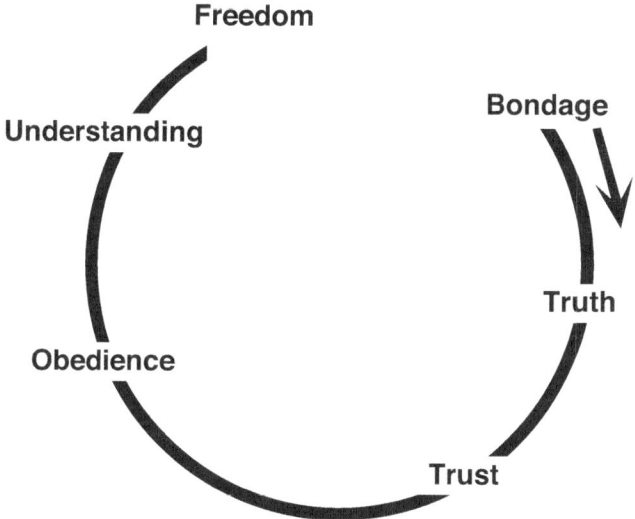

Appendix C - 2

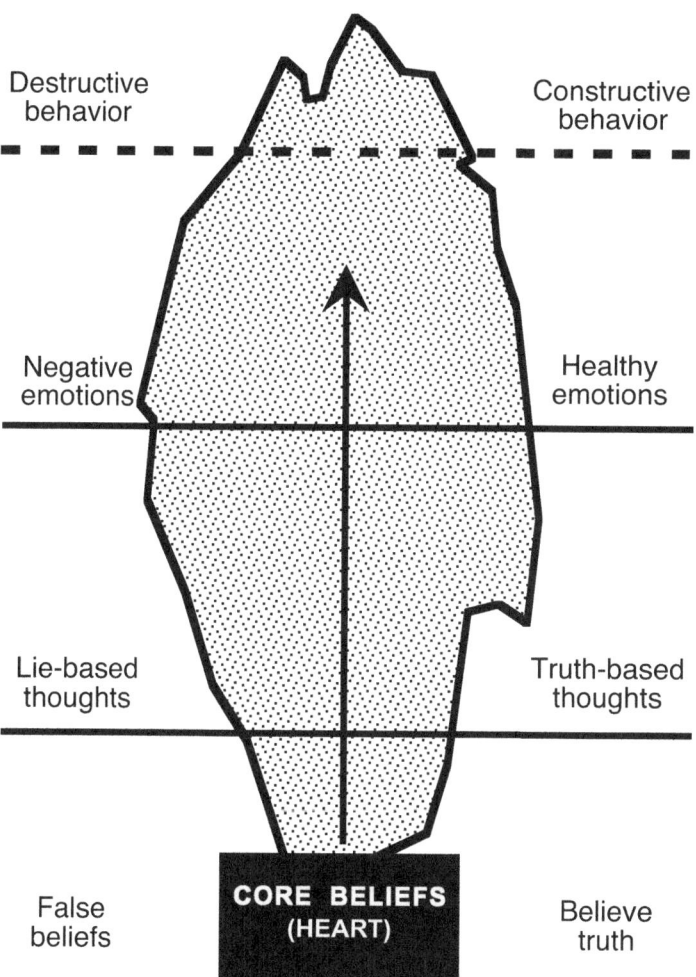

**Under the Surface
Core Belief Systems at Work**

*As a man thinks in his heart,
so is he* (Prov 23:7).

Appendix D - 1
The Power of Sin

The power of sin that indwells us is sometimes referred to as indwelling sin. In his book *What God Wishes Christians Knew About Christianity,* psychologist Bill Gillham does a remarkable job of explaining what exactly indwelling sin is.

He explains that an evil power called *sin* is at work in man. This is not *sins* as we customarily think of them, but a *power* called "sin." This power is Satan's secret weapon against all of humanity.

The power of sin is first seen in Genesis, where God is speaking to Cain as Cain is contemplating murdering Abel: *If you do well, will not your countenance be lifted up? And if you do not do well, sin is crouching at the door; and its desire is for you, but you must master it* (Genesis 4:7). According to Gillham, hidden within this verse is the key to unmasking the devil's means of deceiving us. The Hebrew of the last portion of Genesis 4:7 is literally translated, *"sin is crouching at the door; his desire is for you, but you must master him."* God personifies sin in this verse, unmasking the means Satan uses to deceive us. Personify means to represent as having personality or the thoughts of a living being.

The word *sin* in this verse is not a verb (action word), it is a noun (person, place or thing). It is extremely important to understand that God is not referring to a sinful act here, but a person, place or thing which crouches, which desires Cain (and us), and which can be mastered. God personifies sin (the noun). God is saying that an entity called sin somehow had the ability to influence Cain. Without question, God said that a power which he calls sin was playing a key role as Cain was considering killing his brother. In regard to Cain, God portrays sin as having the ability to persuade Cain, entice Cain, tempt Cain, lead Cain to take matters into his own hands, and suggest to Cain that he solve his problems by rebelling against God.

Another example of what we are talking about is found in Romans 7. Count the actors in Romans 7:15: *That which I am doing, I do not understand; for I am not practicing what I would like to do, but I am doing the very thing I hate."*

How many actors do you see in this verse? Only one—I. However, verses 17 and 20 indicate that there are two actors in the verses that follow: I, plus the power called sin. *So now no longer am I the one doing it, but sin which indwells me. But if I am doing the very things I do not wish, I am no longer the one doing it, but sin which dwells in me is doing it.* There are now two actors in these verses.

Appendix

These verses indicate I am not acting alone when I embrace a sinful thought or commit a sinful act. The power called sin is right there with me.

Gillham concludes "I am not teaching the false idea that I can blame my sins on my mythical, nonexistent sinful nature. That would be a cop-out. The person who takes that unbiblical position projects that blame for his sins on the nonexistent old man who died in Christ, see Romans 6:2-8. That cannot be documented in the text of Romans 6 through 8."

Inspired by the book
What God Wishes Christians Knew About Christianity,
by Bill Gillham
(Eugene, OR, Harvest House Publishers, 1998).

Appendix D - 2

Put Off	**Put On**
Lack of love	Love
Judging	God search my heart
Bitterness	Tender forgiveness
Unforgiving spirit	Forgiving spirit
Selfishness	Self-denial
Pride	Humility
Boasting/Conceit	Esteem others
Stubbornness	Brokenness
Disrespect for authority	Honor authority
Rebellion	Submission
Disobedience	Obedience
Impatience	Patience
Ungratefulness	Gratefulness
Covetousness	Contentment
Discontent	Contentment
Murmuring/Complaining	Praise
Irritation with others	Preferring in love
Jealousy	Trust
Strife/Contention	Peace
Retaliation/Getting even	Return good for evil

Put Off	Put On
Losing temper	Self-control
Anger	Self-control
Wrath	Soft answer
Easily irritated	Not easily provoked
Hatred	Love
Murder	Love
Gossip	Edifying speech
Evil speaking	Good report
Critical spirit	Kindness
Lying	Speaking the truth
Profanity	Pure speech
Idel words	Bridled tongue
Wrong motives	Eternal motives
Evil thoughts	Pure thoughts
Complacency	Zeal for life
Laziness	Diligence
Slothfulness	Wholeheartedness
Hypocrisy	Sincerity
Idolatry	Worship God only
Left first love	Faithful devotion
Lack of joy	Joyful spirit
Worry/Fear	Trust

Appendix

Put Off	Put On
Unbelief	Faith
Neglect of God's word	Bible study/Meditation
Prayerlessness	Prayerfulness
No burden for the lost	Compassion for unbelievers
Burying your talents	Developing your gifts
Irresponsibility	Responsibility
Procrastination	Diligence
Irreverence	Reverence
Inhospitable	Hospitable
Cheating	Honesty
Gluttony	Discipline
Stinginess	Generosity
Lack of moderation	Temperance
Ungodly friends	Godly friends
Temporal values	Eternal values
Love of money	Love of God
Impure morals	Moral purity
Fornication	Abstinence
Lust	Pure desires
Adultery	Marital fidelity

Appendix D - 3

A Counseling Model

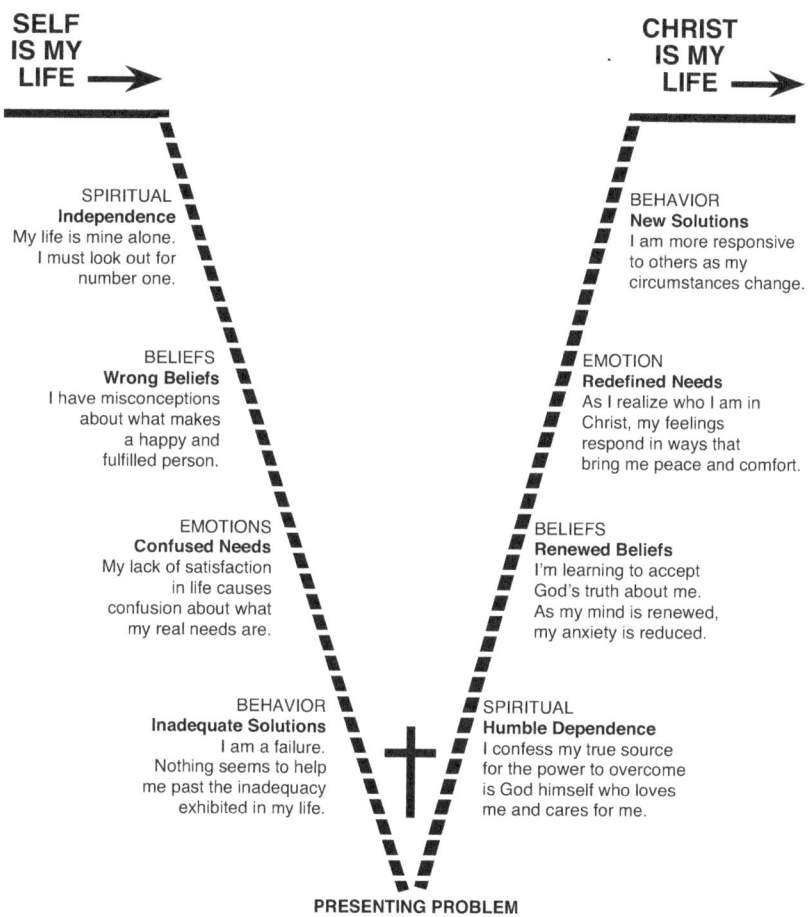

SELF IS MY LIFE →

SPIRITUAL
Independence
My life is mine alone. I must look out for number one.

BELIEFS
Wrong Beliefs
I have misconceptions about what makes a happy and fulfilled person.

EMOTIONS
Confused Needs
My lack of satisfaction in life causes confusion about what my real needs are.

BEHAVIOR
Inadequate Solutions
I am a failure. Nothing seems to help me past the inadequacy exhibited in my life.

CHRIST IS MY LIFE →

BEHAVIOR
New Solutions
I am more responsive to others as my circumstances change.

EMOTION
Redefined Needs
As I realize who I am in Christ, my feelings respond in ways that bring me peace and comfort.

BELIEFS
Renewed Beliefs
I'm learning to accept God's truth about me. As my mind is renewed, my anxiety is reduced.

SPIRITUAL
Humble Dependence
I confess my true source for the power to overcome is God himself who loves me and cares for me.

PRESENTING PROBLEM
The issues that have manifested through my emotional struggles and consequent behavior make me realize the solutions are outside my *self*

Appendix D - 3 (Continued)

THEORY OF RECOVERY

We have developed a counseling model that is designed to treat emotional, psychological and addictive issues from a Biblical perspective. The program is founded upon the belief that God's word contains the answers to our problems and that if we will investigate and act upon what God has to say about the particular problems we are facing, we will find relief from that problem. The key phrase here is to "act upon", so that while the program is clearly Biblical in its scope, it also lends itself to behavioral and reality based theories of recovery and is extremely goal directed in its approach. In other words, it is designed to help clients come to terms with their faulty thinking based upon Biblical principles and to make changes in their lives that are congruent with their new way of thinking. In its simplest form, the model states that, contrary to our usual way of thinking, it is our thoughts about others and ourselves that dictate our reactions to situations in our lives, not the situation itself.

EVENT---THOUGHTS---EMOTIONS---BEHAVIORS

So many of us believe that events in our lives cause us to feel and behave in certain ways. That the things that happen to us cause us to react as we do. But the truth of the matter is that we feel and behave in the ways we do based upon our thoughts and beliefs about the event itself. Based on this theory, an event leads to certain thoughts (usually based on certain past experiences), which, in turn, leads to certain emotions or feelings, which then leads to certain behaviors.

The point, here, is that an event is incapable of causing us to act in a particular manner. When we say, for example, "He really made me angry", we are making an inaccurate statement. In reality, the event (whatever he or she did) triggered a thought process (based on other past experiences) which created an emotion (anger in this case), which, in turn, led to a certain behavior (crying, yelling, sulking, or stomping out of the room, for example).

So you see, we *choose* to act as we do! It may be totally unconscious at the time, but it is still a choice. This is an important concept to understand in that it can be quite liberating to realize that we no longer have to be captive to our emotions. We can *choose* to react differently. What is important here is that until we identify the specific thoughts that are creating our irrational thinking, usually based upon the world's way of doing things, we will continue to act in an irrational manner, causing us great difficulty in life.

INDEPENDENCE

With this as a background, let us look at the diagram for a moment. Most people, including Christians, who come into treatment are living lives of *independence*. By this, we do not mean that they are strong, independent people but, rather, that they have fallen into the trap of living independently of God's peace and assurance. In short, they are living independently of God's will for their lives, and have, in a spiritual sense, chosen to live their lives based upon the world's standards for happiness and success rather than living lives based upon God's standards. By doing so, they are forced to *look out for number one*, while all the time realizing that their life is out of control. The majority of their problems and difficulties are brought about by their own efforts to be in total control of their life circumstances and to be their own resource for living, leaving God totally out of the equation or at least on the sidelines. The Bible calls this living in the flesh.

IRRATIONAL BELIEFS

Referring once again to our Recovery Model, we see that this lifestyle of independence leads inevitably to *irrational beliefs*. When we lead lives that are founded upon the principle of doing things our own way, independent of what God has to say about life and the living of life, it is only natural that our belief systems are going to ultimately fail us. In other words, if our beliefs are based upon the world's system and not upon the truth of God's word, our beliefs will naturally be irrational.

The irrational thinking that leads to wrong beliefs dates back to the fall of man, where Adam chose to do things his own way. Before the fall, man put total trust and hope in God Himself, looking to Him for leadership and trust that could be delivered only by God. But once the fall took place, man was separated from God and left to his own devices. And out of his futile attempts to live life to it's fullest grew pain, hardship, suffering, trials and afflictions. So as we can see, it is extremely important that we learn to think rationally, according to God's principles, for if we fail to do so, we can expect the kind of emotional turmoil in our lives that can lead only to confused needs.

CONFUSED NEEDS

Once our belief systems about ourselves, others and the world around us become inaccurate, *confused needs* will naturally follow. If our perceived needs are based upon faulty, inaccurate beliefs, then it stands to reason that our real needs will be confused. Thinking rationally means thinking appropriately and accurately (based on Biblical principles) about ourselves, about events in our lives, and about situations that we face on an everyday basis. When we think rationally and appropriately, we are in touch with reality and are developing thoughts and attitudes that are consistent with the truth of God. But when we are not thinking rationally, we are left prey to the world and it's systems to define and manipulate our needs for us. Our inaccurate beliefs will distort our real needs and the world system, along with important others around us, will define who we are and how we should satisfy our confused needs.

INADEQUATE SOLUTIONS

As we have just seen, our irrational beliefs will naturally lead to confused needs. Given this, it becomes simple to understand that our attempts to remedy our circumstances must, by definition, be inadequate. Or put another way, what we tell ourselves about our circumstances, and what we believe about a situation will determine how we feel and react to that situation. And if what we tell ourselves is based on faulty information, then we are setting ourselves up for *inadequate solutions.*

Under this scenario, it will seem that everything we try to do in order to help ourselves will end up in failure. No matter how many people we reach out to for help, our needs will still go unresolved. Nothing we do will seem to resolve our dissatisfaction with life and no one will seem to be able to help us. In fact, it will seem that the more we do, the worse it gets.

PRESENTING PROBLEM

Most people struggling with life would agree that this is where they find themselves. This is exactly what most people feel as they enter therapy. Their *presenting problem* is one of continued emotional distress which has led to symptoms such as depression, suicidal thoughts, inferiority, substance abuse, eating disorders, insecurity, inadequacy, guilt, worry, doubt and fear. And in some cases, these problems have been going on for so long that they have begun to manifest themselves in physical conditions such as hypertension, headaches, stomach problems, insomnia, fatigue and chest pains, along with an entire host of other physical symptoms. And most of these people have one thing in common—they are ready for change! They are ready to try something different in order to solve the problems they face.

We want our clients to consider the possibility that where they are right now in their life might be exactly where God wants them to be in order to work his purpose in their life. We want them to consider that perhaps God has allowed them to go their own way, and experience the resulting pain of doing so, in order to show them that what they are doing simply does not work. We want them to consider that God knows full well that they would arrive at this point in their life at this exact time in their life, and that he has prepared a way for them to experience change.

It is our belief that God has a plan for us and one of our primary goals is to help the client find out what that plan is. We are dedicated to the idea of helping individuals understand that God has a better way—that God has the answers to our problems and that he wants to help us find those answers.

It is the goal of this model to aid clients in giving them *hope* and *trust*—the kind of hope and trust that will bring about lasting *change*. Initially *hope*—hope that brings about the client's understanding that God alone has the answers to our problems, and that through Biblical truth, we can begin to realize that God has provided us with practical solutions to our problems. A kind of hope that lets us know that He loves us enough to use difficult circumstances in our lives to change our lives for our own good.

And hope brings about *trust*—trust not only in one's therapist, physician or pastor, but trust in God. A trust that says that God can and will provide answers to those most difficult issues. We can choose to give up our inadequate solutions for God's adequate ones and give him control of our problems, our healing and our lives.

Appendix

And out of this, *change* will be produced—change that helps us realize that our present problems are a result of our false beliefs regarding life, other people and ourselves. The kind of change that helps us understand that our perceived needs and the use of inadequate solutions have resulted in even further conflict. The kind of change that helps us understand that our independence from God is foundational to our inability to live life to it's fullest.

DEPENDENCE

Once we begin to change, we will find ourselves taking on a new spiritual identity. Where once we were leading lives of independence and depending only on ourselves and others to meet our needs, we now take on a new found *dependence*—a dependence on Christ as our real source for power. It is *his* power that helps us in overcoming our difficulties, and we begin to understand that through Christ, we are graciously loved and cared for.

RENEWED BELIEFS

As we become more and more dependent on God, our thought life will begin to change. Where once our beliefs about ourselves and others were distorted, our *beliefs* are now becoming increasingly *renewed*. We are beginning to accept God's truth about ourselves and our problems. We are beginning to understand that we are defined by who God says we are, not by who the world says we are, and not by who we think we are based on past experiences and failures. As this begins to take shape in our minds, we will become less confused and less anxious about our lives, and begin to grow to understand that God loves us just as we are and that his truth will free us. We no longer have to live according to the flesh.

REDEFINED NEEDS

The more our beliefs become renewed, the more we will *redefine our needs*. Where once our needs were confused, based upon irrational beliefs, now our needs are changing and are based upon a new belief system. We are now beginning to understand that what we once thought were our needs are not our needs at all, but rather, a result of irrational thinking. My real needs are something much deeper, and only God has the solutions for them. Once we identify the irrational thoughts that are causing our problems, we can replace them with the truth of God's word and begin to experience relief. Through having our minds renewed by the truth of God, we can change our thoughts, emotions, feelings and even our behavior.

Appendix

NEW SOLUTIONS

And out of this, we will find *new solutions* for our problems. We can now accept responsibility in cooperating with God's ultimate and positive purpose in the very circumstances that seemed to be our problems. We can now see that God's solutions are practical and that they work. By substituting the old ways of thinking with renewed ways of thinking, our lives can be transformed to reflect the logic and rationality of God Himself.

We can now see that Christ came to set us free from our guilt, shame, failure and fear. We are not doomed to live with harmful emotions and the resulting pain of those emotions. God's purpose is to bring healing to all who will come to Him through Jesus Christ and receive the truth. As believers, we have become new in God's sight and he wants us to experience our newness. Our experience of new life is only realized when we aggressively choose to renew our thinking and thereby receive the mind of Christ (Ephesians 4:22-24).

Appendix E - 1

Renewing the Mind from Irrational Beliefs

Ten Often Used Irrational Beliefs
and Their Scriptural Responses

1. I should be loved and approved of by almost every person I know and meet, and live up to their expectations. If others do not approve of me, then I should not approve of myself.
    Matthew 5:11
    John 15:9,18-19
    Colossians 1:21,22
    Matthew 10:35-37
    Galatians 1:9-10
    Romans 8:1

2. I must be highly competent, adequate, intelligent and achieving in everything before I can be happy. When I fail, I should feel badly about myself.
    Romans 12:6
    Ephesians 4:7,11-16
    2 Corinthians 5:21
    2 Corinthians 12:4-30
    Romans 5:1

3. When people act unfairly or wickedly, I should blame them and see them as undesirable and evil.
>   Romans 12:14,17
>   Ephesians 4:31-32
>   1 John 4:9-11

4. It is a terrible catastrophe when I am rejected, treated unfairly and things aren't as I like them.
>   Matthew 5:11
>   John 15:18-19
>   Romans 8:32
>   Jeremiah 31:3

5. Since my feelings are caused by external factors, I have little or no ability to control or change them.
>   Philippians 4:4-8
>   1 Peter 5:7

6. I should be greatly concerned about dangerous and fearful things and must center my attention on them.
>   Matthew 6:25-34
>   Mark 13:11
>   Matthew 10:28-31

7. I can handle difficulties and responsibilities better by avoiding them than by facing them.
>   Galatians 6:9
>   James 1:2-4,12

Appendix

8. I absolutely need something or someone stronger or greater than myself to rely on—something or someone to lean on.
 Luke 18:27
 2 Corinthians 12:9
 Philippians 4:13
 Hebrews 13:5

9. My past remains all important and must influence my feelings and behavior now because it once did. I must be the way I have always been. This is just me!
 Romans 6:6-7
 Philippians 3:13-14
 John 3:3-6
 2 Corinthians 5:17
 Colossians 3:3
 Isaiah 43:7

10. I can achieve maximum happiness by inaction, or by passively enjoying myself.
 Luke 9:23
 Hebrews 12:1-3,12
 Philippians 2:12-16

Appendix E - 2

Renewing the Mind with Positive Confessions

- I am God's child, born again of the incorruptible seed of the word of God which lives and abides forever. 1 Peter 1:23
- I am complete in Christ. Colossians 2:10
- I am the apple of my Father's eye. Psalm 17:8
- I am free from condemnation. Romans 8:1
- I am the righteousness of God through Christ Jesus. 2 Corinthians 5:21
- I am chosen. 1 Thessalonians 1:4
- I am firmly rooted, built up, strengthened in the faith. Colossians 2:7
- I am built on the foundations of the apostles and prophets, with Christ Jesus himself as the chief cornerstone. Ephesians 2:20
- I am a partaker of his divine nature. 2 Peter 1:4
- I am God's workmanship, created in Christ Jesus for good works. Ephesians 2:10
- I am changed into his image. Philippians 1:6
- I am one in Christ! Hallelujah! John 17:21-23
- I have all my needs met by God according to his glorious riches in Christ Jesus. Philippians 4:19
- I have the mind of Christ. 1 Corinthaisn 2:16

- I have eternal life. John 6:47
- I have a guaranteed inheritance. Ephesians 1:14
- I have abundant life. John 10:10
- I have overcome the world. 1 John 5:4
- I have the peace of God which passes understanding. Philippians 4:7
- I have access to the Father by one Spirit. Ephesians 2:18
- I have received the power of the Holy Spirit to do great works. Mark 16:17
- I can do all things through Jesus Christ. Philippians 4:13
- I walk in Christ Jesus. Colossians 2:6
- I have spiritual authority. 1 John 4:4
- I live by the law of the Holy Spirit. Romans 8:2
- I know God's voice. John 10:14
- I am chosen by God himself. 1 Peter 2:9
- I always triumph in Christ. 2 Corinthians 2:14
- Christ is in me—the hope of glory! Colossians 1:27
- I am forgiven all of my sins and washed in the blood of lamb. Ephesians 1:7
- I am a new creation. 2 Corinthians 5:17
- I am the temple of the Holy Spirit. 1 Corinthians 6:19
- I am delivered from the power of darkness and transformed into God's kingdom. Colossians 1:13
- I am redeemed from the curse of the law. Galatians 3:13

Appendix

- I am strong in the Lord. Ephesians 6:10
- I am holy and without blame before him. Ephesians 1:4
- I am accepted in Christ. Ephesians 1:6
- I am blessed. Deuteronomy 28:1-14
- I am a saint. Romans 1:7
- I am qualified to share in his inheritance. Colossians 1:12
- I am victorious. Revelation 21:7
- I am dead to sin. Romans 6:2,11
- I am elect. Colossians 3:12
- I am loved with an everlasting love. Jeremiah 31:3
- I am established to the end. 1 Corinthians 1:8
- I am set free. John 8:31-33
- I am circumcised with the circumcision made without hands. Colossians 2:11
- I am crucified with Christ. Galatians 2:20
- I am alive with Christ. Ephesians 2:5
- I am raised up with Christ and seated in the heavenly places. Colossians 2:12
- I am holy and pure — God's very own. 1 Peter 2:9
- I am the light of the world. Matthew 5:14
- I am the salt of the earth. Matthew 5:13
- I am called of God. 2 Timothy 1:9
- I am brought near by the blood of Christ. Ephesians 2:13
- I am more than a conqueror. Romans 8:37
- I am an ambassador for Christ. 2 Corinthians 5:20

- I am beloved of God. 1 Thessalonians 1:4
- I am the first fruits among his creation. James 1:18
- I am a king and a priest unto God. Revelation 1:6
- I am born of God and the evil one cannot touch me. 1 John 5:18
- I am a joint heir with Christ. Romans 8:17
- I am reconciled to God. 2 Corinthians 5:18
- I am filled with blessings. Deuteronomy 28:2
- I am healed by the wounds of Jesus. 1 Peter 2:24
- I am sealed with the promise of the Holy Spirit. Ephesians 1:13
- I am in the world as he is in heaven. 1 John 4:17
- I am a fellow citizen with the saints of the household of God. Ephesians 2:1
- I am hidden in the Father because Christ has been placed in me and I am in Christ. John 14:20, Colossians 3:3

Whatever is true, whatever is noble,
whatever is right, whatever is pure,
whatever is lovely, think on these things
day and night.
Hold on to the teaching of Christ.
Then you will know the truth
and the truth,
by which you have been made holy,
will set you free
(Philippians 4:8, Joshua 1:8, John 8:31-32).

Appendix F - 1

**The Parallel—
Man and the Tabernacle**

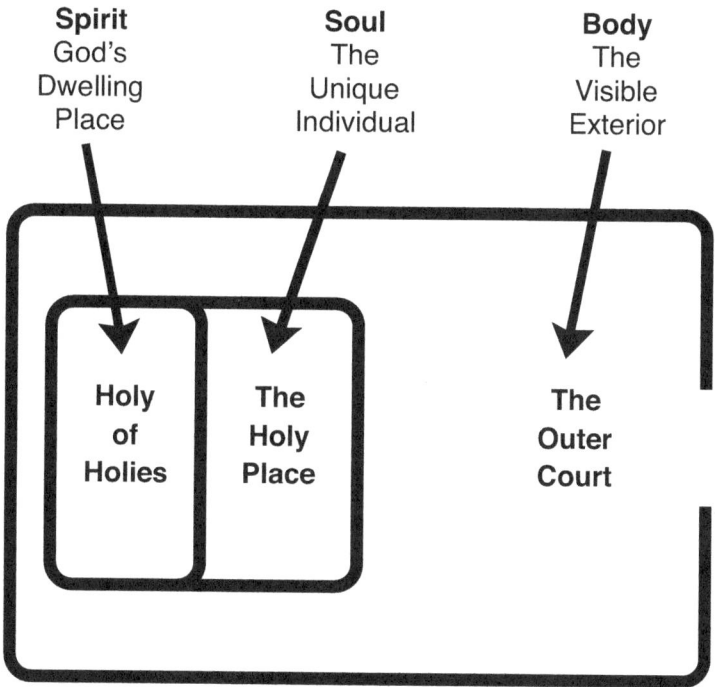

Appendix G - 1

What Happens When Christians Die

The church at Thessalonica was a young church, probably only a few months old when Paul wrote to them. They were being persecuted, and were disturbed about those who were dying before Christ's return. They had questioned Paul regarding what was happening to their friends and family members who had already died—will they miss the gathering? Paul had taught this young church about Christ's return and they knew about eternal life. They had hope. But they were grieved, confused and worried about those who had already died. The question asked by these young believers is one that we often ask today: What happens when Christians die? Paul writes them back saying this: *I would not have you ignorant, brethren, concerning those who are asleep, that you may not grieve as others do who have no hope. For since we believe that Jesus died and rose again, even so, through Jesus, God will bring with him those who have fallen asleep. For this we declare to you by the word of the Lord, that we who are alive, who are left until the coming of the Lord, shall not precede those who have fallen asleep. For the Lord himself will descend from heaven with a cry of command, with the archangel's call, and with the sound of the trumpet of God. And the dead in Christ will rise first; Then we who are alive, who are left, shall be caught up together with them in the clouds to meet the Lord in the air; and so we shall always be with the Lord. Therefore comfort one another with these words* (1 Thessalonians 4:13-18).

Paul calls those he is writing *brethren*—fellow Christians. He tells them that he does not want them to be uninformed and thus grieving about those who have died—those who have *fallen asleep.* Paul addresses death in a unique way by using the Greek word *koimao*, which means a brief, temporary repose. This word is used throughout the New Testament and always means to *fall asleep.* For example, Jesus speaks of the dead Lazarus, *who has fallen asleep* (John 11:11). Stephen's stoning and subsequent death are referred to as his *falling asleep* (Acts 7:60).

Paul wrote to the church at Corinth, *We are of good courage, and we would rather be away from the body and at home with the Lord* (1 Corinthians 5:6). And again, as Paul writes to the church in Philippi, he states, *I am hard pressed.... My desire is to depart from my body and be with Christ, for this is far better. But to remain in the body is more necessary on your account"* (Philippians 1:23).

So, if my body "falls asleep" what part of me goes to heaven? My spirit. Our spirit goes to heaven and

Appendix

spends eternity with the Lord. *And Jesus cried again with a loud voice and gave up His spirit* (Matthew 27:50). *Then Jesus, crying with a loud voice, said, Father, into thy hands I commit My spirit* (Luke 23:46). *And as they were stoning Stephen, he prayed, Lord Jesus, receive my spirit* (Acts 7:59). The saved are either here on earth or with Christ. When we die, our spirit goes immediately to be with Christ. Our body simply falls into sleep.

This temporary sleep, however, is only promised to those who believe that Jesus died and rose again. One of John McArthur's teaching discs explains that Jesus died once and for all in order that he might make death into sleep for us. Christ made sleep the name for death in the dialect of the church. The wages of sin is death—if the penalty for sin has been paid, we no longer face death—only temporary sleep. So, we are to have normal sorrow, but never be without hope. Because we will be gathered together with Christ and experience a reunion. For Christians, partings are just brief. Christians never say a final good-bye.

In Acts 14:19, we find Paul preaching Jesus and being dragged out of the city, and stoned to death. Several years later, he writes about this event. *Fourteen years ago I was taken up to heaven for a visit.... There I was in paradise, and heard things so astounding that they are beyond a man's power to describe or put into words* (TLB). So Paul is able to state in verse

15, *I can tell you this directly from the Lord. That we who are still living when the Lord returns will not rise to meet Him ahead of those who are in their graves* (NLT). Paul answers their question in no uncertain terms. In verses 16 and 17, he describes how this is to take place: *For the Lord Himself will descend from heaven with a loud cry of summons, with the shout of a archangel, and with the blast of the trumpet of God. And those who have departed this life in Christ will rise first. Then we, the ones living who remain [on the earth], shall simultaneously be caught up along with (the resurrected dead) in the clouds to meet the Lord in the air; and so always—through the eternity of the eternities—we shall be with the Lord!* (AMP).

Martin Luther called this, "a call to the church to stand up—to fall into rank." The term *caught up* is taken from the Greek word *harpazdo*—literally meaning to snatch up, to seize or carry off by force—a sudden energy of force that sweeps us up. God will snatch us up and carry us away to be with himself for all eternity.

1 Corinthians 15:42 tells us that at this point we will be given new bodies. *Our earthly bodies which die and decay are different from the bodies we shall have when we come back to life again, for they will never die. The bodies we have now embarrass us for they become sick and die; but they will be full of glory when we come back to life again. Yes, they are weak, dying bodies*

Appendix

now, but when we live again they will be full of strength.... I tell you this strange and wonderful secret; we shall not all die, but we shall all be given new bodies! It will happen in a moment, in the twinkling of an eye, when the last trumpet is blown. For there will be a trumpet blast from the sky, and all the Christians who have died will suddenly come alive with new bodies that will never, never die; and then we who are still alive shall suddenly have new bodies too (NLT).

If this is not enough, there is another bit of good news for the believer in Christ — we will all know and recognize each other when we receive our new bodies. Consider that our resurrected Lord was recognized by Mary Magdalene by the tomb, by the two men on the road to Emmaus and by his disciples. Thomas recognized Christ when he felt his hands and put his own hand into Christ's side.

We must learn to be at peace, comforted with these thoughts.

- Death is not final, as the world has us believe.
- Christ has been victorious over the enemy, over sin, and yes, over death itself.
- God has given us Christ's victory.
- Our penalty for sin has been paid in full.
- When Christ returns, he will take us with him and give us new bodies.
- We will spend eternity with the Lord.

There are a few people that God has chosen by his

grace. And if he chose them by grace, it is not for the things they have done. If they could be made God's people by what they did, God's gift of grace would not really be a gift (Romans 11:5-6, NCV).

Notes

INTRODUCTION
1 Corsini, Raymond. *Current Psychotherapies* (Itasca, F.E. Peacock Publishers, Inc., 1976).
2 Tosi, LeClair, Peters and Murphy. *Theories and Applications of Counseling* (Springfield, IL, Charles C. Thomas, 1987), 14.
3 Ibid. 15.
4 Woolfe, Ray and Dryden, Windy. *Handbook of Counselling Psychology* (London, Sage Publications, 1996), 113–284.
5 Galatians 6:7, *New International Version* (Colorado Springs, International Bible Society, 1984).
6 2 Timothy 3:16–17, *New Living Translation* (Wheaton, Illinois, Tyndale House Publishers, Inc., 1996).

CHAPTER 1
CLIENT-CENTERED THERAPY
1 Rogers, Carl. *Biography from Answers.com* (http://www.answers.com/topic/carl-rogers).

2   Rogers, Carl. *Personality Theories* website (http://webspace.ship.edu/cgboer/rogers.htm).
3   Rogers, Carl. *Selected Carl Rogers Quotes* (http://www.psychology.about.com/od/psychologyquotes/a/rogersquotes.htm).
4   Rogers, Carl. *Biography from Answers.com* (http://www.answers.com/topic/carl-rogers).
5   Rogers, Carl. On Becoming a Person: A Therapist's View of Psychotherapy (London, Constable, 1961), 11.
6   Murdock, Nancy L. *Theories of Counseling and Psychotherapy, A Case Approach* (Upper Saddle River, N.J., Pearson Merrill Prentice Hall, 2004), 110.
7   Rogers, Carl. *On Becoming a Person: A Therapist's View of Psychotherapy* (London, Constable, 1961), 194.
8   Murdock, Nancy L. *Theories of Counseling and Psychotherapy, A Case Approach* (Upper Saddle River, N.J., Pearson Merrill Prentice Hall, 2004), 115.
9   Rogers, Carl R. *Client-centered Therapy*. In Silvano Arieti (Ed.), Volume 3. Supplement to *The American Handbook of Psychiatry* (New York, Basic Books, Inc., 1966), 183–200.
10 Murdock, Nancy L. *Theories of Counseling and Psychotherapy, A Case Approach* (Upper Saddle River, N.J., Pearson Merrill Prentice Hall, 2004), 117.
11 Ibid. 118.
12 Rogers, Carl. *Personality Theories* website

Notes

(http://webspace.ship.edu/cgboer/carl-rogers.html).

13 Rogers, Carl. *Carl Rogers and his Client Centered Approach* (http://www.myshrink.com/counseling-theory.php?t_id=87).

14 Rogers, Carl. *On Becoming a Person: A Therapist's View of Psychotherapy* (London, Constable, 1961), 126.

15 Rogers, Carl. *A Way of Being* (Boston, Houghton Mufflin, 1980), 142.

16 Ibid. 115.

17 Wikipedia Encyclopedia. *Carl Rogers* (http://en.wikipedia.org/wiki/carl_rogers).

18 Corsini, Raymond J. and Wedding, Danny. *Current Psychotherapies* (Itasca, F.E. Peacock Publishers, Inc., 1976), 152–153.

19 Bancroft, Emery H. *Christian Theology, Systematic and Biblical, Second Revised Edition* (Grand Rapids, MI, Zondervan Publishing House, 1961), 198–199.

20 Ibid. 213.

21 Lewis, C.S. *The Problem of Pain* (New York, NY, Harper Collins Publishers, 2001), 78–79.

CHAPTER 2
GESTALT THERAPY

1 Corey, Gerald. *Theory and Practice of Counseling and Psychotherapy* (Belmont, CA, Wadsworth/Thomson Learning, 2001), 193.

2 Simkin, James S. and Yontef, Gary M. *Gestalt Therapy—Current Psychotherapies, Third Edi-

tion (Itasca, IL, F.E. Peacock Publishers, Inc., 1984), 280–281.

3 Corey, Gerald. *Theory and Practice of Counseling and Psychotherapy* (Belmont, CA, Wadsworth/Thomson Learning, 2001), 193.

4 Day, Susan X. *Theory and Design in Counseling and Psychotherapy* (Boston, MA, Houghton Mifflin Company, 2004), 207.

5 Hersen, Michel and Gross, Alan M., Editors. *Handbook of Clinical Psychology* (Hoboken, NJ, John Wiley & Sons, Inc., 2008), 586.

6 Ibid. 585 – 586.

7 Parrott III, Les. *Counseling and Psychotherapy* (Brooks/Cole, a division of Thompson Learning, Inc., 2003), 202.

8 Day, Susan X. *Theory and Design in Counseling and Psychotherapy* (Boston, MA, Houghton Mifflin Company, 2004), 197.

9 Wikipedia Encyclopedia. *Fritz Perls* (http://en.wikipedia.org/siki/Fritz_Perls).

10 Ibid

11 Parrott III, Les. *Counseling and Psychotherapy* (Brooks/Cole, a division of Thompson Learning, Inc., 2003), 205.

12 Corey, Gerald. *Theory and Practice of Counseling and Psychotherapy* (Belmont, CA, Wadsworth/Thomson Learning, 2001), 195-196.

13 Day, Susan X. *Theory and Design in Counseling and Psychotherapy* (Boston, MA, Houghton Mifflin Company, 2004), 196–197.

14 Parrott III, Les. *Counseling and Psychotherapy*

(Brooks/Cole, a division of Thompson Learning, Inc., 2003), 207-208.

15 Binder, Virginia, Binder, Arnold, Rimland, Bernard, Editors. *Modern Therapies* (Englewood Cliffs, NJ, Prentice-Hall, Inc., 1976), 67–68.

16 Day, Susan X. *Theory and Design in Counseling and Psychotherapy* (Boston, MA, Houghton Mifflin Company, 2004), 200.

17 Hersen, Michel and Gross, Alan M., Editors. *Handbook of Clinical Psychology* (Hoboken, NJ, John Wiley & Sons, Inc., 2008), 590–591, and Day, Susan X. *Theory and Design in Counseling and Psychotherapy* (Boston, MA, Houghton Mifflin Company, 2004), 204.

18 Day, Susan X. *Theory and Design in Counseling and Psychotherapy* (Boston, MA, Houghton Mifflin Company, 2004), 205.

19 Simkin, James S. and Yontef, Gary M. *Gestalt Therapy—Current Psychotherapies, Third Edition* (Itasca, IL, F.E. Peacock Publishers, Inc., 1984), 279–280.

20 Hersen, Michel and Gross, Alan M., Editors. *Handbook of Clinical Psychology* (Hoboken, NJ, John Wiley & Sons, Inc., 2008), 586–587.

21 Corey, Gerald. *Theory and Practice of Counseling and Psychotherapy* (Belmont, CA, Wadsworth/Thomson Learning, 2001), 197.

22 Simkin, James S. and Yontef, Gary M. *Gestalt Therapy—Current Psychotherapies, Third Edition* (Itasca, IL, F.E. Peacock Publishers, Inc., 1984), 279–280.

23 Hersen, Michel and Gross, Alan M., Editors. *Handbook of Clinical Psychology* (Hoboken, NJ, John Wiley & Sons, Inc., 2008), 587.
24 Day, Susan X. *Theory and Design in Counseling and Psychotherapy* (Boston, MA, Houghton Mifflin Company, 2004), 206–207.
25 Ibid, 200–201.
26 Ibid. 212.
27 Ibid, 194.
28 Simkin, James S. and Yontef, Gary M. *Gestalt Therapy—Current Psychotherapies, Third Edition* (Itasca, IL, F.E. Peacock Publishers, Inc., 1984). 291.
29 Binder, Virginia, Binder, Arnold, Rimland, Bernard, Editors. *Modern Therapies* (Englewood Cliffs, NJ, Prentice-Hall, Inc., 1976), 70.
30 Simkin, James S. and Yontef, Gary M. *Gestalt Therapy—Current Psychotherapies, Third Edition* Raymond J. Corsini, Editor (Itasca, IL, F.E. Peacock Publishers, Inc., 1984), 286.
31 Binder, Virginia, Binder, Arnold, Rimland, Bernard, Editors. *Modern Therapies* (Englewood Cliffs, NJ, Prentice-Hall, Inc., 1976), 75–77.
32 Day, Susan X. *Theory and Design in Counseling and Psychotherapy* (Boston, MA, Houghton Mifflin Company, 2004), 228.
33 Parrott III, Les. *Counseling and Psychotherapy* (Brooks/Cole, a division of Thompson Learning, Inc., 2003), 221–222.
34 Simkin, James S. and Yontef, Gary M. *Gestalt Therapy—Current Psychotherapies, Third Edi*

tion (Itasca, IL, F.E. Peacock Publishers, Inc., 1984), 314.
35 Corey, Gerald. *Theory and Practice of Counseling and Psychotherapy* (Belmont, CA, Wadsworth/Thomson Learning, 2001), 203.
36 Ibid. 221.
37 Parrott III, Les. *Counseling and Psychotherapy* (Brooks/Cole, a division of Thompson Learning, Inc., 2003), 210.

CHAPTER 3
COGNITIVE THERAPY
1 Murdock, Nancy L. *Theories of Counseling and Psychotherapy, A Case Approach* (Upper Saddle River, NJ, Pearson Prentice Hall, 2004), 220.
2 Lebow, Jay L., Editor. *Twenty-First Century Psychotherapies* (Hoboken, NJ, John Wiley & Sons, Inc., 2008), 44.
3 Beck Institute for Cognitive Therapy and Research (2008, http://www.beckinstitute.org/).
4 Ibid.
5 Murdock, Nancy L. *Theories of Counseling and Psychotherapy, A Case Approach* (Upper Saddle River, NJ, Pearson Prentice Hall, 2004), 245–246.
6 Ibid.
7 Sue, David and Sue, Diane M. *Foundations of Counseling and Psychotherapy* (Hoboken, NJ, John Wiley & Sons, Inc., 2008), 202–203.
8 Lebow, Jay L., Editor. *Twenty-First Century Psychotherapies* (Hoboken, NJ, John Wiley &

Sons, Inc., 2008), 45.

9 Corey, Gerald. *Theory and Practice of Counseling and Psychotherapy* (Belmont, CA, Brooks/Cole Thomson Learning, 2001), 312–314.

10 Beck Institute for Cognitive Therapy and Research, *Cognitive Therapy Today* (Spring 2008 Newsletter, Vol. 13, No. 1, http://www.beckinstitute.org/).

11 Murdock, Nancy L. *Theories of Counseling and Psychotherapy, A Case Approach* (Upper Saddle River, NJ, Pearson Prentice Hall, 2004), 225, 251.

12 Sue, David and Sue, Diane M. *Foundations of Counseling and Psychotherapy* (Hoboken, NJ, John Wiley & Sons, Inc., 2008), 203.

13 Leahy, Ph.D., Robert L. and Dowd, Ph.D., ABPP, Thomas E., Editors. *Clinical Advances in Cognitive Psychotherapy* (New York, NY, Springer Publishing Co., Inc.,2002), 38, 43.

14 Lebow, Jay L., Editor. *Twenty-First Century Psychotherapies* (Hoboken, NJ, John Wiley & Sons, Inc., 2008), 52.

15 Geisler, Norman L. *Baker Encyclopedia of Christian Apologetics* (Grand Rapids, MI, Baker Books, 1999), 741–745.

16 Jones, Stanton L. and Butman, Richard E. *Modern Psychotherapies* (Downers Grove, IL, Intervarsity Press), 209.

17 Lebow, Jay L., Editor. *Twenty-First Century Psychotherapies* (Hoboken, NJ, John Wiley & Sons, Inc., 2008), 55–56.

Notes

18 Sue, David and Sue, Diane M. *Foundations of Counseling and Psychotherapy* (Hoboken, NJ, John Wiley & Sons, Inc., 2008), 203.

CHAPTER 4
BEHAVIOR THERAPY

1 Wikipedia Encyclopedia. *Behavior Therapy* (http://en.wikipedia.org/wiki/Behavior_therapy).
2 Corsini, Raymond. *Behavior Therapy. Current Psychotherapies* (Itasca, F.E. Peacock Publishers, Inc., 1976), 207.
3 Wikipedia Encyclopedia. B*ehavior Therapy* (http://en.wikipedia.org/wiki/Behavior_therapy).
4 Corsini, Raymond. *Behavior Therapy. Current Psychotherapies* (Itasca, F.E. Peacock Publishers, Inc., 1976), 207.
5 *What Is Behavior Therapy?* (http://www.wisegeek.com/what-is-behavior-therapy.htm).
6 Corsini, Raymond. *Behavior Therapy. Current Psychotherapies* (Itasca, F.E. Peacock Publishers, Inc., 1976), 220.
7 Ibid. 215–216.
8 Wikipedia Encyclopedia. *Operant Conditioning* (http://en.wikipedia.org/wiki/Operant_conditioning).
9 Ibid. 2.
10 Corsini, Raymond. *Behavior Therapy. Current Psychotherapies* (Itasca, F.E. Peacock Publishers, Inc., 1976), 215.
11 *Operant Conditioning* (http:/psychology.

about.com/od/behavioralpsychology/a/intro opcond.htm).
12. Wikipedia Encyclopedia. *Operant Conditioning* (http://en. wikipedia.org/wiki/Operant_ conditioning).
13. Corsini, Raymond. *Behavior Therapy. Current Psychotherapies* (Itasca, F.E. Peacock Publishers, Inc., 1976), 216.
14. Wolpe, Joseph. *Psychotherapy by Reciprocal Inhibition* (Stanford, CA, Stanford University Press, 1958), 71.
15. Corsini, Raymond. *Behavior Therapy. Current Psychotherapies* (Itasca, F.E. Peacock Publishers, Inc., 1976), 242.
16. Ibid. 228.
17. Corey, Gerald. *Theory and Practice of Counseling and Psychotherapy* (Belmont, CA, Wadsworth/Thomson Learning, 2001), 269.
18. Ibid. 274.
19. Corsini, Raymond. *Current Psychotherapies* (Itasca, F.E. Peacock Publishers, Inc., 1976), 230.
20. Corey, Gerald. *Theory and Practice of Counseling and Psychotherapy* (Belmont, CA, Wadsworth/Thomson Learning, 2001), 271–272.
21. Geisler, Norman L. *Baker Encyclopedia of Christian Apologetics* (Grand Rapids, MI, Baker Books, 1999), 261–262.
22. Ibid. 262.

Notes

CHAPTER 5
RATIONAL EMOTIVE BEHAVIOR THERAPY

1. Albert Ellis Institute: *A Sketch of Albert Ellis* (http://www.albertellisinstitute.org/aeialbert_ellis_bio.htm).
2. *Albert Ellis Quotes* (www.brainyquote.com/quotes/a/albertelli122035.html).
3. Wikipedia Encyclopedia. *Early Life* (http://en.wikipedia.org/wiki/Albert_Ellis).
4. Ellis, Albert. *Quotations* (Albert-Ellis-Friends.Net:ARationalOasis).
5. Wikipedia Encyclopedia. *Early Theoretical Contribution to Psychotherapy* (http://en.wikipedia.org/wiki/RationalEmotive BehavioralTherapy).
6. Ellis, Albert. *Sex, Love and the Scolding Psychotherapist* (NY Times Week in Review, www.nytimes.com/2007/07/29weekinreview).
7. Ellis, Albert. *The Essence of Rational Emotive Behavior Therapy: A Comprehensive Approach to Treatment* (http://www.rebt.ws/albert_ellis_the_essence_of_rebt.htm).
8. *Albert Ellis Quotes* (www.brainyquote.com/quotes/a/albertelli122035.html).
9. Franklin, Marcus. *Psychology Giant Albert Ellis Dies* (USA Today, February 2007).
10. Ellis, Albert. *A Brief Biography of Dr. Albert Ellis 1913–2007* (July 2007, www.rebt.ws/a/albertellisbiography.html).
11. Ibid.
12. *Albert Ellis Quotes* (www.brainyquote.com/quotes/a/albertelli122035.html).

13 Epstein, Robert. *The Prince of Reason* (Psychology Today, February 2001).
14 Corsini, Raymond. *Current Psychotherapies* (Itasca, F.E. Peacock Publishers, Inc., 1976), 171–173.
15 Ellis, Albert and Harper, Robert. *A New Guide to Rational Living* (Hollywood, Wilshire Books, 1975), 88–186.
16 Corsini, Raymond. *Current Psychotherapies* (Itasca, F.E. Peacock Publishers, Inc., 1976), 167.
17 Kranzler, Gerald. *You Can Change How You Feel: A Rational Emotive Approach* (Eugene, RETC Press, 1974), 25.
18 *Albert Ellis Quotes* (www.thinkexist.com/quotes/albert_ellis/).
19 Ellis, Ph.D., Albert. *Dr. Albert Ellis Has Died* (National Association of Cognitive Behavioral Therapists, www.nacbt.org/Albert-Ellis.htm).
20 McVey, Steve. *Grace Walk* (Eugene, Harvest House Publishers, 1995).
21 Young, Howard S. *A Rational Counseling Primer* (New York, Institute For Rational Living, Inc.). 1974, 7.

CHAPTER 6
PSYCHOANALYTIC THEORY
1 Freud, Sigmund. *The Internet Encyclopedia of Philosophy* (http://www.iep.utm.edu/f/freud.htm), 1.
2 Wallace, William A. *Theories of Counseling and*

Notes

Psychotherapy (Newtone, MA, Allyn and Bacon, Inc., 1986), 34.

3 Murdock, Nancy L. *Theories of Counseling and Psychotherapy, A Case Approach* (Upper Saddle River, NJ, Pearson Prentice Hall, 2004), 34.

4 Wallace, William A. *Theories of Counseling and Psychotherapy* (Newtone, MA, Allyn and Bacon, Inc., 1986), 21.

5 Murdock, Nancy L. *Theories of Counseling and Psychotherapy, A Case Approach* (Upper Saddle River, NJ, Pearson Prentice Hall, 2004), 36.

6 Freud, Sigmund. *The Internet Encyclopedia of Philosophy* (http://www.iep.utm.edu/f/freud.htm).

7 Corey, Gerald. *Theory and Practice of Counseling and Psychotherapy* (Belmont, CA, Thomson Learning, Inc., 2001), 68.

8 Freud, Sigmund. *The Internet Encyclopedia of Philosophy* (http://www.iep.utm.edu/f/freud.htm).

9 Wallace, William A. *Theories of Counseling and Psychotherapy* (Newtone, MA, Allyn and Bacon, Inc., 1986), 38.

10 Freud, Sigmund. *The Internet Encyclopedia of Philosophy* (http://www.iep.utm.edu/f/freud.htm).

11 Ibid. 7.

12 Murdock, Nancy L. *Theories of Counseling and Psychotherapy, A Case Approach* (Upper Saddle River, NJ, Pearson Prentice Hall, 2004), 37.

13 Stewart, William. *A Biographical Dictionary of*

Psychologists, Psychiatrists and Psychotherapists (Jefferson, NC, McFarland & Company, Inc.,Publishers, 2008), 115.

14 Freud, Sigmund. *The Internet Encyclopedia of Philosophy* (http://www.iep.utm.edu/f/freud.htm).

15 Corey, Gerald. *Theory and Practice of Counseling and Psychotherapy* (Belmont, CA, Thomson Learning, Inc.,2001), 71, 72, 87.

16 Wallace, William A. *Theories of Counseling and Psychotherapy* (Newtone, MA, Allyn and Bacon, Inc., 1986), 38.

17 Jones, Stanton L. and Butman, Richard E. *Modern Psychotherapies* (Downers Grove, IL, Intervarsity Press).

18 Shamdasani, Sonu. *Jung and the Making of Modern Psychology* (New York, NY, Cambridge University Press, 2003), 1.

19 Wikipedia Encyclopedia. (http://en.wikipedia.org/wiki/Carl_Jung).

20 Shamdasani, Sonu. *Jung and the Making of Modern Psychology* (New York, NY, Cambridge University Press, 2003), 2.

21 Ibid. 250.

22 *The Jung Page*, 2008. (http://www.cgjungpage.org/index.php).

23 Corsini, Raymond. *Current Psychotherapies* (Itasca, F.E. Peacock Publishers, Inc., 1976), 100.

24 Ibid. 101.

25 Ibid. 107.

26 Wikipedia Encyclopedia. (http://en. wikipedia.org/wiki/Carl_Jung).
27 Ibid.
28 Ibid.
29 Woodward, John B. *Man as Spirit, Soul, and Body* (Pigeon Forge, TN, Grace Fellowship International Publishing, 2007), 18.

CHAPTER 7
REALITY THERAPY

1 Corey, Gerald. *Theory and Practice of Counseling and Psychotherapy* (Belmont, CA, Wadsworth, 2001), 230.
2 Corsini, Raymond J. *Current Psychotherapies, Third Edition* (Itasca, Illinois, F.E. Peacock Publishers, Inc., 1976), 320.
3 Glasser, William. *Modern Therapies* (Englewood Cliffs, New Jersey, Prentice-Hall, Inc., 1976), 52.
4 Corey, Gerald. *Theory and Practice of Counseling and Psychotherapy* (Belmont, CA, Wadsworth, 2001), 232.
5 Parrott III, Les. *Counseling and Psychotherapy, Second Edition* (Pacific Grove, CA, Thomson Brooks/Cole, 2003), 344–346.
6 Corsini, Raymond J. *Current Psychotherapies, Third Edition* (Itasca, Illinois, F.E. Peacock Publishers, Inc., 1976), 323.
7 Ibid. 323.
8 Ibid. 324.
9 Ibid. 324.

10 Ibid. 324.
11 Glasser, William. *Modern Therapies* (Englewood Cliffs, New Jersey, Prentice-Hall, Inc., 1976), 56–57.
12 Corey, Gerald. *Theory and Practice of Counseling and Psychotherapy* (Belmont, CA, Wadsworth, 2001), 8–59.
13 Ibid. 59–60.
14 Ibid. 61.
15 Corsini, Raymond J. *Current Psychotherapies, Third Edition* (Itasca, Illinois, F.E. Peacock Publishers, Inc., 1976), 337.
16 Corey, Gerald. *Theory and Practice of Counseling and Psychotherapy* (Belmont, CA, Wadsworth, 2001), 349.
17 Ibid. 350.
18 Ibid. 351.
19 Glasser, William. *Modern Therapies* (Englewood Cliffs, New Jersey, Prentice-Hall, Inc., 1976), 340.
20 Corey, Gerald. *Theory and Practice of Counseling and Psychotherapy* (Belmont, CA, Wadsworth, 2001), 352.

CHAPTER 8
ADLERIAN THERAPY

1 Murdock, Nancy L. *Theories of Counseling and Psychotherapy, A Case Approach* (Upper Saddle River, NJ, Pearson Prentice Hall, 2004), 68.
2 Stepansky, Paul E. *In Freud's Shadow* (Hillsdale, NJ, The Analytic Press), 9–10.

Notes

3 Stein, Ph.D., Henry T. (Bellingham, Washington, 2008, http://ourworld.compuserve .com/homepages/hstein/).

4 Mosak, Harold H. and Corsini, Raymond. *Current Psychotherapies* (Itasca, F.E. Peacock Publishers, Inc., 1976), 63.

5 Murdock, Nancy L. *Theories of Counseling and Psychotherapy, A Case Approach* (Upper Saddle River, NJ, Pearson Prentice Hall, 2004), 69.

6 Ibid.

7 Stein, Ph.D., Henry T. (Bellingham, Washington, 2008, http://ourworld.compuserve.com/homepages/hstein/).

8 Murdock, Nancy L. *Theories of Counseling and Psychotherapy, A Case Approach* (Upper Saddle River, NJ, Pearson Prentice Hall, 2004), 71.

9 Murdock, Nancy L. *Theories of Counseling and Psychotherapy, A Case Approach* (Upper Saddle River, NJ, Pearson Prentice Hall, 2004), 77, 107.

10 Mosak, Harold H. and Corsini, Raymond. *Current Psychotherapies* (Itasca, F.E. Peacock Publishers, Inc., 1976), 54.

11 Stein, Ph.D., Henry T. (Bellingham, Washington, 2008, http://ourworld.compuserve.com/homepages/hstein/).

12 Murdock, Nancy L. *Theories of Counseling and Psychotherapy, A Case Approach* (Upper Saddle River, NJ, Pearson Prentice Hall, 2004), 70–71.

13 Mosak, Harold H. and Corsini, Raymond. *Current Psychotherapies* (Itasca, F.E. Peacock Publishers, Inc., 1976), 60.

14 Murdock, Nancy L. *Theories of Counseling and Psychotherapy, A Case Approach* (Upper Saddle River, NJ, Pearson Prentice Hall, 2004), 70–72.
15 Ibid, 75.
16 Ibid, 72, 74, 82, 83.
17 Mosak, Harold H. and Corsini, Raymond. *Current Psychotherapies* (Itasca, F.E. Peacock Publishers, Inc., 1976), 66, 77.
18 Ibid, 55–57.
19 Dreikurs, M.D., Rudolf. *Fundamentals of Adlerian Psychology* (New York, Greenberg: Publisher, 1950), 15–16.
20 Ibid. 20, 25.
21 Ibid. 20, 22.
22 Ibid. 26.
23 Stepansky, Paul E. *In Freud's Shadow* (Hillsdale, NJ, The Analytic Press), 248.
24 Murdock, Nancy L. *Theories of Counseling and Psychotherapy, A Case Approach* (Upper Saddle River, NJ, Pearson Prentice Hall, 2004), 76–77.
25 Stein, Ph.D., Henry T. (Bellingham, Washington, 2008, http://ourworld.compuserve.com/homepages/hstein/).
26 Dreikurs, M.D., Rudolf. *Fundamentals of Adlerian Psychology* (New York, Greenberg: Publisher, 1950), 22–23.
27 Murdock, Nancy L. *Theories of Counseling and Psychotherapy, A Case Approach* (Upper Saddle River, NJ, Pearson Prentice Hall, 2004), 83.
28 Ibid, 100.
29 Stein, Ph.D., Henry T. (Bellingham, Washing-

Notes

ton, 2008, http://ourworld.compuserve.com/homepages/hstein/).

30 Meerloo, Joost, Mosak, Harold H. and Corsini, Raymond. *Current Psychotherapies* (Itasca, F.E. Peacock Publishers, Inc., 1976), 79.
31 Seamands, David A. *Healing Grace* (Victor Books, 1988).
32 Stedman, Ray C. *From Guilt to Glory* (Portland, OR, Multnomah Press, 1978).
33 Newell, William R. *Romans Verse by Verse* (Chicago, IL, Moody Press, 1973).
34 Fromke, DeVerne. *Ultimate Intention* (Shoals, IN, Sure Foundation).
35 Seamands, David A. *Healing for Damaged Emotions* (Colorado Springs, CO, Chariot Victor Publishing, 1981).
36 Seamands, David A. *Putting Away Childish Things* (Victor Books, 1982).

CHAPTER 9
SOLUTION-FOCUSED THERAPY

1 Institute for Solution-Focused Therapy (http://www.solutionfocused.net/solution focusedtherapy.html).
2 O'Connell, Bill. *Solution-Focused Therapy, Second Edition* (Thousand Oaks, CA, SAGE Publications, Inc., 2005), 2–3.
3 Pichot, Teri and Dolan, Yvonne M. *Solution-Focused Brief Therapy* (Binghamton, NY, The Haworth Press, Inc., 2003), 12–13.
4 Ibid.

5 O'Connell, Bill. *Solution-Focused Therapy, Second Edition* (Thousand Oaks, CA, SAGE Publications, Inc., 2005), 20.
6 Pichot, Teri and Dolan, Yvonne M. *Solution-Focused Brief Therapy* (Binghamton, NY, The Haworth Press, Inc., 2003), 14.
7 Institute for Solution-Focused Therapy (http://www.solutionfocused.net/solution focusedtherapy.html).
8 Pichot, Teri and Dolan, Yvonne M. *Solution-Focused Brief Therapy* (Binghamton, NY, The Haworth Press, Inc., 2003), 77–80.
9 Ibid. 17.
10 Macdonald, Alasdair J. *Solution-Focused Therapy—Theory, Research and Practice* (Thousand Oaks, CA, SAFE Publications, Inc., 2007).
11 O'Connell, Bill. *Solution-Focused Therapy, Second Edition* (Thousand Oaks, CA, SAGE Publications, Inc., 2005), 29.
12 Lewis, C.S. *The Problem of Pain* (New York, NY, HarperCollins Publishers, 2001), 28–31.
13 Thomas, Major W. Ian. *The Saving Life of Christ* (Grand Rapids, MI, Zondervan Publishing House, 1961), 68–69.

CHAPTER 10
EXISTENTIAL THERAPY
1 Frey, David H. and Heslet, Frederick E. *Existential Theory for Counselors: The Existential Matrix* (Boston, Houghton Mifflin Company, 1975), 1.
2 Corey, Gerald. *Theory and Practice of Counsel-

Notes

    ing and Psychotherapy (Belmont, CA, Wadsworth/Thomson Learning, 2001), 143–144.
3 Ibid. 144.
4 Corsini, Raymond J. and Wedding, Danny. *Current Psychotherapies* (Itasca, F.E. Peacock Publishers, Inc., 1976), 320.
5 Spinelli, Ernesto. *Handbook of Counselling Psychology. The Existential-Phenomenological Paradigm* (London, SAGE Publications, 2003), 182.
6 Corey, Gerald. *Theory and Practice of Counseling and Psychotherapy* (Belmont, CA, Wadsworth/Thomson Learning, 2001), 146.
7 Ibid. 146.
8 Existentialism. Answers.com (www.answers.com/topic/existentialism).
9 Corey, Gerald. *Theory and Practice of Counseling and Psychotherapy* (Belmont, CA, Wadsworth/Thomson Learning, 2001), 146.
10 Ibid. 146.
11 Ibid. 146.
12 Ibid. 153.
13 Existentialism. Answers.com (www.answers.com/topic/existentialism).
14 Murdock, Nancy L. *Theories of Counseling and Psychotherapy, A Case Approach* (Upper Saddle River, N.J., Pearson Merrill Prentice Hall), 2004.
15 Corey, Gerald. *Theory and Practice of Counseling and Psychotherapy* (Belmont, CA, Wadsworth/Thomson Learning, 2001), 150–151.
16 Murdock, Nancy L. *Theories of Counseling and*

Psychotherapy, A Case Approach (Upper Saddle River, N.J., Pearson Merrill Prentice Hall), 2004.
17 Corey, Gerald. *Theory and Practice of Counseling and Psychotherapy* (Belmont, CA, Wadsworth/Thomson Learning, 2001), 143, 145.
18 Ibid. 146–147.
19 Ibid. 148.
20 Ibid. 148–149, 154–155.
21 Ibid. 150–151.
22 Ibid. 153.
23 Murdock, Nancy L. *Theories of Counseling and Psychotherapy, A Case Approach* (Upper Saddle River, N.J., Pearson Merrill Prentice Hall, 2004).
24 Ibid. 189.
25 Ibid. 192.
26 Ibid. 192.
27 Ibid. 192.
28 Ibid. 192–193.
29 Ibid. 193.
30 Ibid. 193.
31 Ibid. 193.

EPILOGUE

1 Jones, Stanton L. and Butman, Richard E. *Modern Psychotherapies* (Downers Grove, IL, Intervarsity Press, 1991), 211.
2 D'Souza, Dinesh. *Imprimis*, Vol. 37, No. 11, Nov. 2008 (Hillsdale College, Hillsdale, MI), 5.

CPSIA information can be obtained at www.ICGtesting.com
Printed in the USA
LVOW01s1745170813

348398LV00016B/1076/P